# Iranian Strategic Influence

# Iranian Strategic Influence

## Information and the Culture of Resistance

W. A. Rivera

ROWMAN & LITTLEFIELD
*Lanham • Boulder • New York • London*

Published by Rowman & Littlefield
An imprint of The Rowman & Littlefield Publishing Group, Inc.
4501 Forbes Boulevard, Suite 200, Lanham, Maryland 20706
www.rowman.com

86-90 Paul Street, London EC2A 4NE

Copyright © 2022 by W. A. Rivera

*All rights reserved.* No part of this book may be reproduced in any form or by any electronic or mechanical means, including information storage and retrieval systems, without written permission from the publisher, except by a reviewer who may quote passages in a review.

British Library Cataloguing in Publication Information Available

**Library of Congress Cataloging-in-Publication Data**

Names: Rivera, W. A., author.
Title: Iranian strategic influence : information and the culture of
 resistance / W.A. Rivera.
Description: Lanham : Rowman & Littlefield, [2022] | Includes bibliographical
 references and index.
Identifiers: LCCN 2021040623 (print) | LCCN 2021040624 (ebook) |
 ISBN 9781538164679 (cloth) | ISBN 9781538164693 (paperback) |
 ISBN 9781538164686 (ebook)
Subjects: LCSH: Information warfare—Iran. | Iran—Foreign relations—1979-1997. |
 Iran—Foreign relations—1997- | United States—Foreign relations—Iran. |
 Iran—Foreign relations—United States. | Iran—Strategic aspects.
Classification: LCC DS318.83 .R58 2021 (print) | LCC DS318.83 (ebook) |
 DDC 327.5507309/04—dc23
LC record available at https://lccn.loc.gov/2021040623
LC ebook record available at https://lccn.loc.gov/2021040624

*Para Tí,*
*Unto Thee*

# Contents

| | | |
|---|---|---|
| Acknowledgment | | ix |
| Introduction | | 1 |
| 1 | The History of Resistance | 15 |
| 2 | The Ideology of Resistance: Adaptive Resistance | 29 |
| 3 | The Structure of Resistance: Designed Redundancy | 43 |
| 4 | Strategic Influence | 53 |
| 5 | How Iran Does Influence | 67 |
| 6 | Resistance in Iran's Near Abroad | 81 |
| 7 | Lebanon: The Hizb'allah Model | 83 |
| 8 | Iraq | 107 |
| 9 | Syria | 153 |
| 10 | Conclusion | 179 |
| Notes | | 225 |
| Bibliography | | 227 |
| Index | | 233 |
| About the Author | | 235 |

# Acknowledgments

Many thanks to the editors at Rowman and Littlefield, who walked this first-time author through the process with care. Many thanks also to the reviewers whose notes were invaluable in shaping this final product. I am grateful, too, to the many friends and family members who read versions of this work and provided feedback and encouragement. Caroline Elizabeth Levine provided very valuable support as a research assistant, proofreader, and other support functions, for which I am very grateful. I am especially grateful to Jeannie Johnson and Marilyn Maines who saw value in my work early on and helped bring it to fruition. And, of course, to the great team of advisors and friends from the University of Delaware, especially Daniel Greene, Bahram Rajaee, and Stuart Kaufman. Dr. Kaufman's work on Symbolic Politics and social mobilization inspires and shapes much of this effort. Thanks, also, to David Sallach, of the University of Chicago, my mentor, friend, and guide.

# Introduction

What is Strategic Influence? Strategic Influence is the use of the elements of national power—diplomatic, military, economic, *with and through information*—to shape the information and operational environment in order to erode the will of the enemy. For countries such as Russia, China, and Iran information is the main currency of their strategy, even if their main goal is to dominate a region—hegemony. Because the cost of militarily occupying a land is so high and often comes with international sanction, the "new" way of war is predicated on building narratives, activating identities, mobilizing proxies, and disorienting targets through the use of information in service of strategic goals. Strategic Influence is not limited to the cognitive domain as its effects are tacit, physical and kinetic action, and economic power can also be leveraged in its execution. The Grand Strategy of the actor may be traditionally understood as hegemony, balancing, or revisionism, but the main strategy deployed is meant to influence local populations to create new strategic landscapes while eroding the will of the adversary. Strategic Influence is about influence because even military assets are used in support of the narrative. Strategic Influence is about strategy because it is orchestrated at the highest levels of government, integrates strategic and tactical lines of effort, and with whole of government approaches, is developed and deployed with the intent to achieve a strategic end.

Strategic Influence involves the interleaving of various levels of analysis, often including competing issue areas, and various time frames. I use the term *strategic policy* to denote the way actors develop, execute, evaluate, and revise foreign, economic, and security policies to achieve strategic ends. Policy generally addresses methods to overcome obstacles and achieve desired ends identified to be in the interest of the actor. The identification of interests, of course, in turn, depends on the perceptions, history, geography, economic goals, and security concerns, given by a set of circumstances according to that actor's identity and values. Strategic policy, then, becomes the way in which strategic actors, nations, and others design and implement their influence strategies, where these strategies/policies reflect the nation's self-identity and projected goals across time, issue area, and level of analysis.

To identify Iran's influence strategies accurately, it is imperative, therefore, to understand Iran's Strategic Culture, perspective on its own identity, perceived role in the world, and its historical and contemporary challenges and goals. To do so means attempting to think as Iran's leadership thinks, to understand their history as they do, to understand, ultimately, their mythmaking and myth-propagation as foundations for their Strategic Influence. Myths are key to Strategic Influence, because the mobilization of audiences is in large part why Strategic Influence is used; myths create narratives, themes, and frames that enable influence. Therefore, understanding foundational myths, cultural myths, and the like, which are the very stuff of influence, enables a more accurate representation of Iran's influence strategies. The result of this effort is a model—a more or less formal, constructed, representation—of Iran's Strategic Influence policymaking. To do so is necessary whether one's goal is to engage, coopt, or defeat Iran's Strategic Influence. And to do so is not to believe, but to understand, Iran's projected perspective. Putting aside debates about what their authentic perspective is and focusing on what they project their perspectives are and how those perspectives support their Strategic Influence is essential to success.

For Iran there are two main drivers in this strategic policymaking process—adaptive resistance and designed redundancy. First, I found the term *resistance* used throughout the discourse of Iran's political elite. As such, I use it throughout this work to refer to Iran's orientation to the outside world. This idea is developed, in greater detail, in chapter 3, "The Ideology of Resistance." The Islamic Republic of Iran was born from revolution, but the revolution was more than just a replacement of the local ruling elite; it was an act of resistance against the global order. At that time, the global order was bi-polar, and resistance was encapsulated in the slogan, "neither East nor West" (Arjomand 2009, 23). From that time forward there has been a strong anti-U.S. and anti-Western ideological strain captured in the term "Westoxification" (Arjomand 2009, 79).

Resistance permeates the political discourse and the policy agenda. In a profound sense, the rhetoric and praxis of the Iranian revolutionary regime have developed as a rejection and counterweight to Western, primarily U.S. power. Their rhetoric—that is, their use of history, victimization—and their praxis—that is, their use of political and military proxies—are in service of influence strategies designed to humiliate the United States and reconstruct the regional and global order. Understanding the depth and breadth of the strength of anti-Western sentiment is critical to developing a more efficacious orientation toward the Iranian political elite.[1]

Yet, to say that Iran is a revisionist power intent on changing the status quo in the Middle East and beyond is not to say that they are radical or irrational. On the contrary, their approach to Strategic Influence requires them to be pragmatic: to take victories where possible and to turn defeats into rhetorical victories where necessary. Further, their ideological focal points at any given time are reflective of their goals and the current, usually local, political realities on the ground. That is, their resistance is ideological, but it is adaptive. This characteristic of Iran's Strategic Culture goes beyond rhetoric; the form and substance of their decisionmaking structure are also adaptive, albeit consistently anti-Western and revisionist.

To gain a better sense of the breadth and depth of this anti-Western ideology—adaptive resistance—this work examines Iran's history, ideology, and the policy decisionmaking structure. This is because there is still widespread misunderstanding concerning Iran's leadership and Strategic Culture. This work offers a new typology of the factions whose competition drives strategic policy decisionmaking, yet also generates consensus. This new typology is elaborated in chapter 4, "The Structure of Resistance." Since factional alignments determine policy outcomes, understanding them is critical to countering Iran's strategy. In addition to a new typology of the factions, chapter 4 also offers an examination of the formal and informal institutions through which factional competition captures the strategic policy decisionmaking agenda. In Iran, the informal institutions—vehicles through which faction leaders exert influence—convert the formal institutions of government into playing fields for their power competition.

Through the examination of Iran's history, ideology, and structure of resistance a more thorough and nuanced view of Iran's strategic decisionmaking process will emerge. It will become clear that Iran's decisionmaking is characterized by an intricate and multilayered structure of checks and balances—designed redundancy. Designed redundancy serves two key purposes. First, it is designed to obfuscate the decisionmaking process to the outside world to prevent external interference. Second, by dispersing powers throughout the system, designed redundancy works to prevent any one institution or faction from taking over the entire system. Two outcomes of this designed redundancy are consensus decisionmaking and, since consensus is desirable if not necessary in most cases, the ability for key actors to veto. As such, designed redundancy also makes the Iranian system resistant to change, even as its external strategic policies are adaptive.

Consensus, however, can often be easy to derive and maintain, resistant to change, and antithetical to U.S. interests or desires. For example, even those actors Western media outlets refer to as "reformers" strongly defend Iran's right to a peaceful nuclear program, including domestic enrichment. In this case, as in other cases of technological advancement, economic development, and national interests broadly defined, there is widespread agreement among the political elite and often public sentiment supporting it. Part of this is the belief that the United States is an enemy of Iran and is trying to keep it from progressing. Part of it is predicated on an understanding of Iran's historical role as a leader of human rights, mathematics, science, and technology. Thus, Iran's history, too, is a field of contestation, of creating and re-creating national identity, and therefore, strategic interests and policy. History may not be determinative, but it is certainly indicative, which is why chapter 1 is a historical overview.

These two defining characteristics of Iran's strategic policy making—designed redundancy and adaptive resistance—are prominent in Iranian Strategic Influence. Who is driving policy is not always clear to outsiders, and it is not always clear which factions have formed a consensus, or which factions oppose it. It is not always clear, either, whether the forces of change, such as the signing of the Joint Comprehensive Plan of Action (JCPOA, often referred to as the Iran deal or the nuclear deal) were a rapprochement with the West or an adaptation designed to gain more influence for Iran to achieve their revisionist end goals—or both. These uncertainties, although the ideology of the observer may collapse them with a certainty all their own, are very much designed and create disorienting effects. Disorientation, along with narrative building based on myths, activating identities, and mobilizing proxies are the ways in which Strategic Influence works. This work will unpack how Iran is using these Strategic Influence campaigns to achieve their grand strategic end of regional hegemony.

This work defines hegemony in terms of influence, not military or economic domination. Iran seeks to be able to control effects in Iraq and Syria through its proxies as it does in Lebanon through Hizb'allah. They are also actively seeking ways to supply Hizb'allah and establish another front in their war against Israel. These are the strategic objectives that are captured in the term *hegemony* for Iran's near abroad. By knowing how Iran's history, ideology, and structure are used to evoke memories and emotions concerning oppression, resistance, and ultimately triumph the United States will be better able to understand, coopt, deflect, and defeat Iran's strategic influence campaigns and learn from that effort how to deploy similar techniques against near-peers Russia and China.

## WHY IRAN?

From a geopolitical point of view, Iran is an important player both regionally and internationally. Geographically, it borders the vital Persian Gulf, the

Middle East, the Caucasus, Southwest Asia (Afghanistan), and the Central Asian States. Strategically, it competes for control of the vital Strait of Hormuz in the Persian Gulf, through which at the time of this writing 21 percent of the world's oil passes (U.S. Energy Information Administration 2019). Their ideological orientation and discursive practices as well as material support for resistance movements/terror groups keep them at the center of such important dialogues as the Middle East peace process and even U.S.-Venezuelan relations. And, of course, there remains the question of its nuclear ambitions.

Given perceived U.S. interests in the regions where Iran operates, it is difficult to understate the importance of Iran from the point of view of the United States. "Today, the pursuit of U S. interests and the quest for regional stability in Iraq, Afghanistan, the Persian Gulf, the Caspian Sea, and Central Asia-leads in numerous and overlapping paths squarely back to Iran" (Rajaee 2004, 160). The recent signing of the JCPOA and subsequent U.S. withdrawal continue to cast doubt on Iran's ability to integrate into the global economy, and the recent execution of Iran's senior architect of its Middle East strategy has exacerbated tensions between the United States and Iran to a heightened degree. A 2010 report by the Rand Corporation accurately summarizes the Iranian threat in this way: "Iran's regional ambitions and its confrontation with the international community over its nuclear program have made it one of the most pressing foreign policy issues for the United States. After reviewing a range of global threats, the 2006 National Security Strategy of the United States of America warns, 'We may face no greater challenge from a single country than from Iran'" (Thaler et al. 2010, 1). The U.S. withdrawal from the JCPOA may have put the nuclear issues at play yet again. And the Trump administration's emphasis on Iran's malevolent behavior—proxy wars—brought Iran's behavior in Lebanon, Iraq, Syria, and Yemen front and center in U.S.-Iranian relations and international attention. The current National Security Strategy of the United States offers this, "Iran, the world's leading state sponsor of terrorism, has taken advantage of instability to expand its influence through partners and proxies, weapon proliferation, and funding" (2017).

Across decades the U.S.-Iran relationship has been framed in terms of threat and hostility. Further, the U.S. narrative, culminating in the 2017 National Security Strategy, is that Iran is a malignant actor intent on regional instability and antagonism toward the United States. "The power of these frames is tremendous, which is evident in the public discourse on the issues. Very few citizens today know that the first hostile action in U.S.–Iran relations came from the American side or that relations between these countries were not always bad" (Malici and Walker 2017, 5). Is it possible to have a more nuanced view of U.S.-Iran relations, one that recognizes (better, anticipates) certain threats, but does not make cooperation impossible? Clearly, Iran remains an important country with an increasingly important role in important regions; getting Iran "right" means understanding their background, history, and ideology, and it also means looking closely at what their practices are as they expand their influence—one of the purposes of this book.

Yet trying to get U.S.-Iranian relations "right" must also take into account other strategic players such as China, Russia, India, and Turkey (C. G. Cordesman 2011; Wright 2010) and the increasingly important Iranian-Saudi cold war (Wehrey 2009). India imported "705,000 barrels per day (bpd) in May, their highest level since October 2016, according to data from shipping and industry sources, despite the threats of fresh U.S. sanctions" (Verma 2018). Iran's crude exports to India are second only to Saudi Arabia's, and India is careful to balance these relationships. However, after sanctions were put in place by the United Nations Security Council (UNSC) in 2010 India refused to go along with extra sanctions put in place by the United States and its European allies. Initially, India stopped using the Asian Clearing Union to pay for Iranian oil, in an effort to comply with U.S. wishes, but "by September of 2011, India had resumed payments to Iran by using other financial intermediaries" (C. G. Cordesman 2011, 14). Further, India has invested millions of dollars in Iran's Chabahar Port. India has no land route to the Central Asian States (CAS), given the hostile relation with its northern neighbor Pakistan. Chabahar is a port in Southeastern Iran where India ships its goods for transport to the CAS. The importance of this to India's economy was acknowledged by the United States, which exempted India from Iran-related sanctions. India's need for oil and its commercial relationship with Iran are too complex, long-standing, and ingrained to be easily broken.

Turkey and Iran, once great regional rivals, significantly increased trade and military cooperation since the AKP's accession to power and its adoption of the Zero Problems with Neighbors foreign policy approach. Turkey occupies the unique position of being both a regional power and a member of NATO. Its recent decision to host U.S. anti-missile satellite systems complicates its relationship with Iran. Yet, trade between the two countries rose to $10 billion in 2008 and continues to rise (Cordesman 2011, 19) to a target of $30 billion as of 2019 (Karadeniz 2019). In addition, both countries have a growing problem with their Kurdish population, a problem exacerbated by the Syrian civil war, the removal of Saddam Hussein, and the establishment of the Kurdish autonomous region in northern Iraq (Wright 2010, 164). Yet while they have opposing strategic interests in the Syrian civil war and the survival of the Assad regime, they have a mutual interest in defeating the threat posed by the Islamic State of Iraq and the Levant. As of this writing, the United States has announced its withdrawal from Syria, leaving Turkey to finish the fight against ISIL. Turkey has met with Russia and Iran to plan the future of post-ISIL Syria numerous times and has been in open conflict with Iranian proxies in Northern Syria. The level of cooperation between Turkey and Iran is a source of concern to those who would isolate Iran, yet there is significant tension as well. The complications in Turkish-Iranian strategic relations, like Indo-Iranian affairs, afford both opportunities and challenges for U.S. policymakers.

China and Russia are two global actors with long and deep economic, political, and security relations with Iran. As both are permanent members of the UNSC, they often block actions against Iran led by the United States. As major trade partners, they often act to protect Iran, yet they have voted for four rounds of sanctions against Iran in the UNSC. This dual-track approach to Iran was described by China's Foreign Ministry, referring to the most recent round of sanctions, "The Security Council not long ago adopted the 1929 Resolution on the Iranian issue. China believes that the resolution should be earnestly, accurately and fully implemented, instead of being arbitrarily interpreted and expanded" (Cordesman 2011, 15). China is now Iran's largest trading partner, and it imported about 9 percent of its crude oil from Iran in 2015 (Wright 2010, 182). And more recently, "Iran's crude oil and condensate exports averaged 2.5 million b/d in 2017, about 0.2 million b/d higher than the 2016 average. China and India accounted for about 43% of all Iranian exports in 2017, and Turkey and South Korea took substantial volumes during the year" (EIA 2019). Further, China sees the flow of oil from the Middle East as central to its national interest and therefore sees a strategic partnership with Iran as beneficial, not just necessary. Iran and China signed a twenty-five-year strategic partnership agreement to deepen ties in the military, economic, and energy sectors (Erdbrink, 2016; Lt. Col. Davis, 2020).

Russia's cooperation with Iran had gone farther and deeper than China's. Russia is officially opposed to Iran attaining nuclear weapons. Nevertheless, it is Iran's largest arms provider, works closely with Iran with regard to Syria, and is working with Iran and Qatar to develop the Gas Exporting Countries Forum.[2] It is also cooperating with Iran's plans for nuclear energy including fueling Iran's Bushehr nuclear power plant. Further complicating cooperation with the West is the development of an anti-missile shield being deployed in Turkey and Eastern Europe. The stated aim of this shield's deployment is to protect Europe and Israel from Iranian attack, yet Russia sees this as a potential threat and has warned that it will focus its nuclear arsenal against these shields, and threatened withdrawal from the recently signed START deal with the United States (*The Guardian* 2011).

These multifaceted, complex relations often work in Iran's favor as they rely on the national interests of partner countries that contravene the policies of the United States and its allies. Most recently, of course, is the Iranian-Russian cooperation in Syria. While Western media report that Iran and

Russia are working to support Assad, it is more likely that they are leveraging power to be the key decision makers in a post–civil war Syria. Goals would include blocking U.S. influence in Syria for Russia and Iran and keeping the Saudi influence at a minimum for Iran. Nevertheless, mutual interests in Syria and in other areas do not negate a history of confrontation and conflict and a geographic proximity that makes both actors, at the least, wary of each other.

Perhaps more challenging still is the complication of the Iranian-Saudi cold war. This relationship has implications for Yemen, Bahrain, Lebanon, Iraq, Syria, and the Persian Gulf countries, and for the Middle East peace process as well (Wehrey 2009). Both countries see themselves as leaders of the Islamic world and see each other as rivals. Yet, according to findings by RAND, the key driver of their tension is regional hegemony and the role of the United States in the Gulf (Wehrey 2009, xii). According to this view, Iran paints Saudi Arabia as a proxy of the United States and the United States as an imperial, "arrogant" power, suppressing Muslim rights. In this vein, support of Hamas is as much a discursive attack on Saudi Arabia as it is a direct challenge to Israel. In other words, Iran takes on the mantle of the defender of Muslims in the Middle East and accuses Saudi Arabia as being a lackey of the West.

Given Iran's geographical location, its vast energy resources, its strategic partnerships, and its ideological, economic, and military resistance to the West, it is a key player in the three regions it abuts. Further, Iran is very vocal and has support among the Non-Aligned Movement in the UN and has global friendships that buffer it against U.S. sanctions. Brazil continues to trade heavily with Iran. Iran is active in giving aid and establishing trade in Africa as well. For all of these reasons Iran is an important country. Getting Iran "right" is critical to global security and U.S. national interests, yet there is as much misunderstanding concerning Iran as there is agreement about its importance. Without understanding Iranian decisionmaking and the cultural and historical influences that shape this decisionmaking, the perception of Iranian actions that precipitate them, the Iranian reaction to them, continued U.S. sanctions, and the political discourse of some among the West lead to an escalation of tension. Simply put, there is no consensus answer to the following question. "What will be the reaction of the Iranians, who are governed by a cultural code that is not that of America or Britain, to the threat of force?" (Polk 2009, 16)

## A CHALLENGING PUZZLE

Iran remains a challenging puzzle to scholars and practitioners alike. Some hold that this is partly due to Iran's deliberately confusing power structure

(Rakel 2009, 105; Green, Wehrey, and Wolf 2009, 1; Thaler et al. 2010, 74). Others believe that this is because of a tendency of Western observers to try to fit Iran into a simplified, parsimonious, rational model (Ansari 2003, 53; Polk 2009, 206–207; Malici and Walker 2017, 3). In my estimation, both explanations make valid points. Iran's power structure is complex, in part deliberately so, and many of our Western, rationalist, parsimonious models cannot capture the nuances, complexities, or cultural factors that shape Iranian decisionmaking.

However, this is detrimental to all parties concerned. I disagree with Ansari's point that "Iran has been and remains the benefactor of a systematic failure of key Western policymakers to understand it" (Ansari 2003, 53). Rather, this lack of understanding has led to a ratcheting up of rhetoric, sanctions, and an ever-increasing possibility of armed conflict. Further, even the Iranian elite, for whom the above claim might be truer than it is for the average Iranian citizen, suffer the consequences of sanctions and conflict, as members of the Iranian elite are often specifically targeted by sanctions. Understanding the Iranian decisionmaking processes, the key players, and their interactions can help break the impasse that seems to be leading inexorably to conflict, even after the signing of the JCPOA. Why do the Iranian decisionmaking elite continue down the path of confrontation at such a high economic and security cost?

Misunderstanding and misinformation about Iran are prevalent and this confusion is dangerous. "The more that political actors and observers in the United States talk about the Islamic Republic of Iran, the more apparent it becomes that little is known about this uniquely complex polity. . . . [T]he Iranian system is cumbersome, unwieldy, complex, and hard to understand—all of which constitute *an attribute not a flaw*, of the system's design" [Emphasis added.] (Green, Wehrey, and Wolf 2009, 105). From the point of view of many, Iran's complexity is a flaw. But as stated above this is largely driven by a desire for simplicity; Iran's complexity is in large measure a deliberate buffer against internal instability and external enemies. Green et al. are right in seeing this complexity as an attribute and not a flaw, in my estimation.

By making decisionmaking a complex process with multiple inputs from different institutions and actors, the Iranian system is designed to prevent any one actor or group from taking control and dominating strategic policy. And by making each component of the system competitive yet reliant on the other parts of the system Iran has, so far, been successful in buttressing its political system from external shocks. Being able to capture and understand these complexities of the Iranian system is an essential task for scholars and policy practitioners, however difficult it may be. If refashioning our tools, models, and modes of thinking are necessary to achieve this task, then so much the better for it. Although there is widespread consensus on Iran's strategy toward Iraq and even Syria, for example, it is still necessary to understand the history, ideology, and structure of Iran's elite and political culture, particularly if influence strategies are to be designed to counter Iran's growing influence. In fact, this work concludes with examples of Strategic Influence campaigns against Iran and its campaigns in Lebanon, Iraq, and Syria. The example campaigns I propose are general sketches but show how such campaigns rely on Iran's history, ideology, and structure to weaken the Iranian elite's grip on the Iranian people. I also show ways to counter Iran's efforts to use commonalities between their culture and those of their target audiences to further their goals. No successful campaign can be launched without knowing, understanding Iran's history and ideology, but also their complex structure of strategic decisionmaking.

Iran has a unique combination of formal and informal governing institutions. The formal institutions are divided into republican institutions and the religious oversight bodies: the formal republican institutions include the presidency and the parliament, who stand for regular elections, and the formal religious oversight institutions include the Council of Guardians that vets all electoral candidates for revolutionary credentials. The informal institutions include the Bonyads, constitutionally mandated autonomous charitable organizations that report directly to the Supreme Leader and control between 20 and 40 percent of the Iranian economy (Molavi 2006, 176; Polk 2009, 153). The Bazaari, the merchant and commercial class, maintain a great deal of influence throughout the system, but are primarily supportive of factions that work to increase trade. And, of course, there is the vast clerical establishment, including seminaries, mosques, and Friday Prayer Leaders. Often the informal institutions have more power than the formal ones and this makes analysis difficult. "The very informality of the system makes the examination of Iranian decisionmaking exceedingly difficult because back-channeling maneuvering and bargaining are, by nature, hidden from public view" (Thaler et al. 2010, 74).

A further complication occurs because both the formal and informal institutions become sites of contestation for the various factions that dominate Iranian policy formation. Being in a certain position in a formal or informal institution is often the result of being a member of a certain faction. More, the power of the position held is often based upon the person holding that office and upon the factional connections that the person can bring to bear. Because these factions are fluid, with membership moving from faction to faction, with new factions emerging and old factions receding from the powerful elite, "It would be virtually impossible to construct a precise organizational table detailing all the informal networks and their interrelationships—especially difficult from afar, but challenging even from Tehran" (Thaler et al. 2010,

39). While this is a daunting challenge, it is one that is worth attempting in order to understand this complex and important state.

Further, it is important to move away from the idea that Iran is a retrogressive state that seeks to suppress its people and maintain the lifestyle of centuries past that is only true of only some among the elite. Others among the elite and the population see Iran as a progressive state that spends a great deal of its fortune on scientific and technological development. "Since the Islamic revolution, the country has a low illiteracy rate, a high rate of higher-educated people, and, especially, a large number of highly educated women. The younger generation, aware of its personal needs and longings are not afraid to articulate them, is very critical of the Iranian government" (Rakel 2009, 105). This presents an opportunity for the United States to engage in discourse with the Iranian people that I discuss at length in the conclusion.

As Rakel has pointed out, Iran is also the site of competing discourses that often shape the factional alignments. The *velayat-e faqih* (the guardianship of the jurisprudent) ideology, implemented as the official ideology of state by Khomeini, was controversial even then. Khomeini and the adherents of *velayat-e faqih* "understood the concept of the ruling jurisprudent to mean that, in the absence of the Twelfth Imam, the best-qualified Shi'a cleric would wield power" (Buchta 2000, 15). While all the major players today pay homage to the Supreme Leader and his office, the *velayat* concept does not enjoy widespread appeal from the populace and is widely rejected among the clergy, both inside and especially outside Iran.

An ideology of resistance, however, does enjoy widespread support among the Iranian political elite. From its inception, the Islamic Republic of Iran has portrayed itself as a revisionist power intent on breaking the "domination" of the "arrogant" powers in the "Muslim world." Related ideological strains are nationalism; military, technological, and scientific prowess; and, of course, Islamism. Religious ideological currents have long histories in Iran where it is often a unifying force in a nation that is only slightly Persian majority. In contemporary Iran, Islamism is also a contested ideology, as we will see in greater detail below. For some, Islamism is equated with clericalism, for others it has a strong sense of nationalism attached to it, while for others it is universal and perennial, and for some others still it is the roadmap to which democratic governance should look. While it would be erroneous and dangerous to downplay the role of Islamism in Iran, there is also a strong sense of being Iranian that is inculcated. Nationalism and Islamism sometimes conflict. And sometimes they are both used to serve the larger discourse of resistance. In its ideological war with Saudi Arabia, for instance, Iran speaks in pan-Islamic terms, while Saudi Arabia refers to Shi'a Iran. In seeking regional hegemony (if such be its goal) Iran is handicapped by its Shi'a religion and Persian nationality, something Saudi Arabia uses against it. On the other hand, Iran portrays itself as resisting the United States and Israel and supporting others who do so as well (Thaler et al. 2010, 19).

Pragmatism is another strong ideological current in Iran, and it manifests itself in public appeals for tolerance, trading with the world, and finding some accommodation with the West. And, of course, there is the reform-minded democratic ideology that manifested in protests against Ahmadinejad's 2009 reelection. However, in my estimation, it is a mistake to equate these ideological discourses with factions. Within each discourse space there are various factions, and these factions may seek to combine these discourses in unique ways. For example, Ahmadinejad, like most members of the political elite, is an Islamist. Ahmadinejad believes that the Hidden Imam will return from Occultation when the conditions are right and that faithful Muslims must work to create those conditions. He has made it clear that he means an Islam that is universal and powerful. While he is a millennialist Islamist, he is also a nationalist. Thus, he and his then chief-of-staff Esfandiar Rahim Mashaei can speak about Iranian Islam to the dismay of the clerical ruling elite, who speak in terms of pan-Islamism. It is the mixture of the broader discourses that are analyzed below in offering a taxonomy of the factions.

Therefore, to understand Iranian Strategic Influence it is necessary to understand the layers of its strategic context, its formal and informal institutions, its discursive practices, and its factional alignments. Fundamentally, these complex interactions are indeed difficult to map if one is attempting to account for each piece of the puzzle at any point in time, let alone across time. However, strategic contexts, such as the fall of the Taliban and Saddam Hussein and the Syrian Civil War, the U.S. withdrawal from the JCPOA, subsequent sanctions regime, and the execution of Qasem Soleimani, present clear challenges and windows of opportunity that galvanize the Iranian elite. Foregrounding Iran's Strategic Culture by showing the relationship between Iran's History, Ideology, and Structure in strategic context to illuminate Iran's Strategic Influence is the primary motivation of this work.

## STRUCTURE AND USE OF THIS WORK

Chapters 1 to 3 of this book provide context and a broader and deeper understanding of Iran's strategic culture. While each component in chapters 1 to 3 may not be obviously present in the cases I examine after, they are critically important in order to get inside the mind of the decisionmaking elite and therefore vital in any attempts to influence them. Chapter 1 provides historical context. While Persia is an ancient land, the Islamic Republic of Iran began in 1979. This presents a challenge. Continuities exist in some form, and these will be presented. However, given the scope and scale of this work only those continuities and ruptures that are directly applicable to this analysis will be reported. In a more general historical work, it would be possible to delve more deeply into more of the interesting events, advancements, and discourses that shaped Persian and Iranian identities. However, the events, advancements, and discourses reported here are focused on shedding light on contemporary drivers of strategic policy.

Chapters 2 and 3 give the ideological and structural context for contemporary strategic decisionmaking. The discussion of ideology is not meant to be a broad, theoretical approach, but rather a consideration of the notions of resistance that generate policy preferences. This narrow scope, however, covers a great deal of the rhetoric and practice of the Islamic Republic pertinent to the issue areas and regions discussed below. The discussion of structure is essential to understanding how policy is framed, selected, executed, and evaluated. The unique mix of formal and informal institutions, as well as the unique mix of republican and religious institutions brings to sharp relief the idea of designed redundancy. However, it is impossible to understand Iran's decisionmaking without understanding the various and powerful factions that make-up the political elite. Their competition for power produces and disrupts consensus decisionmaking, converts formal institutions of government to fields of contested meaning and power, and reduces strategic policy outcomes, in certain cases, to factional competition.

Since this work focuses on Iran's Strategic Influence it is essential to have a clear understanding of what that term means; this is the subject of chapter 4. Influence can have many varying meanings in different contexts. In marketing versus international security, the term *influence* has not only some commonalities but also differences. This chapter explains my usage of the term *influence*, offering a theoretical underpinning and definition of the term. To achieve this definition of influence I examine Department of Defense doctrine and academic literature. I juxtapose influence to authority and governance and I examine mobilization theory as the immediate objective of influence. I then examine Iran's influence strategy in light of these theories. Chapters 1 to 3 focus on Iran's strategic influence in Lebanon, Iraq, and Syria, respectively. Iran is careful to portray itself, the United States, Daesh, and other actors in consistent ways, generating narratives, and motivating behaviors that align with its strategic objectives. Its use of information is central to achieving proxy mobilization and regional influence.

The book is designed so that it can be read from beginning to end. However, it could also be useful to read the first three chapters and then take on one of the case studies. It could also be fruitful to read the issue areas independently to combine this work with other general studies or research on diplomacy, or proxy warfare, or some related work. My intent is to enable scholars, students, and analysts to read the book for deeper understanding or sections of the book for information. Ultimately, my goal is to inform U.S. policymaking toward Iran and maximize the benefits of the various windows of opportunity that emerge periodically, as well as to inform our policy posture toward Iran more generally. It is my hope that my execution meets my intent.

## Chapter 1

# The History of Resistance

From the great Persian empires of lore, through the 1979 Iranian Revolution, and up to today, the recreation of Iranian national identity through ideological discursive practices has been a defining characteristic of Iranian politics and strategic policy. "A case can be made that in the 20th century Iranians have been afforded, or have produced, more opportunities to recreate themselves in a bombastic and dualistic fashion, energetically vacillating between extremes of contentious Islamism and secularism, pre-Islamic and Islamic imagination, and avid anti-imperialism" (Farhi 2008, 13). This crafting of national identity has been set against a background of foreign influences, invasions, and humiliations: the Greeks under Alexander (early fourth century BCE), the Parthians (third century BCE), the Romans (first century BCE), the Arabs (651), the Turks (1071), the Mongols (1221 and 1258), and, in modern times, the Ottomans, Russia, Great Britain, and the United States. Countering this history of humiliations is the memory of the great empires of Cyrus (549–530 BCE), Darius (522–486 BCE), Xerxes (486–465 BCE), the Sasanians (224–651), and the Safavids (1501–1722).

The mix of religion and politics in Iran, too, has a very long tradition. As early as 230 BCE the Parthians used Zoroastrianism to unify their newly conquered land: "Emphasizing a return to the Zoroastrian religion . . . the Parthians restored the symbols of 'Persia,' its original alphabet and calendar, and brought to the fore what Iran had never before had, a sort of national church, *Mazdaism*" (Polk 2009, 16). Zoroastrianism over the centuries had become so central to the Persian identity that "it certainly had an important impact on Shi'a Islam. In effect, what it did was to allow the Iranians to proclaim themselves true Muslims but to do so in a way that retained their traditional distinction from the Arabs and their more recent distinction from the Ottoman Turks" (Polk 2009, 39). The Safavids used Shi'a Islam as a unifying and identifying discourse in contradistinction to the larger Sunni Ottoman Empire (Polk 2009, 39–41; S. K. Farsoun and Mashayekhi 1992, 59).

The twin discourses of national and religious identity, then, have a long history in Iran. National identity has generally been built on the dual pillars of Persian greatness in military prowess, poetry, art, philosophy, and language on the one hand and fear and suspicion of foreign powers on the other. Religion has been used to unite a people made up of various ethnic and linguistic backgrounds. What the Iranian Revolution of 1979 did most effectively was to unite these two strains through the discourse and structure of the *velayat-e faqih*—the guardianship of the jurisprudent. This theory holds that the Supreme Leader, or *Rahbar*, is acting in place of the Twelfth Imam, who is in occultation and will someday return as a Messiah (Wright 2010, 12). But what the *velayat-e faqih* system, or *nizam,* accomplished in uniting themes of national pride and religion was built upon a long history of resistance.

## THE ORIGINS OF RESISTANCE

Given its geography, Iran has been the land of nomads, invaders, and settlers from various surrounding areas since ancient times. Given its topology, these nomads, invaders, and settlers were able to exist in relative isolation for very long periods of time. Where agriculture was possible many villages and towns sprung up but existed in relative isolation from the rest of the country. There were very few big cities in Iran's early history, and the combination of geography and topology engendered little unity. "Because of the discrete separation of so much of the population, Iran became a patchwork of ethnic, religious, tribal, and other groupings, all of whom seemed to find constant reasons for conflict with their neighbors" (Pollack 2005, 17).

Maintaining cohesion in a multilingual, multiethnic, multi-confessional land is not an easy feat and Iran was no exception; to the contrary, conflicts were arduous and long-standing. It was for this reason that the Parthians used the Zoroastrian religion in an early effort to unite Persia. They were able, through establishing a national religion, to produce a unique Persian identity. This Persian identity, based on common religious practice, language, and culture, took hold to such a degree that subsequent invaders, one after another, adopted Iranian ways, unable to get the Persians to abandon their identity. This was certainly true of the Muslim invaders. "Unlike many other lands of the Islamic empire, Arabic did not entirely supplant Persian as the language of the masses—the elites learned it, but most of the population continued to speak variations of Pahlavi, the Persian tongue of the Sassanids. Moreover, the Muslim conquerors actually adopted a great deal from their Iranian subjects" (Pollack 2005, 21). This was also true of the Seljuk Turks, who conquered Iran in the early twelfth century (Pollack 2005, 21; Polk 2009, 29). This is not to say that the Muslim, Seljuk Turks, and other invaders did not impact Iranian culture through language, art, and, of course, political and military domination; it is to say that the distinctive Persian identity thrived despite the many invasions, some of which were brutal and destructive, adopted some of the invaders' ways, but adapted them so that they were more Persian than not.

Medes, Persians, and Arabs, and other peoples who spoke related languages such as Kurds, Lurs, and Bakhtiari, also invaded and settled across Iran. The Arabs occupied territory along the Persian Gulf from ancient times but by the seventh century CE came as conquerors. Spreading elements of their culture, such as their script and religion, throughout Iran and into Central Asia. Turks and Mongols followed suit in the tenth and eleventh centuries. "The nomadic Turkmens who stayed mainly in the northern parts of Iran and eastern Anatolia . . . formed the basis of the Safavid Empire, but they were not alone. Along the southwestern and southern areas of Iran were various other Turkish-speaking peoples, such as the Qashghai, Khamseh, and Afshar" (Polk 2009, 46). While the Arab invader mostly settled in urban areas, these later invaders remained nomadic largely because so much of Iran was not inhabitable save for nomadism. The various invasions, the semi-hostile terrain, the absence of a central identity or authority, all made Iran divided and vulnerable to further attacks.

But it was the Mongols that brought the most devastation to Iran. "Hulagu Khan, smashed across Iran in 1258 to capture the still-partly Persian Baghdad, killing perhaps 800,000 people and ending the Abbasid caliphate. . . . Most of the famous old cities of Iran were virtually annihilated by attack after attack—Herat, for example, was sacked six times between 1270 and 1319—and in the wake of the armies came famine and pestilence" (Polk 2009, 30). The effects of these invasions across the wide-open central steppes of Iran continue to linger and were only exacerbated by more modern violations of their sovereignty (Polk 2009, 30; Pollack 2005, 22).

In the early sixteenth century one of the great Persian dynasties—the Safavids—rose to power. The Safavids, like the Parthians before them, would bring unity to Iran through religion. That is, while Islam was already the religion of the people of Iran, the Safavids would make it the religion of the state. However, they did so favoring Shi'a over Sunni Islam. They did this for two reasons. First, the Safavid's wanted their empire to be distinct from the Ottoman Sunni Empire to Iran's west. Second, the similarities between Zoroastrianism and Shiism presented a great opportunity to foster national unity. According to Polk, "To judge by the popular literature, festivals, and other habits, the ancient religion of Iran, Zoroastrianism, still deeply colored Iranian culture. . . . In effect, what it did was to allow the Iranians to proclaim themselves true Muslims but to do so in a way that retained their traditional distinction from the Arabs and their more recent distinction from the Ottoman Turks" (2009, 38–39). Thus, when Ismail of the Safavids, conquered the Turkmen capital of Tabriz, he forced the denizens to adopt Shiism (Polk 2009, 39; Pollack 2005, 22).

For the Iranian nation adopting Shiism resonated with Zoroastrianism in two significant ways. First, Zoroastrianism had a practice called "weeping of the Magi," a form of collective memory and mourning over past failures (Rose 2011). That is, one of the central narratives of Zoroastrianism was ritualized into regular practice in order to reinforce national identity. The "weeping of the Magi" carried over into the practice of Ashura, an annual remembrance of the massacre of Husain by the Umayyad dynasty. One of the early divisions in Islam came with the death of its founder Muhammed. Some believed that a family member should succeed him, while others believed that a council of elders should elect his successor, according to tribal custom. Those who believed in family succession supported Ali, a cousin of Muhammed. Ali was passed over, however, and two other men would serve as Caliph before Ali would assume the role. However, Ali was assassinated in office. The Umayyad dynasty was then established. Its first Caliph Yazid I ordered the arrest of Husain, Ali's son, and when he refused to surrender, he, along with seventy companions, was killed; that collective memory is "atoned" for, annually, by Shi'a faithful at the festival of Ashura.

The second significant impact Zoroastrianism had on Shiism is its hierarchical clerical structure. The term *mullah* is fairly familiar to most Western audiences; it is roughly equivalent to a village priest. In the early periods of the Safavid Dynasty most of the population could not read and those men who could were chosen to teach the Qur'an and lead prayers. However, more formal education would gain one the title of Mujtahid, that is, roughly, a professor of the Qur'an, one who could interpret and teach. In time, above a Mujtahid would come the rank of Ayatallah, meaning sign of God, or, even higher, the rank of Grand Ayatallah. A practice would emerge that a Grand Ayatallah would be followed by many other clerics and would be recognized as a Marjah al-Taqlid, that is, as someone worthy of emulation.

It is perhaps one of the greatest ironies in Iranian history that the Shahs empowered the clerics to unite Iran and that clerics would then use that power to take political power away from the Shahs. The hierarchical structure of Shi'ism and its vast organizational reach throughout the country made it both a necessary force to be reckoned with and in some domains even more powerful than the Shahs. That is, since religion was central to the Iranian identity even then, it gave the clerics a pronounced prominence. Along with this prominence was the organizational system of the Mosque, which enabled narrative building through sermons and resource collection and distribution. In time the clerical elite were responsible for education, adjudicating marriage and hereditary law, and even elements of positive law. In other words, they functioned, with recognized authority, in domains the Shahs thought belonged to the state.

This tension between the Shahs and the clerics would be a consistent theme throughout Iranian history from the Safavids onward and would have a significant impact on modern and contemporary religious-political relations. These tensions, of course, would come to a full-blown crisis in the Islamic Revolution of 1979, where the themes of religion, political unity, and resistance would merge. This, of course, would become the ideology that informs their Strategic Influence. That it began under the Safavids as a path toward national unity and contradistinction to other powers is either one of the great ironies of history or the fulfillment of some historical or providential imperative.

## THE MODERN HISTORY OF RESISTANCE

The Qajar dynasty ruled Iran from 1785 to 1925 (Abrahamian 2008, 9). Much of that modern history prefigures contemporary Iranian history, particularly as it pertains to the struggles of the political elite to maintain territorial integrity and national unity and to wrest control from the powerful clerical class. Some of the key issues, such as control of the courts, education, social services, and other functions of a modern state, were controlled by the clerical elite. As Iran entered the modern state system, they attempted to "modernize." These attempts brought them into direct conflict with the powerful clerical elite. It should be noted that while there were significant material interests at stake for the clergy, they secured income from running schools, from seminaries, from religious taxes, and from other services, there was more at stake here than just money. The rhetoric and praxis of "modernity" as myth and narrative were anticlerical. In Iran during the Qajar dynasty, modernity and Islamism were diametrically opposed.

Another factor that pressured the Shahs of this period was the growing merchant class and the external forces of Great Britain and Russia and their economic, political, and occasional military incursions. While the local merchants benefited initially from foreign trade, cash-strapped Shahs often made concessions to powerful foreign nations, leaving the local merchant classes dependent on foreigners. A position the merchant class grew to resent, creating for the Shahs yet another source of resistance to their modernization efforts. Both the merchant and clerical elites would come together to resist the Shah in the great Tobacco Revolt, described below.

Further, the Shahs did not have a strong central military; they relied on tribal contingents and tribal leaders. "These tribes, it was generally agreed, could now easily 'out-gun' the regular army. As Nasser al-Din Shah bemoaned, 'I have neither a proper army nor the ammunition to supply a regular army'" (Abrahamian 2008, 12). Further still, a Shah without the support of the clerics—the *ulama*—could not maintain power, national unity, or domestic peace. Thus, "Shahs found that approval of the *ulama* was often necessary to prevent civil war because military force alone could not legitimate their rule" (Polk 2009, 73). To gain this approval, the Qajars used religious language, adopted religious titles, and "shrouded themselves in a religious aura" (Abrahamian 2008, 15). Therefore, in attempting to unite Iran and legitimate their own authority, Shahs consistently empowered the *ulama*.

The difficulty the Shahs experienced with the *ulama*, however, went deeper than the occasional disagreement over policy. In fact, the operative assumption the *ulama* worked with was that the government was, in fact, illegitimate and corrupt, as any government that is not of God must be. The best any man-made government could hope for was an accommodation with an *ulama* that saw that government as illegitimate. As opposed to Sunni jurisprudence, which acknowledged the legitimacy of government powers, "denial of legitimacy has been an almost equally prominent feature of Imami Shi'a juristic literature. Denial of legitimacy however has only rarely been associated with revolution or rebellion and it may be demonstrated that the Imami jurists were, no less than their Sunni counterparts, concerned to provide, within the structure of the Shari'a, a means of accommodation with defacto powers" (Calder 1982, 3).

The mainstay, as Polk noted, was that the twelfth Imam was the only legitimate ruler and that any other leader was standing in his place. Therefore, the *ulama* were the mediators of the law, interpreting the "rightness" and "wrongness" of laws and policies based on their reading of the Qur'an. The "area of accommodation" (Calder's term) meant that the de facto authority of the state along with the de jure illegitimacy of the state required the mediation of the clerical class. "Further, it was precisely by this ability to register a greater or lesser degree of support to actual rulers that the fuqaha' were able to exercise real influence on governmental policies" (Calder 1982, 6).

But with the rise of the modern state came the need to centralize authority, have more-or-less formal trade and diplomatic relationships with other powers, sometimes greater powers, and the need to defend one's territory and sovereignty. This is part of what drove Qajar Shahs to insist on more power to enforce their rulings and therefore less dependency on the *ulama*. "Because the Shahs refused to acquiesce in this restriction of their role, and as they came to be perceived by the increasingly politically active population as the allies of non-Muslim foreigners who aimed to subvert the country and destroy the faith, they came to be viewed as mere tyrants. This gap between government and the people, led by the *ulama,* went through a series of stages in which the reach of the religious establishment grew, while that of the Shahs declined" (Polk 2009, 74).

The two primary external actors in this drama were Great Britain and Russia. Both were involved in imperial competition—the Great Game for Central Asia and the Sub-Continent (Polk 2009, 78; Abrahamian 2008, 36). Both recognized Iran's strategic location, but neither was focused on Iran, per se. However, "In 1781, Agha Muhammad managed to dislodge the Russians from their foothold on the Iranian Caspian coast and two years later stormed back into the breakaway province of Georgia" (Polk 2009, 78). Some four decades later the Russians thoroughly defeated Iran's forces and imposed the Treaty of Turkmenchay in 1828, which "called for the repatriation of Caucasians, now theoretically Russian citizens, so the head of the Russian treaty supervision mission in Tehran determined to flush them out of Iranian households" (Polk 2009, 79). In response, crowds stormed the Russian enclave and even after being fired upon, continued to kill as many Russians as they could, giving life to a new form of Iranian nationalism.

This fusion of nationalism and religious identity, begun by the Parthians and adopted by the Safavids, was coming into conflict with the needs of the modern state and the need to bring Iran into the modern world. Yet the seeds of this religious-nationalist unity also contained a deep suspicion of foreigners and a jealous protection of the prerogatives of the *ulama*. Whether these forces are inherently antithetical is not, here, the point. That the particular type of religious-nationalist unity that previous dynasties fused was in sharp conflict with how the Qajars, and later the Pahlavis, interpreted the need for modernization and governance is the point. These forces came to a head in the Tobacco Revolt of 1890.

Nasir ad-Din Shah sold a monopoly of the Iranian tobacco trade concession to an English company for £15 million. This brought the merchants who would lose revenue and the *ulama* who were suspicious of the Christian West together in protest against the trade deal. The protests drew a sharp and brutal response from the Shah, including ordering troops to fire on demonstrators and exiling religious leaders. The *ulama* fired back. "A religious order, a fatva, was issued by the supreme authority, the Marja-e Taghlid, making the use of tobacco a mortal sin while the concession was in force and the foreign salesmen were active. All over Iran, the match went out; with one accord, the entire nation gave up its addiction to tobacco" (Polk, 2009, p. 85). The Shah, having no alternative, canceled the concession. This show of force on the part of the *ulama* forced the Shah's hand and exacerbated the economic crisis of the government, which further weakened the Shah and contributed significantly to the Revolution of 1905. "The revolution's long-term causes were rooted in the nineteenth century; its short-term ones were triggered in 1904–05 by an economic crisis brought about by government bankruptcy and spiraling inflation" (Abrahamian 2008). In a familiar pattern, the merchants and *ulama* protested and the government responded with force. And as we saw with the Tobacco Revolt, it was the *ulama* who brought the greatest pressure on the Shahs and forced change.

In June 1906, the *ulama* threatened to go on strike and deprive the Iranian people of religious services. Sayyed Abdallah Behbehani and Sayyed Muhammad Tabatabai organized and led a group of seminary students in a procession to the holy city of Qom. Once there, they were joined by Sheikh Fazlollah Nuri, the other senior mojtahed. "The three threatened to move en masse to Karbala and Najaf, and thus deprive the country of religious services unless the shah dismissed both Naus and the governor, resolved the Kerman crisis, stopped the bank construction, and, most important of all, established an Adalat Khaneh (House of Justice)" (Abrahamian 2008, 1941). On August 5, the Shah signed a proclamation for nationwide elections to elect a Constituent Assembly—the *Majles*. And once again the power of the clerical class led the merchants and others in forcing the Shah to cede power.

But perhaps most significant of all was the oil concession. A few years prior to the Tobacco Revolt a French geologist named Jacques de Morgan discovered the presence of large oil deposits in Iran. He went to William K. d'Arcy, an English entrepreneur who funded further exploration and ultimately contracted another concession from the cash-starved Iranian government. "The original area of the concession was vast—nearly two-thirds of Iran—and was to run for 60 years. D'Arcy's group, which grew into the Anglo-Iranian Oil Company (AIOC), was to pay Iran 16 percent of its net profits" (Polk 2009, 95). It was not until 1912, though, that oil began shipping through the Persian Gulf. This would fuel the British Navy throughout the First World War and bring Iran and Great Britain closer, to the exclusion of Russia.

The Russians were still in Iran, however. In 1920 the Shah, with British prodding, decided to get rid of all the Russian officers. It was there that the British saw Reza, a senior officer of the Iranian army. "The British decided to build the Qazvin contingent into the nucleus of an Iranian security force and began to provide it with arms and training and paid its salaries and expenses. To command it, they picked Reza. With British encouragement, Reza marched on Tehran. There, the British assisted him by preventing the newly formed Swedish-officered gendarmerie (which outnumbered his force about four to one) from opposing him and by 'advising' the Shah to accept his advent as a successful coup d'état" (Polk 2009, 101). Reza Pahlavi ascended the Peacock throne.

While Iran was never colonized by a European power, these military and economic interventions into their domestic affairs were precursors to the neocolonialism we see at play today. Forcing military and economic dependency is the very stuff of colonialism, even if it is done without outright military occupation. For further example, "During the second half of the nineteenth century, Britain and Russia imposed their banks upon Iran and began indirect exploitations by acquiring 'concessions' to collect taxes and to extract and market raw materials and agricultural products, in exchange for an often paltry sum paid to the Qajar Shah's dynasty" (Rostami-Povey 2010, 23). Perhaps it was this that drove the Shah to seek a more distant and neutral sponsor-state.

One interesting development early in Reza's reign was his desire to move away from the British as well as the Russians. He sought an external balancing power. With the defeat of the Germans, he turned to the United States. This would be the beginning of the U.S.–Iranian strategic alliance that would last until the 1979 revolution and be the stuff of animosity for both sides for decades after. But it was another of Reza's moves that may have been a more direct cause. Shah Reza went after the *ulama*. "After using the *ulama* to avoid pressure to establish a republic, Reza not only dropped them from his entourage but embarked on a program to halt all their traditional activities— administration of the law, granting of public charity, and provision of education—from which they received the bulk of their income" (Polk 2009, 104).

Again, there was this imperative of the Shah to forge a modern state, with control of the courts, education, and so on in the hands of the government and not in that of the religious elite. While the Shah was relatively successful early on, he ultimately displeased the British, who deposed him, exiled him to South Africa, and replaced him with his young son Muhammad Reza Pahlavi. Although the Shah took over for his father in 1941, he didn't face his first major challenge until the Mossadeq affair in 1951–1952. At the heart of that matter was the Iranian oil concession to Great Britain. "The figures suggest why: From the beginning of production in 1911 to 1950, Iran received 9 percent of the total value of oil exported while the British government received approximately 36 percent and other (foreign) shareholders about 4 percent. In any given year, Iran never received more than 17 percent of the value of the oil produced from its fields" (Polk 2009, 110).

Mossadeq chaired a committee in the Iranian parliament that recommended the nationalization of the oil industry. The *Majles* seemed to be on the side of the Iranian people while the Shah appeared to be on the side of foreigners. In fact, he was seen as a personification of the Iranian spirit of national pride. "After decades of corrupt rule by the Shahs of the Qajar dynasty and subjugation to foreign powers followed by Reza Shar's authoritarianism and arbitrary rule, Mossadegh was the 'man on horseback' the Iranians had been waiting for. Together with his National Front he defined what Iran desired to be in the post-World War II era" (Malici and Walker 2017, 69). Because of this Polk can say with confidence, "It was the fate of the AIOC [Anglo-Iranian Oil Company] concession that made Mossadegh Iran's first democratically elected prime minister" (2009, 111). The British response to the threat of nationalization was predictable: "they threatened to invade Iran, sanctioned it, boycotted its oil on the world market, and froze its financial assets" (Polk 2009, 113). But when this did not move Iran, they approached the Eisenhower administration and together plotted the coup to overthrow Mossadeq.

Mohammed Reza Shah returned to power, and from that point forward was America's man. He was part of the U.S. strategy to keep the Soviets out of the Middle East and to guarantee the free flow of oil through the Persian Gulf. The Shah felt secure enough in his reign to continue his father's modernization efforts, removing the *ulama* from their roles as judges, teachers, and other key roles that were also their primary means of income. "Muhammad Reza Shah regarded them with a mixture of contempt and fear. He once described to me their leaders, the *mujtahids,* as 'lice-ridden, dirty old men.' But he recognized that the Iranian people revered them as the anchors of their lives—in the accepted phrase, the *marja-e taghlid* ('resource of emulation') in a sea of tempestuous change" (Polk 2009, 119).

His general attitude toward the clergy was intensified toward Grand Ayatallah Ruhollah Khomeini, the future first Supreme Leader of Iran, because of Khomeini's vociferous objection to the Shah. Khomeini was placed under house arrest and was also imprisoned on numerous occasions and was ultimately exiled. But Khomeini's words resonated with the populace and he remained a popular and important figure even in exile. "Khumayni's radical attitude to Islamic law is perhaps best seen in his assumption that divine law represents an effective alternative to constitutionalism or republicanism; and that indeed it excludes these other forms of governmental organisation: divine law precludes human laws . . . Khumayni however did not set out to analyse or write a historical treatise: his purpose was hortatory, to inspire loyalty and to assert an identity; not to investigate differences but to assert unity and solidarity" (Calder 1982, 13).

The Safavids used Shiism to unite a multiethnic and multilingual people. Khomeini appealed to that same unifying force. He also appealed to the notion of collective memory and sacrifice, as well as to the authority of the *ulama*, those twin pillars of Zoroastrianism cum Shiism. "Divine law, Islamic government and just faqih are images which fuse together in an ideal Utopian apocalyptic world" (Calder 1982, 17). Resistance to an illegitimate government was built into Shi'a jurisprudence, which even the Shahs appealed to for national unity. Resistance to outside forces was likewise built into the Iranian national ethos. The organization, authority, and power of the *ulama*, again at times promoted by Shahs, until the modernization campaigns of the Qajars and Pahlavis, enabled them to promote revolution as they had done before. The Revolution of 1979 was a culmination of forces, including powerful religious symbols, collective myths and narratives, as well as power interests that had been at work for centuries. What was new was the implementation of the *velayat-e faqih* system, the governance of the jurisprudent, a system that placed the highest-ranking cleric as Supreme Leader of Iran.

## THE CONTEMPORARY HISTORY OF RESISTANCE

The Islamic Republic of Iran (IRI) is a revolutionary state. This is true in two distinct and important ways. It is certainly true that the ruling elite took power through an armed and popular revolution and established its current system to implement revolutionary ideals. But Iran is also a revolutionary state in the sense that it seeks to disrupt, usurp, and replace the existing international political order. This manifests itself both in the ideology it embraces and broadcasts and in its governmental structures. The ideology and structure of resistance examined below provide important clues as to what motivates Iran's Strategic Influence.

Since it burst upon the international scene in 1979, the IRI had had to face dramatic challenges from within and outside. During most of the 1980s, Iran faced a wave of assassinations intended to weaken or displace the regime (S. K. Farsoun and Mashayekhi 1992, 1). At the same time, it was facing an existential threat in its war with Iraq. It is hard to overestimate the impact that this dual threat, at the very beginning of its political life, had on Iran's leadership. The displacement of the imperial-era elite, the conflicts bred by the revolution, and the harsh crackdown by Khomeini loyalists are among the deep divisions that were not resolved before the Iran-Iraq War. Many of these divisions persisted throughout and after the war and many were exacerbated by it. By the end of the 1980s however, the political elite in Iran had survived the internal attacks with their hold on power consolidated through judicial and extra-judicial executions (Arjomand 2009, 24). They had survived the Iran-Iraq War despite overwhelming odds and Saddam Hussein's support from Saudi Arabia, other Gulf states, and the West.

The 1990s, however, brought fresh challenges. To the east, Iran faced the newly formed and highly radical Taliban. The Taliban, a Salafi fundamentalist group, considered Shi'a Iran apostates and therefore enemies. To the West, Iran faced a hostile Saddam Hussein. On a regional scale, it had to contend with Saudi Arabia, whose wealth and status as keeper of the holiest sites of Islam presented formidable challenges. Additionally, the IRI's support of Hizb'allah and Hamas perpetuated a deep animosity with Israel. Yet another major regional actor who was hostile to Iran was Hosni Mubarak of Egypt. Their relationship soured considerably when Anwar Sadat's assassin was honored in Iran by having a street named after him. Each of these regional rivals was allied, to some degree, with the United States. The United States increased its pressure on Iran during this time, employing tactics such as the sanctions regime started by Clinton, the U.S. military domination of the Gulf with the no-fly zones in Iraq, and a permanent presence of around 20,000 troops in the region by the mid-1990s.

In 2001, the first of these restraints was removed by the U.S. invasion of Afghanistan, which led to the toppling of the Taliban. The second restraint was removed by the U.S. invasion of Iraq in 2003, which led to the toppling of Saddam Hussein's Baathist Party. While clearly unintended consequences, the effect of these U.S. wars was to remove two of the most important regional-systemic constraints from Iran's strategic environment. More recently, the upheavals in North Africa, the so-called Arab Spring, are interpreted by the Iranian elite as further evidence that the tide of public opinion and power is shifting in their direction. "Iran's recent assertiveness is not merely a result of feeling the same type of isolation and sense of siege it experienced during the revolution and the Iran-Iraq War. Rather, it is also due to the fact that Iranian elites and power centers have perceived a changed regional environment that favors Iranian power" (Thaler et al. 2010, 18–19). They are *adapting* to changes in their environment through the deployment of ideological and material resources. As I will demonstrate below, ideological discursive practices and strategic decisionmaking culture are key to understanding the ways in which Iran's Strategic Influence has adapted to this changing landscape.

One of Iran's main strategic goals is to displace U.S. power in the Middle East. To remove this constraint from the strategic landscape, "Iran must first weaken, discredit, and, if possible, humiliate the United States while at the same time successfully promoting its own influence and power as an alternative" (Thaler et al. 2010, 17). That is, to achieve their strategic ends, the IRI must ultimately be focused on weakening America's position in the region, including its standing as regional hegemon. Degrading U.S. power and prestige is essential to Iran's elite because they see themselves locked in an existential battle with the United States. Iran's Supreme Leader remains convinced, as do other members of the elite, that America's genuine goal in imposing sanctions is regime change. Competition with Israel and Saudi Arabia is secondary, as these states, from the Iranian point of view, are proxies of the United States. And as Thaler has pointed out, one of the most important ways that Iran can achieve the goal of defeating the United States in the region is by humiliating it.

Iran claims success against both Israel and the United States through its Lebanese proxy Hizb'allah. In 1983 an attack on a U.S. Marine's barracks killed 241 troops and led to the withdrawal of U.S. troops from Lebanon. Hizb'allah also claimed victory in driving Israel out of Lebanon in May 2000 and again for fighting it to a standstill in their 2006 war. Iran seems to be replicating this model in Iraq and Syria through its support of the Popular Mobilization Forces and other Shi'a militias. Moqtada al-Sadr's group in Iraq was an essential component of the then prime minister Maliki's coalition government and used its veto power to prevent a deal to keep U.S. troops in Iraq after the December 2011 deadline, despite efforts by both Secretaries of Defense Gates and Panetta and Secretary of State Clinton (Wilson 2011; Knights 2011).

To what extent Iranian influence affected these negotiations will probably never be clear, but the IRI claims that they drove the United States out of Iraq just like the way they drove America and Israel out of Lebanon.

They seek through proxies and asymmetric warfare to make the cost of U.S. presence so high that the United States withdraws; the withdrawal is then portrayed as a defeat and humiliation of the "arrogant, hegemonistic" United States at the hands of the resistance. Iran, therefore, funds and arms proxies, and uses its diplomatic resources to create a discourse of U.S. humiliation to lay claim to regional hegemony and to restore its honor by defeating its great nemesis. Moreover, it sees the United States as playing the same game against Iran. "In sum, Iran's perception of itself is shaped by a long history of victory and defeat; it sees itself as a once-great power humbled and humiliated by the West, particularly the United States" (Thaler et al. 2010, 20). This self-perception gave rise to an ideology of resistance, the subject of chapter 2, and a unique political structure, the subject of the subsequent chapter 3.

*Chapter 2*

# The Ideology of Resistance
## *Adaptive Resistance*

Iran has a long history of both glorious empire and achievement, but also persecution and victimization. This collective memory, this shared history, paved the way for the 1979 revolution, although arguably not in quite the way that most participants expected. In addition to Khomeini's charismatic power and the strong organization of the religious institutions, what gave Khomeini impetus was the blending of the religious and nationalist identities that his *velayat-e faqih* system embodied. That is, Khomeini was able to mobilize mass *resistance* through the deployment of historical and national identity myths to build a system of *resistance*. This system was built in *resistance* and for *resistance* clearly, but it was meant to be resistance against more than just the Shah. It was meant to serve as symbolic and actual resistance to others, to the West, especially the United States.

*Resistance* against *Oppression* is the key theme of the IRI's ideology. It predated Khomeini's rise to power and could be found in the writings and lectures of Ali Shariati, a sociologist with strong ties to Western thought. "Among his western intellectual mentors, Shariati was most excited by the writing of Franz Fanon, whose *The Wretched of the Earth* so touched him and his friend that they translated it from French into Persian. It was from Shariati and his friends' translation of the title of this book as *Mostazafin-e Zamin* that Khomeini borrowed his rallying cry in support of the oppressed and dispossessed" (Crooke 2009, 94). But the recognition of *oppression* does not always result in *resistance*. It was Khomeini's charisma and leadership, his exhortation to revolution, and his ability to take the teachings of Shariati and merge them with Shi'a theology to go from mobilization to revolution. "This is the essence of 'political Shi'ism.' It does not represent a formal process; it is not about conversion from one sect to another; and it is not a process linked directly to the Iranian government or managed directly by it. Political

Shi'ism, loosely, is the concept of mobilization and of activist revolutionary ideology mooted by Sayyid Qutb; taken up and adapted by the Najaf nexus; translated into popular mobilization by Shariati; and taken to a revolutionary conclusion by Khomeini" (Crooke 2009, 108).

The revolution in question was not just against the Shah and his political order; it was also a revolution against the United States and its hegemony in the Middle East and beyond. But given America's overwhelming power, resistance had to be adaptive to circumstances, seeking opportunities, and being strategically patient. In the empirical chapters I show how Iran attempts to capitalize on opportunities and how they wait for these opportunities—the essence of strategic patience—all in the name of adaptive *resistance*. Resistance required adaptation to changing circumstances, while maintaining ideological consistency, and waiting for the best opportunities to act. This is what I refer to as adaptive *resistance* in service to the formal ideology of the state the *nizam*—the *velayat-e faqih system*.

## THE *VELAYAT-E FAQIH* SYSTEM

For Iran's first Supreme Leader Grand Ayatallah Ruhollah Khomeini, "The qualifications essential for the ruler derive directly from the nature and form of Islamic government. In addition to general qualifications like intelligence and administrative ability, there are two other essential qualifications: knowledge of the law and justice" (Algar 1981, 49). In his view, then, justice entailed economic justice and freedom from oppression. "Through the political agents they have placed in power over the people, the imperialists have also imposed on us an unjust economic order, and thereby divided our people into two groups: oppressors and oppressed" (Algar 1981, 49).

There are two key points embedded in this quote. First, Khomeini was appealing to a long history of Shi'a jurisprudence. "The potential opposition implicit in the juristic theory of niyaba 'amma was rarely stressed but some kind of modus vivendi was advocated, varying from positive support for the relatively just and tolerant (but still 'illegitimate,' ja'ir/zalim) ruler to dissociation and dissimulation (taqiyya) under the obviously unjust or intolerant ruler (Calder 1982, 5). That is, Khomeini was appealing to a strain of Shi'a theology, though rarely stressed, that warranted opposition to unjust rulers. But Khomeini was not just appealing to theologians, but recalling the theme of oppression that defines the Shi'a identity and warrants resistance. "The events associated with the martyrdom of Imam Husayn are at the heart of Shiite spiritualty and religious culture. Indeed, as the Kufan practice of commemorating the events of Karbala began to spread across the wider Shiite community, so too did the Shiite community begin to form an identity and system of belief that differed from the ruling Sunni majority" (Ostovar 2016, 25). Khomeini's hortatory, therefore, was both theological and populist simultaneously. Further, it is important to bear in mind that Iranian memory of the United States does not begin in 1979; it dates to (at least) the 1952 coup against Prime Minister Mossadeq, who attempted to nationalize the oil industry and was toppled. This led the way to the Shah's resumption of power, suppression of democratic and economic rights as oil was sold to Western interests at a great economic loss to the Iranian people. And it should also be noted that Khomeini was adamantly opposed to the Saudi monarchy for these same reasons, among others.

The *velayat-e faqih* frame appeals to Islam as a unitive discourse, but also as an Islamic-nationalist discourse expressed as a rejection of imperial domination. Khomeini built a power base predicated on religious faith and a long memory of repression. His revolt against the Shah was also a revolt against Western imperialism. This revolt had widespread support, as did the slogans "Death to the Great Satan" and "Neither East nor West," which were manifestations of the deep resentment toward *gharbzadegi*—Westoxification (Boroujerdi 1992, 34). Western culture was seen as ruinous, and, as such, "the majority of both religious and secular Iranian intellectuals have turned toward, nativism, traditionalism and Islamism" (Algar 1981). Further, from its inception, the IRI eschewed a provincial sense of nationalism in favor of a broader Muslim identity—the *umma* and an ideology of *resistance*. "Shia beliefs and mythologies form important foundations of the Islamic Republic's ideology. Its historical sense of grievance, for example, is heavily influenced by Khomeini's interpretation of the Shia as dispossessed, betrayed, and humiliated by the powerful and corrupt. Islam becomes a tool of resistance; it is, as Khomeini often argued, the champion of all oppressed people" (Juneau 2015, 89).

Note the necessary and foundational correlation between this anti-Western religious-nationalist theme and the theme of resistance. If the United States is the Great Satan, then *resistance* is the religious/civic duty of every able-bodied member of the *umma*. The Revolution, predicated on the *velayat-e faqih* religious-nationalist discourse, "greatly influenced Iran's strategic culture and identity by formalizing its sense of victimization while introducing a radical Shi'a ideology of *moqavamat* [resistance] against *zolm* [injustice] . . . Iran's leaders proudly viewed their revolution as belonging to the entire world—or at a minimum, to the entire Islamic world" (Thaler et al. 2010, 13). Juneau makes the point that a state that has been humiliated and oppressed does not necessarily have to choose resistance; in fact, only a few do so. Further, it does not necessarily follow that resistance needs be violent; rather it could be a peaceful resistance. The difference, according to this view, is the regime's identity. For Iran, "This identity is rejectionist: Iran is a limited-aims revisionist rejecting the U.S.-dominated status quo. Revolutionary Iran has built its identity as the champion of the resistance to, and rejection of, the U.S.-dominated order" (Juneau 2015, 85). Thus, the *velayat-e faqih* became a political-cultural-ideological frame and continues to shape policy-making in substantial ways.

The *velayat-e faqih* ideology, implemented by Khomeini as the official ideology of state in the 1979 Islamic Revolution, was controversial even then. Khomeini and the adherents of *velayat-e faqih* "understood the concept of the ruling jurisprudent to mean that, in the absence of the Twelfth Imam, the best-qualified Shi'i cleric would wield power" (Buchta 2000, 15). While all the major players today pay homage to the Supreme Leader and his office, the *velayat-faqih* concept does not enjoy widespread appeal from the populace and is widely rejected among the clergy, both within and outside Iran. An ideology of resistance, however, does enjoy widespread support among the Iranian political elite. From its inception, the IRI has portrayed itself as a revisionist power intent on breaking the "domination" of the "arrogant" powers in the "Muslim world."

Related ideological strains are nationalism; military, technological and scientific prowess; and, of course, Islamism. Religious ideological currents have long histories in Iran where it is often a unifying force in a nation that is only slightly Persian majority. In contemporary Iran, Islamism is also a contested ideology. For some, Islamism is equated with clericalism, for others it has a strong sense of nationalism attached to it, while for others it is universal and perennial, and for some others still it is the roadmap to which democratic governance should look. While it would be erroneous and dangerous to downplay the role of Islamism in Iran, there is also a strong sense of national identity. Nationalism and Islamism sometimes conflict. And sometimes they are both used to serve the larger discourse of resistance. In its ideological war with Saudi Arabia, for instance, Iran speaks in pan-Islamic terms, while Saudi Arabia refers to Shi'a Iran. In seeking regional hegemony (if such be its goal) Iran is handicapped by its Shi'a religion and Persian nationality, something Saudi Arabia uses against it. On the other hand, Iran portrays itself as resisting the United States and Israel and supporting others who do so as well (Thaler et al. 2010, 19).

Below I offer a new taxonomy of the factions, based on their ideological dispositions predicated on the *velayat-e faqih* system. All members of the elite, all elected officials, must publicly support the *nizam*. However, different factions have different ways of interpreting the system based on their ideology. Thus, even pragmatic factions, like the expediency faction, have to frame their rhetoric in terms of the system and resistance. They speak about openness to the West, while simultaneously speaking about resisting Western dominance. These ideological practices as frames, discourses, and myths help organize the factional taxonomy I offer and will help demonstrate a major part of the motivation behind Iranian Strategic Influence. Therefore, before I delve into the factions and their orientations, I will first explain the theoretical frame I used to conduct this analysis.

## THE FACTIONS

Why is a book about Iran's foreign policy—specifically its Strategic Influence policy in its near abroad—going into Iran's domestic political processes, its ideology, factionalism, and the structure of its political elite? Iran's history and ideology motivate and provide content for their Strategic Influence campaigns. They rely on shared histories of *oppression* and ideologies of *resistance* to achieve success in their near abroad. However, to understand how they do so and how to counter their strategies it is absolutely essential to understand their makeup, the competing forces within their elite, and the structure they seek to export. One need not be a neoclassical realist to agree with Juneau that "to better understand foreign policy, one must take domestic factors into consideration" (Juneau 2015, 4). But more specific to this work, "Students of Iran have long recognized the impact of domestic politics on the country's foreign policy. Factional politics on their own, however, cannot account for broad foreign policy trajectories. It is Iran's rising power that shapes the country's behavior: benefiting from a window of opportunity, Iran assertively sought to seize the openings it faced" (Juneau 2015, 92).

All of the politically relevant factions in Iran adhere, at least publicly, to the *nizam*; public disavowal of the governance of the jurisprudent would result in a disqualification from public office and an eviction from the power elite. Further, it is an open question as to whether reform movements in Iran intend the same thing as Western scholars and practitioners do when they deploy terms such as *democracy, representation,* and *openness*. In attempting to understand the factions in practice, it is advisable to view them in terms of their leaders, their alignments with and against others, and their discursive practices. It is essential to keep in mind that these factions, their alignments, and their discursive practices are fluid. In other words, it is best to be guided by the empirical evidence within specific time bounds. However, the themes that bind and divide these various factions are persistent.

For example, both Thaler et al. and Rakel accept the conservative/reformer divide as a way of organizing the factions in Iran.[1] This is problematic from both historical and practical perspectives. Historically, the content of meaning of these terms change. "Since the start of the twentieth century, the boundaries between conservative and liberal-democratic Islam in Iran and beyond have been in a state of constant flux, buffeted by social, political and economic winds" (Rostami-Povey 2010, 41). Practically speaking, a look at the principlist faction belies this simple categorization. The principlists are considered among the more powerful of the "conservative" factions. Former president Ahmadinejad attempted to loosen restraints on dress codes and other symbols of clerical rule. The term "conservative" when referring to Iranian politics is not commensurate with relaxing Islamic dress codes. This results in a serious classification error. Is Ahmadinejad a conservative or a reformer? The politics on the ground simply do not fit neatly into these imposed categories. Ahmadinejad is certainly an Islamist, but he is not a clericalist as the *Velayat* system demands. Because of this, some of the principlists distanced themselves from Ahmadinejad's allies and joined in the chorus calling his group "deviants" (Aramesh 2011). The term *deviant* is used to mean straying from the path, but is also meant to insult, humiliate.

But from what are the "deviants" accused of straying? Because *velayat-e faqih* remains the central ideological tenet of the IRI, attempts to move away from clerical rule is deviation to a high degree. Here is another example from the Ahmadinejad period. "For some time now, opponents of President Ahmadinejad have been referring to Esfandiar Rahim-Mashaie, the president's Chief of Staff, and his close associates as the 'deviant faction' because conservatives and principlists believe that Mashaei and his men[2] have deviated from the principles of the conservative movement, such as a strong commitment to Velayat Faqih and clerical Islam" (Aramesh 2011). Seemingly opposed to the central ideological system among the political elite, the so-called deviants have earned the ire of the clerical establishment, the Revolutionary Guard, and even other principlists. This is particularly interesting for Iran watchers because a significant majority of clerics have never adhered to the *velayat-e faqih* system. The majority of clerics are Quietists; they see the role of the clerical establishment as guiding and advising, not ruling and governing. Yet, Ahmadinejad's faction, by attacking the clerical establishment, pushed them toward the anti-deviant coalition.

On November 18, 2011, the principlists held a gathering attended by tens of thousands of supporters. While the meeting was primarily about fostering unity in anticipation of the upcoming parliamentary elections, the principlists felt the need to distance themselves from this "deviant" current. The spokesman for the group, Ali Akbar Velayati, personal adviser to the Supreme Leader on foreign policy issues and member of the Expediency Council and the Supreme Council of the Cultural Revolution, said the principlists wanted "true principlists and those who are 'loyal' to the system and the revolution [to] take control of the parliament" (MEHR News 2011). To emphasize the point, the motto of the gathering was "wisdom and unity under the umbrella of velayat" (MEHR News 2011).

Until the *velayat-e faqih* system is supplanted, it is a logical place to start in describing the factional politics that shape and are shaped by ideological practices. The *nizam* instantiates the duality of Islamic governance and an expanded notion of nationalism—a dual discourse with a long history in Iran. "Iranian identity is bifurcated, split between the pre-Islamic traditions of Zoroastrianism and Manichean millennium before Islam, and the Islam-influenced developments of the last 1,300 years" (Milani 2010). The *nizam* is also predicated on republicanism—representative government. What we see in the factional alignments in Iran today are groupings that stress one of these three features of the *velayat-e faqih* system. As such, the logical re-categorization that I use here, using the official name of Iran thematically, groups the factional types as Islamist (primarily, but not exclusively clericalist), Republican, and Nationalist—the Islamic Republic of Iran.

The Islamists are the most powerful of the three types and also come in different varieties. The strongest current of Islamism in Iran today is clerical. Clerical Islamist thinking is heavily dependent on the *Velayat* system as it gives them their raison d'etre. There are Islamists who blend some of the nationalist discourse with the Islamist discourse and seek a more active international role and opposition to the West. There are Islamists who seek a more modified approach intended to increase trade and dialogue with the West, but still maintaining the current system. And there are those who see spreading the Revolution as an Islamic duty. There is wide agreement that the domestic and social policies that are in place are largely to be left in place. They are mostly in agreement that the republican institutions are in place to affect the policies that the ruling clerics have identified as in the strategic interests of the IRI, although one faction among the clerical Islamists maintains that the Republican institutions should be dismantled (Laura Secor 2007; Daniel Brumberg 2010). They compete with the nationalists for the support among the poor, the rural, and the bureaucracy, and through control of such informal institutions as the Society of Seminary Teachers of Qom, the Friday Prayer Leaders, and the Haghani Circle they attempt to unify the clerical establishment and society. As we saw in the historical summary above, the religious elite seek to maintain their control over education, social mores on marriage, hereditary rights, and charities. As typifications, these three currents are not precisely the factions that one sees in operation, but they do represent, in broad strokes, the ideological discourses to which they appeal, each appealing to segments of the population and rooted in the *velayat-e faqih* system.

In Iran, even the Republicans (sometimes referred to in the West as reformers) are often clerics, such as former president Khatami, and current president Rouhani (who is often called a reformer). But this does not mean that they are clericalist; rather, they prefer a more democratic, representative form of government within the *Velayat* system. However, those who stress the importance of the republican institutions and the democratic process, be they clerics or not, have a different vision for Iran, deploy different discourses, and appeal to different segments of the population. In addition to the obvious elevation of the democratic process over clerical or autocratic rule, they favor more openness to the West, a looser interpretation of Islamic dress code, and greater economic liberty, although with strong socialist principles. There is a natural constituency for this approach among the more educated and urban populations, and the vast Iranian diaspora in Europe and the United States.

Nationalism appeals to broad segments of the population, even to some who favor the republican ideology. The principal difference is that nationalists are not necessarily tied to the democratic process, greater openness to the West, or greater freedoms economically, although these issues form an important divide among nationalists. Generally, this ideological current seeks a strong central government, control of the economy to achieve nationalist ends, often utilizes strong anti-Western rhetoric, and is predicated, in large measure, on the idea that Iran/Persia has a long and glorious history which gives Iran the right and the responsibility to be a regional and even global power. Its tendency is to be autocratic, to appeal to the military, the Pasdaran (the Revolutionary Guard), and Basij forces, and through redistributive policies (using oil wealth) to the poor, the rural populations, and the bureaucratic cadre of middle managers that run the government. Further, they tend to stress good governance and strong management skills.

**Islamists**

The *Principlists* are the largest and most influential Islamist-clericalist faction in Iran today. They organized the United Principlist Front as a vehicle for fielding candidates for the Majlis election, held in March 2012 and secured a majority of seats. In the February 2016 Majlis election the Principlists lost their majority retaining only 80 seats out of the 290-seat body. Interestingly, the non-principlist factions joined together to form a coalition called the "List of Hope." The coalition brought together Green Party movement leader former president Ayatallah Khatami, current president Rouhani, and parliament speaker Ali Larijani. This coalition marks a significant shift, as it indicates a united front against the principlists who named their coalition "Principlists Grand Coalition." The Principlists also lost their outright majority in the Assembly of Experts, the body that selects the Supreme Leader. That body has a total of eighty-eight seats and is directly elected by the people by region. Of the eighty-eight seats the List of Hope coalition won fifty-nine seats; however, many of those were clerics supported by the Principlist faction as well (Majlis Monitor 2016). The Principlists enjoy the support of the Supreme Leader. They also have the support of two of the most important nongovernmental institutions—the Association of Combatant Clergy and the Society of Seminary Teachers of Qom. The principlists enjoy support from the Pasdaran as well. The Pasdaran is certainly not monolithic in worldview or interests, but they tend to support various principlist factions (Thaler et al. 2010, 69).

As noted previously, the principlists have joined other Islamist factions to marginalize Ahmadinejad and his followers as "deviants" because of their perceived attacks on the clerical establishment. "Mahdavi-Kani, the 77-year-old [then] head of the Society of Militant Clergy, member of the Assembly of Experts, and traditional conservative icon, has supported principlist figures opposed to the Ahmadinejad administration. Mahdavi-Kani has strongly criticized Ahmadinejad for his handling of the economy and has asked Ahmadinejad 'not to presume the clergy . . . [are] tools' or 'attempt to undermine the status of the clergy and elders'" (Thaler et al. 2010, 72). While Ahmadinejad has not been in office since 2013, he remains an important national figure and his faction continues to attract adherents. In the run-up to the 2017 president election, Ahmadinejad declared his intention to run again, only to be rebuked by the Supreme Leader.

While most of the powerful clerics are principlists and tied closely to the Supreme Leader, *the Expedients,* formerly led by Ayatallah Ali Akbar Hashemi Rafsanjani, is a different type of Islamist faction. Rafsanjani who passed away in 2016 at age eighty-two was a confidante of Khomeini, and was instrumental in securing the Supreme Leader position for Khamenei. He served as speaker of the Majlis (1980–1989), president (1989–1997), head of the Assembly of Experts until his ouster in 2011, was a member of the Council of Guardians, and was the head of the Expediency Council. During his presidency, Rafsanjani was known to be a proponent for clerical rule, free trade, and using coercive means against dissenters. He was often described as the richest man in Iran.

Like many of the other Ayatallahs in the leadership, Rafsanjani, an Islamist and clericalist, enjoyed a powerful base of his own. He had a vast network of patronage due to his various positions and wealth. His policy preference for some openness to the West is predicated on commercial interests and access to technological advancement. Despite his use of force against protesters during his presidency, he openly criticized the Ahmadinejad administration for doing the same. Rafsanjani and Ahmadinejad were bitter rivals and their battles have been public and have involved the Supreme Leader. Despite major setbacks caused by his battles with Ahmadinejad, Rafsanjani remained a powerful figure with many followers until his death. The decline of Ahmadinejad helped Rafsanjani regain some lost ground, and this enabled him to work with reformers and others to promote one of his faction members to prominence—President Rouhani. Prior to his election as president,

Rouhani ran the Center for Strategic Research, a Rafsanjani think tank. Rouhani's election to president is a great boon to the Rafsanjani faction (of which he may now be the head) as was (seemingly) the recent signing of the JCPOA. The Expedients enjoy support among the *Bazaari* merchant class, some students, the urban middle classes, and technocrats.

I refer to Rouhani and his faction as Expedients to distinguish between a new and rising faction, which I refer to as the *Pragmatists*. As of 2010 when Thaler et al. reviewed the factional alignments of the Iranian political elite, the most recent analysis prior to this one, the Larijani brothers were seen as supportive of the principlist camp and with friendly relations with Rafsanjani. However, events since then indicate that the Larijani brothers are a new faction with intentions to compete for status and power; they too are Islamist and clericalist. Ali Larijani is currently the speaker of the Majlis. He has also served as chief nuclear negotiator with the IAEA, secretary of the Supreme National Security Council, Head of the Islamic Republic of Iran Broadcasting (an appointment made by the Supreme Leader), and is a former Pasdaran member. Like Ahmadinejad and Qalibaf, former mayor of Tehran, men in their fifties and representative of the veterans of the Iran-Iraq war, he has strong revolutionary credentials and an impressive résumé. His brother Ayatallah Sadeq Larijani served as head of the Judiciary.

The Larijanis are close to the Supreme Leader and are supportive of the *velayat-e faqih* system and its concomitant clerical rule. They have great wealth and like Rafsanjani have a broad base of support among the *Bazaari*. They also have support from some elements of the Pasdaran. However, they seem to have a great deal of support from the clerical establishment as well. Part of what has made them such a force in recent events is that they have been at the forefront of the pushback against Ahmadinejad and Mashaie's brand of millennial-nationalism. Further, the Larijanis enjoy support among the educated urban middle class and students. Dr. Larijani is author of four books on Immanuel Kant.

## The Republicans

The *Republican* groups, often referred to as reformers, include the important Association of Combatant Clerics (not to be confused with the Association of Combatant Clergy), the Islamic Iran Participation Front (IIPF), and the Mojahedin of the Islamic Revolution Organization (MIRO); these groups and others have come together to form the Green Movement. Key members of the Association of Combatant Clerics are Hojjat-el Islam Seyed Mohammad Khatami, former president of Iran (1997–2005) and Ayatallah Mehdi Karoobi, former chairman of the Majlis (1989–1992 and again 2000–2004) and presidential candidate in 2005 and 2009. IIPF's secretary general is

Mohsen Mir-Damadi and one of its founders was Mohammad Reza Khatami, brother of the former president. MIRO is headed by Mohammad Salamati and has a socialist economic platform coupled with a democratic process political platform. These groups united under the candidacy of Mir Hossein Mousavi in the 2009 presidential election and in the subsequent protests known as the Green Movement.

Mousavi, former prime minister (1981–1989, the position was abolished with the constitutional reform of 1989) also served as Foreign Minister (1981) and was one of the architects of the 1979 Revolution. Mousavi was supported by Khomeini in his prime ministership against the wishes of the then president Khamenei, the current Supreme Leader. After Khomeini's death, Mousavi fell out of favor with both Khamenei and Rafsanjani and withdrew from politics, outside of being an adviser to Khatami during his presidency. Both Mousavi and Khatami have repeatedly stated that Iran's right to nuclear technology is non-negotiable, but that it has no intention of developing weapons. This is the official position of the government of Iran and is often articulated by the Supreme Leader.

What the republican-leaning groups seek is openness to the West in terms of political dialogue and economic relations. Khatami famously created the initiative known as the "Dialogue Among Civilizations" seeking normalization of relations with the West and expansion of ties with other countries as well. Just as famously, U.S. president George W. Bush's inclusion of Iran in the axis of evil weakened Khatami's outreach and humiliated him before the inner-circle political elite. Bush's inclusion of Iran in the axis of evil, precisely as Khatami was arguing for greater outreach to Washington and the West, exacerbated tensions between the republican factions and the principlists who saw Khatami as weak and humiliating Iran in the eyes of its mortal enemy, the United States.

Where the republican-leaning factions run into the greatest difficulty with the Islamists is in their views of social policy. Republicans generally favor a more open social environment, a greater role for women in politics and society, and a relaxation of the religious laws that affect daily life. In 2009, the principlists and other factions united to defeat the Republicans and have since subsequently blocked them from access to the power elite. Mousavi remains under house arrest and the Green Movement appears to have either dissipated or merely gone underground—that only time will tell. The Supreme Leader's approval of Rouhani was in part an effort to get the Republican factions more securely in the system.

## The Nationalists

Abadgaran, a fairly new coalition organized in 2002, largely comprised former Pasdaran members, and is one of the more important of the Nationalist groups. Its full name is the Developers of Islamic Iran (*abadgaran-e Iran-e eslami*); this partly captures its commitment to Islam as well as its engineering and management expertise, and also its economic ties to the Pasdaran's various construction and engineering projects. Many of its members have mid- to senior-level positions in the bureaucracy. Ahmadinejad was closely associated with this faction, which is headed by Emad Afroogh and Gholam Adel. Both Afroogh and Adel are members of the Majlis. Adel's daughter is married to Supreme Leader Khamenei's son, Mojtaba. Adel moved his allegiance from Ahmadinejad to the principlist camp, movement consistent with Ahmadinejad's fall from favor with the Supreme Leader and other status-bearing elite. However, Abadgaran remains a potent force, even if no longer an independent faction. They are nationalists in that they place Iranian history and Iranian security at the forefront of their policies. As we have seen, the "key ideas singular to Shiism in the Islamic world—like the concept of a messiah (Mahdi), and millenarian optimism—are in fact a reincarnation of pre-Islamic Iranian ideas and concepts drawn from Zoroastrianism and Manichean philosophies" (Milani 2011).

The 1979 Revolution attempted to eradicate the pre-Islamic history from memory, but to no avail. Therefore, Ahmadinejad's and Mashaei's pleas to recall the national greatness of pre-Islamic Iran, including praising Cyrus, have angered the clergy and have been seen as "something akin to sedition" (Milani 2011). What is worse from the perspective of hardline clerics is the reference to Iranian Islam. "In the first days of the Islamic revolution, key clerical figures in the regime, particularly the infamous Khalkhali—a favorite disciple of Khomeini, who appointed him head of the revolutionary courts— went on to call Cyrus a 'Jew boy' and a 'sodomite.' Meanwhile, in spite of an increasingly louder chorus of critics, some from the highest echelons of clerical power in Iran, Mashaei continued to wax eloquent about Cyrus, Iranian nationalism, and Iranian Islam" (Milani 2011).

Nationalistic claims gain wide support among the populace, particularly when coupled with populist slogans and redistribution. Further, the clerical regime is not particularly popular and the *velayat-e faqih* system, while still dominant in the political system, remains widely unpopular among the people, as well as most clerics. For this reason, the clerical establishment, those who benefit the most from the *nizam* and those who do not support the *Velayat* system, see this brand of nationalism as a direct threat. Chief among them is the Supreme Leader; his turning away from Ahmadinejad has opened the floodgates of criticism and attacks that led to Ahmadinejad's fall.

Another powerful leader in the nationalist camp is the former mayor of Tehran, Mohammad Baqer Qalibaf, who ran for president against Ahmadinejad in 2005, and heads a group of technocratic young nationalists (with ties to the principlist camp), which is made up of former Pasdaran officers.

General Ezzatollah Zargami is head of the very powerful Islamic Republic of Iran Broadcasting and a member of the Supreme Council of the Cultural Revolution, General Mohammad Bager Zolqadr is Deputy Chairman of the Supreme National Security Council, and both men are supporters of Qalibaf.

Qalibaf, like many others in his growing cadre of followers, is a former Pasdaran officer, served in the Iran-Iraq war, is in his fifties, and is moving from positions of executing policy to positions of determining policy. This rising group of former officers are protective of the revolutionary mission of Iran, but are also practical managers and are cautiously interested in opening Iran to the West, primarily for economic reasons (Hourcade 2008). As opposed to Ahmadinejad's group, their version of nationalism is not necessarily hostile to the clerical elite; for instance, they maintain loyalty to the Supreme Leader but do want a change in the way Iran deals with the outside world. Indeed, part of the criticism against Ahmadinejad is that his rhetoric is harmful to Iran not only with the West but regionally as well (Hourcade 2008). The revolutionary credentials that come from fighting the Iran-Iraq war, being loyal to the Supreme Leader, and the rising power of these young nationalists make them a powerful force for the near future.

Factions deploy ideological discursive practices to win support among the people and to recruit among the elite. They also do so to define the strategic landscape and dominate the political discourse. This is clearly so in the case of their nuclear program. Even where there was large-scale agreement among the elite on the nuclear program, enrichment should occur in Iran, it is Iran's right to enrich and develop nuclear technology, Iran should enjoy all the rights that attend being a signatory to the Nuclear Non-Proliferation Treaty, and so on, there was factional competition on the details of the Paris Agreement of 2004 and the 2009 Geneva Accord, such that both deals were scuttled (Rivera 2016).

However, factional competition is not only based on discursive practices but also the use of official power. As such, the faction leaders seek to get their members appointed to key positions and in doing so attempt to capture the policy-making structure. However, given the complexity—designed redundancy—of Iran's strategic decisionmaking structure, this is a very difficult thing to accomplish. That structure, which I refer to as Designed Redundancy, is the subject of the next chapter. As Iran competes for Strategic Influence across the Middle East there is often deployment of these discursive practices, appeals to common history, common religious experience, the need for technological and military prowess, and the competition between religious conservatism and relaxed social mores. These resonate because of local conditions in Lebanon, Iraq, and Syria more so than because of Iran's experience, but they are ripe for Iranian influence. Where there is greater similarity in the way Iran builds up its proxies both militarily and politically.

*Chapter 3*

# The Structure of Resistance
## Designed Redundancy

The broader discourses that are rooted in the cultural frame of the *velayat-e faqih* system, while inculcating a strong sense of resistance against the West and a strong Islamist-Nationalist ideological identity as a reflection of Iran's history, provide constraints and opportunities to factional rivalries but were also instrumental in the construction of the Iranian constitution and the structure of the government. Institutionally, what emanated from these ideas was a mix of republican and religious bodies responsible for policy formation and oversight. Thus, the Iranian system has formal republican institutions such as an elected presidency, parliament, and a constitutionally independent judiciary, which are, however, subject to religious oversight by the Guardian Council, which vets all candidates for office for revolutionary bona fides, for example.

However, since the *velayat-e faqih* system places the *Rahbar*, the Leader, as the highest authority, it is often the informal groupings that form around him that are more relevant to policy formation than the actual positions in government (Rakel 2009; Thaler et al. 2010; Green, Wehrey, and Wolf 2009). Thus, the system, in addition to fostering competition between the republican and religious formal institutions also fosters competition between the informal groupings surrounding key players among the elite—factions. Further, Iran's factional system requires consensus decisionmaking because the power to innovate is weak but the power to block innovation is strong (Thaler et al. 2010, 38).

Designed redundancy as a characteristic of Iran's strategic policy structure is manifest in three distinct features that renders it, in its totality, a unique political system. First, there is a mix of formal and informal institutions that influence policy preferences as each institution can potentially wield a veto or play spoiler. The remainder of this section uses this first divide as an organizing principle. The second feature, also represented here, is the replication of responsibilities. There is a built-in redundancy to the key security and policy decisionmaking bodies. For example, there is the regular army and then the Revolutionary Guard. There is the Supreme National Security Council and then the Supreme Leader's Council on Foreign Affairs. Some see this as a handicap, others as an evolutionary and adaptive element necessary for Iran's survival. Lastly, it is important to note the duality of the republican institutions and the religious oversight institutions. These three twin features of designed redundancy make Iran's governance system unique, difficult to comprehend, and even more difficult to influence.

## FORMAL INSTITUTIONS

The Supreme Leader is at the heart of this complex system. He appoints the head of the armed forces and six members of the twelve-member Council of Guardians (*Shoraye Neghban*). The other six members are approved by the Majlis (the parliament) from a list of recommendations from the head of the judiciary, who is, himself, appointed by the Supreme Leader. The Guardian Council vets all candidates for any electoral office, including the Assembly of Experts and all legislation. This body is charged with guaranteeing the Islamic revolutionary ideology of the system and providing strong limitations on the democratic process in keeping with the principles of the *velayat-e faqih* (Buchta 2000, 59).

The Assembly of Experts (*Majlis Khebregan*), also chaired by Ayatallah Jannati, comprises eighty-six senior clerics; these seats are geographically allocated. Each candidate for this high office is vetted by the Guardian Council and elected by popular vote to eight-year terms. Ayatallah Ahmad Jannati is also the chairman of the Assembly of Experts. According to Iran's constitution the assembly can remove the Supreme Leader if they find him incompetent. It would also be up to them to select a new Supreme Leader should the current Supreme Leader die, become incapacitated, or is removed from office. As the men who are officially charged with replacing the Supreme Leader, these men are themselves carefully vetted by the Guardian Council on five criteria, they must (1) be faithful, trustworthy, and possess moral integrity; (2) possess enough knowledge of *fiqh* (Islamic Jurisprudence) to recognize those Islamic jurisprudents who fulfill the necessary conditions for assuming the office of leader; (3) possess social and political skills and be familiar with the problems of the day; (4) be loyal to the system of the Islamic Republic of Iran; and (5) not have declared himself politically or socially opposed to the existing order at any time in the past (Buchta 2000, 60–61). In this case, each member is elected by popular vote, but in order to run for office they must meet very strict standards. Here the overlay of religious oversight and democratic governance converge in a clear way.

The presidency functions much like any modern head of government. He is responsible for the day-to-day operations of the government and presides over a cabinet that consists of various ministries. The president is also the chairman of the Supreme National Security Council (SNSC). He is elected, after vetting, for no more than two consecutive four-year terms. The president and the Supreme Leader can be at odds, as was the case with Khatami and his reformist agenda. They can also be simpatico, as was the case with Ahmadinejad, who received public support from Supreme Leader Khamenei immediately after Ahmadinejad's controversial 2009 reelection. However, this does not always mean that the president, even Ahmadinejad, is subservient and without power. "A good example of this is Ahmadinejad's assertion that Iran's nuclear program is a national right. Painting the issue as a fundamental matter of sovereignty and independence makes it difficult for anyone (including Khamenei) to compromise with the international community" (Thaler et al. 2010, 26–27). There was also a great deal of pushback from the Supreme Leader against the Joint Comprehensive Plan of Action (the JCPOA, more commonly known as the Iran nuclear deal). Nevertheless, Rouhani successfully negotiated with the five permanent members of the United Nations Security Council (UNSC) and Germany, while positioning the JCPOA well within the ideological framework of Iran. The Supreme Leader ultimately supported the signing of the JCPOA, even if only reluctantly and with reservation.

This reiterates the power of the ideological discourses and factional competition. The successful articulation and deployment of discourses have great power because of the need to be consistent with revolutionary, resistant, and Islamic principles and because of the need for public legitimacy. The president presides over the government through various ministries and officials. However, each of those ministries has an official representative from the Supreme Leader's office whose primary responsibility is ensuring that the Supreme Leader's views are represented and to report back to the Supreme Leader any activity that is not in keeping with those wishes. Here we see a redundancy that is meant to maintain ideological fervor and purity.

The Majlis is Iran's parliamentary body. It consists of 290 members and is chartered to propose legislation, review and approve government budgets, ratify treaties, and provide oversight on the executive branch. There have been ten parliamentary elections since the revolution and one notable trend is the drop of clerical members of the body. The first Majlis had 131 clerics, the 2008 Majlis, dominated by hard-liners, had only 42 (Wright 2010, 21). The 2016 Majlis sets a historical precedent. "After the second round of elections a record 17 women will become lawmakers in the 290-seat parliament—one more than the number of clerics, which has hit an all time low" (AFP 2016). The Speaker as of May 28, 2020, has been Muhammed Bagher Qalibaf, former mayor of Tehran. Every law passed by the Majlis must be reviewed by the Guardian Council for vetting according to the constitution and Islamic principles. The Guardian Council vets Members of Parliament before they run and legislation before it is passed; here the designed redundancy feature of religious oversight is also very clear. Maintaining revolutionary zeal requires oversight and effort.

Recognizing the possibility of governmental paralysis should the Majlis and the Guardian Council not be able to resolve disputes, and the inherent threat this paralysis could pose to the system, Khomeini approved the creation of the Assembly to Discern the Interests of the System (Majma'e Tashkhise Maslehat) as part of the constitutional reform of 1988—the Expediency Council for short. The Expediency Council is a unique institution in that it consists of representatives from both the formal and the informal governance systems. The principal aim is to guarantee the viability of the system by maintaining unity, while resolving conflicts of governance. There are permanent members appointed by the Supreme Leader and temporary members are asked to serve when a particular issue arises in which they have some expertise. The Expediency Council was chaired by Ayatallah Rafsanjani since its inception until his recent passing. The current chair is Sadeq Larijani. The name of the council is revealing, as its mission is to expedite the survival of the system as Islamic resistance. In other words, this is an overt institutional expression of the adaptive resistance that I am attempting to foreground here.

The judiciary in Iran is declared by the constitution to be independent. The head of the judiciary is appointed by the Supreme Leader. Its primary responsibility is the enforcement of Islamic and positive law and it appoints six lay members to the Guardian Council. It should be noted that the other members of the Guardian Council are appointed by the Supreme Leader and this mechanism allows him great influence in the selection of the other six members. While the Supreme Leader appoints the head of the judiciary, the president appoints the minister of justice, subject to Majlis approval. This is yet another designed redundancy between the president and the Supreme Leader, as well as the presidency and the parliament. The minister of justice can investigate crime, but the judiciary prosecutes criminals. In a system where the formal institutions are governed by set rules and procedures this may appear fairly streamlined, but in a system where factions compete for power having one faction control the presidency and another the judiciary produces competition.

The SNSC is chaired by the president and is directly responsible to the Supreme Leader. It has penultimate authority in establishing strategic national security and foreign policy, including cultural, economic, and other matters that may impact national security. "In addition to the president, formal members of the SNSC include the ministers of foreign affairs, interior, and intelligence; the chiefs of the IRGC and Artesh; the heads of the legislative and judicial branches; the Chairman of the Guardian Council, and two personal representatives of the Supreme Leader" (Thaler et al. 2010, 31). Other members are asked to serve when the issue under review pertains to their area of expertise.

However, this does not tell the entire story. In 2006 the Supreme Leader created the Strategic Council on Foreign Relations (SCFR) as an advisory body. It was established "to help global decisionmaking, and to seek new horizons and scopes in foreign relations of the Islamic Republic" (Fulton 2011). According to its first chairman, Kamal Kharrazi, "All foreign relations issues on a strategic level are with the framework of the responsibility of the [SCFR] and it has nothing to do with executive matters" (Fulton 2011). The reaction of the Ahmadinejad administration is also telling. Gholam-Hossein Elham, administration spokesman at the time, "attempted to downplay the significance of the SCFR by telling reporters within twenty-four hours of its creation that the SCFR had 'no executive and practical duties'" (Fulton 2011).

Yet the SCFR is seen as a shadow foreign policy council that conducts diplomatic missions independent of the executive branch. Velayati, former foreign minister for both Khamenei, during the prime ministership of Mousavi, and Rafsanjani, was appointed special adviser to the Supreme Leader when incoming president Mohammad Khatami replaced him. During Rafsanjani's presidency, Velayati's loyalty to Khamenei was a source of friction (Fulton 2011). Today, Velayati serves on the SCFR and often conducts diplomatic missions on behalf of the Supreme Leader.

The designed redundancy of the strategic policy structure of Iran as a manifestation of the *velayat-e faqih* system produces a complex system of republican institutions that are overseen by religious authorities. For example, the popularly elected members of the Majlis must have their legislation approved by the Guardian Council. However, to ensure that deadlock doesn't ensue, there is the Expediency Council to arbitrate. On the one hand, there is the regular army—the Artesh. On the other hand, there is the Revolutionary Guard—the Pasdaran. On the one hand, there is the bureaucracy that supposedly is responsive to the president and his ministers. On the other hand, there is the vast army of "advisers" that the Supreme Leader dispatches to these ministries to affect his will or report on deviance from the system. The *nizam* guarantees the ultimate authority of the Supreme Leader. This is entrenched in the 1979 constitution. It is enacted through the religious supervisory bodies of the Guardian and Expediency councils

(Rakel 2009, 109). And it is evidenced in the Supreme Leader's ability to weaken presidential authority. That is, the Supreme Leader as the ultimate authority has yet to be effectively challenged within Iran. Both Presidents Khatami and Ahmadinejad have attempted to institute reforms (from decidedly different political perspectives) only to be stymied by the power of the Supreme Leader.

The system is designed so that "multiple institutions that perform identical or similar functions—and therefore compete with each other for resources and status—has generated a diffuse and complicated system. In theory, this multifarious, redundant design prevents any one center of power from gaining undue influence over the entire system and ensures the overall survival and security of the regime and the central position of the Supreme Leader" (Thaler et al. 2010, 21). The Supreme Leader distributes resources and status and, as such, prevents any one institution, individual, or faction from dominating the system. With regard to strategic policy this is especially true as the Supreme Leader has the power to declare war, to mobilize troops, and to dismiss many senior position holders in the IRI. "These senior positions include the head of the judiciary, the head of state radio and television, the supreme commander of the Islamic Revolutionary Guards Corps (IRGC or Pasdaran), the supreme commander of the regular military and the security services, and the clerical jurists in the Council of the Guardian" (Rakel 2009, 109). But it is through the granting of status that the Supreme Leader maintains equilibrium in the face of challenges from both internal factional rivalries and to external shocks to the system.

Focusing on the formal institutions of government can lead one to the false conclusion that decisionmaking is virtually impossible, given the institutional balancing/competition at play. However, it is clear that "the relative influence an institution has in policymaking depends not only on the constitutional powers ascribed to it but also on the influence of the personality in charge" (Thaler et al. 2010, 21). As Buchta puts it, "A further important characteristic of Iran's political system is the fact that prominent individuals are often more powerful than their formal positions would indicate. Thus, to gain an understanding of the internal dynamics of the system, it is more useful to view the bonds of patronage and loyalty among various individuals than to view the system's ideological, formal, or bureaucratic characteristics" (Buchta 2000, 7). The informal institutions are where power politics play out, they are the playground where the informal factions compete and the Supreme Leader functions as the "balancer-in-chief" (Juneau 2015, 92). It is also where discursive practices shape outcomes that are then carried out through the formal institutions and to Iran's near-abroad. While this is a generalization, it is not an exaggeration, by much. The next section describes the informal institutions and how they operate.

## INFORMAL INSTITUTIONS

Much like the formal structure, the informal structure has the Supreme Leader at its center. The other key men function as gatekeepers of their respective domains and networks. Each network seeks to perpetuate its power base through patronage and financial support. This is facilitated by gaining control of not only formal institutions of government but also key informal groupings, or by elevating the status of informal groupings by gaining the recognition of the Supreme Leader.

The factions control key assets such as revenue streams, media outlets, and clerical organizations. The Bonyads, charitable organizations with large endowments; the Pasdaran, the informal name of the Islamic Revolutionary Guard Corps; and the Bazaari, the merchant class, represent the key revenue streams (Molavi 2006; Keddie, 2003; Khalaji 2007). The Bonyads, semi-official charities, control a large sector of the economy as well (Molavi 2006). They report directly to the Supreme Leader, and often their chief officers are appointed by the Supreme Leader, and each of the Bonyads has a special representative of the Supreme Leader. High-ranking current and former members of the Pasdaran own companies that are directly linked to the all-important energy sector (Khalaji 2007). The Bazaaris represent the commercial and merchant classes. These informal institutions are not monolithic and there are members of each that support different factions. Nevertheless, a more open approach to trade with the West is a stated goal of the Bazaaris, generally speaking, while it is not in the interest of the Pasdaran. For the Pasdaran this openness would mean allowing more companies to compete for development contracts. These are general themes, and there are many counterexamples.

The media outlets and clerical organizations are key to understanding some of the discursive practices in Iran. The Supreme Leader appoints the head of the Islamic Republic of Iran Broadcasting (IRIB) Company. There are various other official and semi-official news outlets and websites that are associated with key members of the elite. Keyhan online is headed by Hossein Shariatmadari, a close ally of the Supreme Leader. Khabar Online is a widely read online news source that is pro-Larijani. The Islamic Republic News Agency (IRNA) is run by Ali Akbar Javenfekr, one of Ahmadinejad's allies. MEHR news is closely associated with the Pasdaran. Media outlets help shape the discursive practices of the elite and are often used to bolster claims of one group against the other, as well as to humiliate opponents.

Clearly, the clerical establishment is a powerful group in the IRI. Yet warnings about assuming a monolithic orientation must be doubled when it comes to this large, important, and disparate grouping. There are powerful clerical groupings that are very supportive of the *velayat-e faqih* system and its Islamist goals, for example, the Haghani Network and the Combatant Clergy

Association. But there are also groupings that are critical of the system and agitate for reform, such as the Association of Combatant Clerics, headed by former president Mohammad Khatami. The Shi'a clergy are largely unsupportive of the *velayat-e faqih* system, therefore extra effort has been made by the regime to control seminary education and religious discourse more generally. As such the Association of Seminary Teachers of Qom and the Friday Prayer Leaders have come under more direct control of Khamenei in recent years.

Between the media outlets and the religious institutions discourses can propagate very quickly, which is why the Supreme Leader attempts to control them tightly through direct appointments, representatives, and in some cases, judicial overview. It is often the factional competition that drives coercive moves against media outlets and those who run them. What is portrayed as anti-free speech and anti-press crackdowns by the West is often an attempt to gain control of certain informal institutions by one faction against another. Further, there is a special court for the clergy whose head is appointed by the Supreme Leader. The great extent that the regime goes to in order to control the media and religious messaging indicate the power of discursive practices.

For Khamenei, what is crucial is to maintain control of the discourses and a balance among the various actors and factions to keep the system working and his power base secure. This is a self-reinforcing loop. That is, the more the other players have to rely on Khamenei as a broker, the stronger his position. Through various means the Supreme Leader signals his approval or disapproval of certain players among the elite, which triggers reactions from the others. Recognition by the Supreme Leader can elevate an outsider into the inner circle, and denial of recognition can remove elite status in many cases. Therefore, the designed redundancy not only makes it difficult for outsiders to understand precisely where decisions are being made, whether in the formal or informal institutions, whether in the Majlis or the Guardian Council, or whether the president has out-maneuvered the Supreme Leader, but it also makes it very difficult for any one faction to gather and maintain enough power to substantially threaten the Supreme Leader and the *velayat-e faqih* system.

## SUMMARY

Resistance history reveals a long line of Shi'a and Muslim grievance accompanied by a narrative that the Iranian Revolution is restorative of the great Islamic empires of lore. With a renewal of Islamic governance came an opportunity to develop science, technology, military prowess, and other forms of greatness long denied to Islamic countries by an "arrogant, hegemonic West."

This history empowers an ideology of resistance that is rooted in a particular interpretation of Islamism, but which transcends Islamic lands and reached out to all the oppressed. The ideology of resistance is a call to all oppressed peoples to stand against the power of the West. Thus, relationships in Africa, Asia, and Latin America are predicated on trade and scientific cooperation, but deeply rooted in resistance—at the least in establishing a counter-narrative and alternatives to Western-dominated international institutions and rules. This history and ideology made manifest in the revolutionary zeal of the Islamic Republic of Iran produced a rule system—*velayat-e faqih*—that placed the Supreme Leader—*Rahbar*—at its center and a system of government that is both adaptive and redundant and thereby resistant to outside influence and internal domination. It also produced a system of governance—as well as a system of government—that is based on consensus and therefore emboldening of factional alignments.

Through the historical, ideological, and structure chapters this work has sought to highlight three key features. First, the concept of resistance, not always clearly defined, is powerfully present in practice, in ideological rhetoric, and has deep historical roots. We shall see below how Iran creates a culture of resistance and uses it to expand its influence. Second, that this fundamental truth of resistance, though essential to Iran's rhetoric and strategy, is in fact, adaptive. In order to survive, the Iranian leadership seeks opportunities, tries to make the best of failing policies, picks battles carefully, and in its own way adheres to red lines so as not to provoke too massive a response—the core of its asymmetric policy. The third major point here concerns the designed redundancy of their system. This is, as stated, partly in place to confuse outsiders, but it is also there to keep internal factions competing for power, leaving the Rahbar as the central node in a complex network.

Historical, Ideological, and Structural modes of resistance are the essence of the Islamic Republic of Iran and the twin pillars of its influence strategies—designed redundancy and adaptive resistance. One may not always find all of these elements at the forefront of analysis or reporting on Iran, yet they are always present, even if in the background. Any attempt to understand Iran's behavior without this background will lead to error, often significant error. In the case studies in the following chapters, there will be examples of how Iran replicates these modes of resistance in Lebanon, Iraq, and Syria. These three modes of resistance are the essence of the revolutionary (revisionist) zeal of Iran, as resistance is the essence of their Strategic Influence, the subject of chapter 4.

*Chapter 4*

# Strategic Influence

The preceding chapters explain the stuff (historical, ideological, and structural) of Strategic Culture that Iran uses to empower its narratives, discursive practices, tropes—in short, its Strategic Influence. This chapter explores the following questions: What is Strategic Influence? How does the United States approach Strategic Influence? How does Iran approach Strategic Influence? Why "do" Strategic Influence; why does it matter? And lastly, how does Iran do Strategic Influence? These questions, taken in order, serve two interrelated purposes. First, they funnel chapters 1 to 3 into Strategic Influence—that is, the History, Ideology, and Structure of Resistance are shown to be fodder for Iranian Strategic Influence policymaking. Second, this chapter bridges these concepts and the empirical work of the subsequent chapters.

The importance of Strategic Influence cannot be understated in the contemporary world. The ability to mobilize proxies, to activate, and to (potentially) radicalize identities and the ability to sow confusion among rivals are just some of the maneuvers with which contemporary warfare must contend. To understand Iran's Strategic Influence goals and approaches, this chapter examines U.S. Department of Defense's strategic communication, influence, and information doctrine, and academic definitions of influence, I then introduce mobilization as a goal of influence. These approaches coupled with chapters 5 to 7 are then used to unpack Iran's influence goals and approaches in practice.

## THE IMPORTANCE OF INFLUENCE

"It is impossible not to communicate" (JDN-2-13 and Joint Chiefs of Staff 2013, 1). So begins the Joint Doctrine on Strategic Communication. In our words, in our silence, in our action, in our inaction, we are always communicating. This raises the following salient questions. Who, then, interprets, shapes, and gives meaning to what we communicate, and to what effect? "Not synchronizing communication activities and operations results in conflicting messages, reduces credibility, directly impacts communication effectiveness, and allows the adversary to undermine our credibility and narrative" (JDN-2-13, 2013, 1). Every strategic actor is, in this way, constantly communicating. This is true beyond social media. It is true in how states position troops, ships, and so on. It is true in what states leaders visit. It is true in many ways of varying importance to different audiences and times.

Because of this, "Discussing and providing context about the joint forces' operations and actions is in the national interest and is one method of building and maintaining trust, credibility, and support" (JDN-2-13, 2013, 1–3). Strategic communication is designed to influence audiences to understand the intent of action/inaction, it creates a narrative that gives meaning to events. This narrative, pitched in terms of national myths, is key to how audiences react, and that reaction can have very important strategic effects. This is more than just winning hearts and minds, although that should not be underestimated either. This is about something much more central to conflict. "Commanders and their staffs should identify adversary support and bring every capability to bear in an effort to affect, undermine, and erode that support and the adversary's will. Note well, that eroding the will of the enemy often involves *mobilizing audiences*, by evoking memories and passions. The main effort for winning the battle of wills, particularly in operations characteristic of irregular warfare (IW), will likely occur in and through the information environment" [Emphasis added] (JDN-2-13, 2013, 1–8). It is in this sense, this battle to erode the adversary's will, that influence is at its most important.

It is here that a reliance on hard power, kinetic action, and economic sanctions can often backfire, hardening wills instead of undermining or eroding them, unless these "hard" tactics are part of an influence campaign. The adage that if one has a hammer the entire world is a nail seems particularly salient here. Reliance on kinetic action and economic sanctions seems to make sense for a power that has plenty of both. However, since the ultimate goal is to erode the enemy's will, these approaches, although readily at hand, may be contraindicated. Indeed, it goes a long way toward answering one of the most important questions strategists are asking. After seventeen years of war against violent extremism why is it that we win every battle, but cannot win the war? Why is it that after over thirty-five years of increasingly hard sanctions against Iran, its influence in the region is increasing? It is one of the driving contentions of this work that we are not "winning" because we are not fighting the right war, have not identified the right goals, and have no clear articulation of what "winning" is (these points will be taken up in-depth in the conclusion).

In short, the United States has no national influence strategy. This is in sharp contrast to rivals such as China, Russia, and Iran. "The IRI has traditionally pursued a mixed soft/hard power national security strategy that prioritized soft power over hard power. This is because its leaders believe in the primacy of the moral, spiritual, and psychological dimensions of statecraft and strategy, and not because it is a failed hard power 'wannabe.' Likewise, Iran's apparent decision to eschew a large, balanced conventional force structure may reflect an approach to national security that places greater emphasis on guile than on brute force, and on soft power than on hard power" (Eisenstadt 2015, 12). In the space of kinetic conflict, it is clear to Iran and other actors that no conventional force they could build will ever be a match for the U.S. military. However, they have mastered the asymmetric approach where low-cost improvised devices inflict heavy losses militarily, but more importantly, *erode U.S. will*. Further, they are far less concerned about the United States or regional adversaries invading them because of their Revolutionary Guard and Basij units that are spread throughout the country and are trained specifically for local asymmetric defense of their homeland.

It is most interesting that where Iran recognizes its greatest vulnerability is precisely where we lack the strategic vision to press our advantage. They fear that the United States will influence their population, particularly their youth, and turn the Iranian population against the ruling elite. For the hard-line clerics this would mean losing the earthly and spiritual battles against the Great Satan, the United States. "Thus, according to hard-line Assembly of Experts member Ayatallah Mohammad Taghi Mesbah Yazdi, 'If we are defeated in hard warfare, the afterlife reward will be awaiting us, but defeat in soft warfare means losing worldly and afterlife salvation'" (Eisenstadt 2015, 12). If this is, indeed, the Iranian elite's greatest fear, should it not be the U.S. government's greatest motivation?

The end of this chapter will lay out Iran's Strategic Influence goals and approaches. Here, the intent is to sharpen the mind around this foundational question—why does influence matter? It matters because undermining and eroding an adversary's will is the heart of "winning" any conflict. It matters because increased kinetic lethality cannot win when a population has turned against you. It matters because the slow, constant, and cumulative effect of asymmetric warfare coupled with successful narratives, saps not only the best army's will, but the will of the people whose support is necessary for success, both locally in theater and domestically. It puts, or it should put, Strategic Influence, therefore, at the heart of our national strategy. It certainly is at the heart of Iran's national strategy. Before exploring Iran's Strategic Influence goals and approaches in depth, the next section unpacks what Strategic

Influence is from the U.S. government, Department of Defense, and academic approaches.

## DEFINING STRATEGIC INFLUENCE

What is Strategic Influence? The working definition proposed here is this. Strategic Influence is the use of the elements of national power—diplomatic, military, economic, *with and through information* to erode the will of the enemy by shaping the information and operations environment to generate desired strategic effects. These effects could include galvanizing domestic audience support for operations, eroding confidence in foreign governments' domestic audiences, mobilizing proxies to act and speak in ways commensurate with one's strategic goals, sowing confusion among the enemy—all of these, and others, are ultimately about eroding the adversary's will to fight. For countries such as Russia, China, and Iran information is the main currency of their strategy, even if their main goal is to dominate a region. Because the cost of militarily occupying a land is so high, the new way of war is predicated on building narratives, activating identities, mobilizing proxies, and disorienting through the use of information in service of strategic goals. The Grand Strategy of the actor may be traditionally understood as hegemony, balancing, or revisionism, but the main strategy deployed is meant to influence local populations to create new strategic landscapes. Strategic influence is about influence because even military assets are used in support of the narrative. Strategic influence is about strategy because it is orchestrated at the highest levels of government and is developed and deployed with intent to achieve a strategic end.

### U.S. Department of Defense Approaches

As noted above, "It is impossible not to communicate. In this age of interconnected global communication networks and social media platforms, everything the joint force does sends a message" (JDN-2-13, 2013, 1). And further, "Every act of government has a psychological impact. The movement of a carrier battle group from one end of the Mediterranean Sea to the other, for example, has a direct psychological impact on the countries in the area it departed and the countries near its new location. It may also indirectly influence other audiences around the world" (Gough 2003, 1). This action, the moving of a carrier battle group will have several meanings, some intended, others not. Any ambiguity or vagueness in the messaging is an opportunity for adversaries to shape the narrative and dominate the messaging. "The movement of the carrier becomes part of a Strategic Influence campaign when its movement was deliberately directed and timed with White House and Department of Defense (DoD) press conferences, with State Department diplomatic endeavors, and with other government actions to magnify the psychological effect" (Gough 2003, 2). This messaging effort by the U.S. government is absolutely necessary as a foundation for Strategic Influence. It is partly offense, shape the message directly and clearly. It is partly defense, deny the opportunity to adversaries to exploit ambiguity or vagueness.

Strategic influence is about shaping the understanding of events such that the movement of a carrier from point A to point B is not left for others, with potentially hostile intent, to interpret and frame those events for target audiences. For instance, the U.S. government uses various tools to coordinate information. They include "public affairs, political warfare, political advocacy, public diplomacy and psychological operations" (Gough 2003, 2). With Gough, however, I must contend, "Public diplomacy by itself is not Strategic Influence. Psychological operations are not Strategic Influence. None of these components can be conducted in isolation in the 21st Century. Strategic influence constitutes the orchestrated combination of them all" (2003, 2). What would constitute Strategic Influence, then? It requires "coordinating and synchronizing themes, messages, images, operations, and actions to support strategic communication-related objectives and ensure the integrity and consistency of themes and messages to the lowest tactical level through the integration and synchronization of all relevant communication activities. . . . This integration ensures maximum trust and credibility with relevant audiences, stakeholders, and publics" (JDN-2-13, 2013, 1–2). These themes and messages, with which kinetic actions and operations must be coordinated, communicated to relevant audiences, stakeholders, and publics are part of the information environment.

To conduct influence operations the DoD distinguishes the following elements. First, there is the information environment. "The information environment is the aggregate of individuals, organizations, and systems that collect, process, disseminate, or act on information . . . and is, therefore, the principal environment of decision making" (JDN-2-13, 2013, 1–2). The information environment comprises three dimensions—the physical dimension, the informational dimension, the cognitive dimension (FM-3-13 and Department of the Army 2013, 2; JDN-2-13 and Joint Chiefs of Staff 2013, 1–2).

The physical is made up of key decision makers, infrastructure, and systems that enable information movement and processing. The Internet, broadly speaking, is a useful example. We can map the various systems and infrastructure that bring Wi-Fi, cable, or other services to your home, but also the major players such as Twitter and Facebook, and also the key influencers on those sites. In this sense, it is not about the information being sent, but it is about the tangible assets—the infrastructure—that enable the dissemination of information. The information dimension, in military terms, is "where information is collected, processed, stored, disseminated, and protected. It is the dimension where the C2 of modern military forces is exercised and where the commander's intent is conveyed. Actions in this dimension affect the content and flow of information. The informational dimension links the physical and cognitive dimensions" (JDN-2-13, 2013, 1–2). The cognitive dimension is how humans receive, interpret, process, create, think about, visualize, discuss, understand, and decide. It is the human mind as infrastructure and the collective mind of an audience that is at play here. Here we have such vital factors as culture, language, religion, gender, and so on. These factors impact how decision makers decide, how populations react, and so on.

To impact the information environment, at a higher level, requires the deployment of the recognized elements of national power, which include diplomacy, information, military, and economics. Strategic influence requires that the diplomatic, military, and economic elements of national power, and all whole of government approaches, work with and through information to achieve Strategic Influence effects (FM-3-13, 2013, 2–3). Simply put, "The Department of Defense supports national-level strategic communication by ensuring its military objectives synchronize with and complement other United States Government information and communication efforts" (FM-3-13, 2013, 2–4). These definitions and concepts, at first glance, may appear fairly simple and rather obvious. However, they bear some thought. The distinction between information, diplomacy, economics, and military is largely overstated. Rather, it is the information contained in military maneuvers, economic activity, and diplomacy that matters. Further, all elements of national power rely on information, are information, and trade in information.

Take the example given above concerning movement of a carrier from point A to point B; that movement relies on information, contains information, and trades information—that is, it communicates. The purpose of influence operations is to shape that communication to serve national interests. The same is true of diplomacy. The debate about whether to move the U.S. embassy from Tel Aviv to Jerusalem was in large part about what that communicates to the world—what information the action contains. But it is also true of the economic domain where the decision to invest, prices, and/or exchange rates each relies on information, contain information, and trades in information. It is precisely because they are information-based that humans can understand them, think about them, discuss them, and come to decisions about them. Therefore, to the question, what is in the information environment, ultimately the answer is everything. What pieces of information matter to any particular actor at any point in time is dependent upon that actor's history, ideology, and the structure of their decisionmaking bodies that construct interpretive frames, which enable and disable processing information effectively. To further refine this concept of the information space, I will turn to some academic approaches to influence. In academia there are three terms that frame this discussion: soft power, hard power, and smart power. Below, I will unpack those terms and then relate them to Strategic Influence.

## Academic Approaches

According to Wastnidge, there are three key elements to the development and deployment of soft power. They are a country's culture, where their culture is shared or valued; their foreign policy, where it is legitimate and seen to have moral authority; and their political values, as in democracy promotion for the United States (2015, 364). Of course, Wastnidge is relying on Joseph Nye's definition of *soft power*. "Soft power is the ability to affect others to obtain the outcomes one wants through attraction rather than coercion or payment. A country's soft power rests on its resources of culture, values, and policies" (Nye 2008, 94). The connection between soft power and influence is direct and strong. The desired outcome of influence is also the desired outcome of soft power. "If I can get you to want to do what I want, then I do not have to force you to do what you do *not* want" (Nye 2008, 95).

The problem with Nye's approach is that he saw soft power as independent of hard power, and he privileged soft power as a superior form of power. "Soft power is not *merely* influence, though it is one source of influence" [Emphasis added] (Nye, 2008, 95). However, we cannot take for granted that soft power exists independent of hard power. Wastnidge explores two critiques of soft power. "Lukes sees the notion of soft power as blunt because it fails to distinguish between the 'different ways in which people's interests can be influenced and the battle for their hearts and minds engaged' (Lukes, 2007, 95). Hence there is a lack of distinction between processes that are disempowering and those that are empowering in their effects" (Wastnidge 2015, 366).

While influence seeks to erode the adversary's will to fight and degrade the adversary's support among the population as a way to achieve this, it also seeks to empower local populations to choose alternate modalities of political expression. The distinction between empowering and disempowering processes is important in considering influence strategies. To empower certain behaviors and to disempower others is precisely the point of Strategic Influence. To do so by defining events, behaviors, terms, and so on, is the gist of influence. Further, the rejection of coercion and payment can be seen as problematic as well. Sometimes these tactics are necessary to achieve the strategic goal.

Another facet of soft power—attraction—is also subject to criticism. Mattern challenges the notion of attraction as being distinct from force (2005).

"As I argue here, this is problematic because neither of the most prominent assumptions—attraction as natural and attraction as constructed through persuasive argument—are feasible or logical in the context of world politics. In fact, as I argue, in the context of world politics it makes far more sense to model attraction as a relationship that is constructed through representational force—a nonphysical but nevertheless coercive form of power that is exercised through language" (Mattern, 2005, 583). Mattern offers this definition of representational force, it is "a form of power that operates through the structure of a speaker's narrative representation of 'reality.' Specifically, a narrative expresses representational force when it is organised in such a way that it threatens the audience with unthinkable harm unless it submits, in word and in deed, to the terms of the speaker's viewpoint" (2005, 586). Mattern distinguishes representational force—nonphysical—with physical forms of harm, although the two are often mixed. The reason physical harm comes to certain "others" is because they have not yielded to "representational force."

In truth, Russia, China, Iran, and the United States deploy a combination of soft and hard power at various times to achieve strategic ends. One can consider this "smart power," but it is far more accurate to consider this Strategic Influence. The problem with the smart power construction is the same as above. Smart power treats the elements of soft and hard power as distinct, when they may not be and very often are not. Every kinetic move contains information and that every information move informs behavior. The distinction between information and behavior is analytical rather than real.

> If we wish to identify the meaning(s) of any sign, we should look not to the sign as a thing-in-itself (as the immanentists would have us do), nor to its use (as Wittgenstein suggests), but to the responses to that sign. To argue that a sign has a certain, "true" meaning reflects the judgment that one response is more appropriate than all others. Such judgments are only made by someone for some purpose. If meaning is not immanent in the event, it becomes a creation, a possession of human beings. The quest for meaning involves the effort to devise appropriate responses. To find the world meaningful is to know how to respond to it. To belong to a community of shared meaning consists of responding to one another according to mutual expectations. To create a community requires controlling the range of response to situations encountered in common. (Sederberg 1984, 2)

First, we must understand that a sign can be a behavior, an event, a semantic token, or a symbol. Here, we can think about the events of 9/11. The targets of those terror attacks were certainly symbolic—the Twin Towers and the Pentagon—of U.S. power. That is, al-Qaeda was not just sowing destruction through kinetic action, but they were communicating through symbolic action simultaneously. Yet, it was the president's reaction, the way he framed those attacks, that gave them the meaning that lead to the Global War on Terror. The meaning ascribed devised the *appropriate* response—the War on Terror. Both Osama bin Laden and President Bush used kinetic action and symbolic communication to influence audiences. Clearly, they had very different messages, and to some degree, they were playing to different audiences, but also to some degree to the same audiences. But the framing, symbols, and messages cohere in Strategic Influence and depend on communities of shared meaning.

"The communities of shared meaning of which we are a part are never completely stable or coherent, for they are the products of our shifting patterns of response. But neither are our individual selves perfectly coherent or autonomous; rather, they too are artefactual in nature, beset with inconstancies, and reflect the network of meanings of which we are a part" (Sederberg 1984, 7). Bush's famous question, why do they hate us, referred to a community of shared meaning, two really—they and us. The us—the United States—was a reference to an America where democracy, freedom, and other political values were shared and understood. "They" hated "us" because we are a community of shared meaning and those meanings are foreign, hostile, and incompatible with their shared meanings.

Thus, Seberberg provides a "new" definition of politics that is directly tied to the definition of Strategic Influence adopted in this work.

> Politics consists of all deliberate efforts to create, maintain, modify, or abandon shared meanings in the attempt to overcome the alienation produced by the loss of a sense of organic unity. To establish shared meaning, mutual response must be structured. Response may be shaped through the application of various forms of power from logical or moral suasion, through bribery, to coercion. The use of coercion, though, indicates the failure of other means to limit response. In turn, if coercion fails, the effort to establish shared meaning necessarily fails, for no other recourse remains. (Sederberg, 1984, 7)

Because politics, domestic and international, is about establishing meaning, Strategic Influence is the essential means by which strategic ends are achieved. Coercion, here, is not just kinetic action but also the type of representational force for which Mattern argues. That is, coercion can be kinetic, verbal, or symbolic. Likewise, suasion need not be based solely on attraction but can be undergirded with force. This is an essential component of Iranian Strategic Influence, as we will see below, as they dispute American claims to standing for democracy and freedom and attempt to redefine the role of the United States in the Middle East and elsewhere as being "hegemonistic" and "arrogant" and "imperialistic."

"Politics, defined as the deliberate effort to control shared meaning, becomes an arena of ceaseless conflict in which the contenders struggle to impose their respective meaning upon one another. No shared meaning so established would be especially stable, however, as the oppressed would strive to free themselves from relationships in which they have no voice and from which they are alienated. The legitimacy of such arrangements would be in continuous dispute" (Sederberg, 1984, 56). This is, in large measure, as accurate a description of Middle Eastern politics and U.S.-Iranian relations as is available. The contestation of meaning between the United States and Iran may vary slightly from administration to administration, but the ability to fundamentally change the meanings at play, a necessary step to change the political relationship, remains out of reach. It should be noted that attempts to shape the political or strategic landscapes through coercive kinetic force alone is rarely successful. This is because the meanings that shape the political are not arbitrary, but rather usually deeply ingrained in the culture—the communities of meaning—of that national unit. And these cultures—communities of meaning—have ready-made roles and rules that prescribe responses.

Strategic influence must engage the culture in question through messaging, symbolic interaction, and create cooption, cooperation, competition, and even conflict where necessary to change the meanings inherent in a culture that condition responses. In other words, to get the desired behavioral responses and strategic objectives, Strategic Influence must utilize the shared meanings of the target community. To ground these doctrinal and academic approaches to Strategic Influence, the next section examines mobilization literature as it is the primary goal of Strategic Influence. That is, we influence populations to mobilize them in such a way that erodes the will of the enemy. The notion of deploying myths that we saw at play in the history section above is unpacked theoretically here before being examined in case studies below.

## GOALS OF STRATEGIC INFLUENCE

In general, the goals of Strategic Influence include building narratives, disorienting targets, activating identities, and mobilizing proxies. These are also congruent with what some think of as Gray Zone warfare or Hybrid Warfare. Narratives are built to extend the range of influence communities—that is, communities real and virtual who are predisposed to believing and repeating tropes delivered by the influencer. It is also often the case that even if people are arguing against your narrative, you are still dominating the conversation. These narratives along with maneuvers such as feints are meant to disorient the adversary. The term *disorientation* bears consideration. The idea is that one is not facing the right direction, fighting the right fight. Concentrating on amassing troop strength and kinetic lethality when the battle is about influence, for example, could be evidence of disorientation. Concentrating on amassing troop strength and kinetic lethality as part of Strategic Influence, however, is indicative of understanding the current fight against opponents such as China, Russia, and Iran. The idea of activating identities and mobilizing proxies are intertwined. Proxies are often mobilized because their identities have been activated and the mobilization of proxies often activates identities. Nevertheless, they can be and often are distinguished in analysis and practice. Russian incursions into Crimea showed both these elements. It was to Russian-speaking Crimeans that narratives were directed to activate their Russian identity and get them to act against the Crimean government. Their activation was soon followed by the mobilization of proxies, militias. Naturally, this is a story we will see repeated in the empirical chapters below. The goals of Strategic Influence, however, can be summed up in one word—mobilization. Narratives, identity, proxies, motivation, and disorientation are all part of mobilization theory, to which I now turn.

Three major approaches for understanding social mobilization are securitization theory, contentious politics, and symbolic politics. Together they present a robust picture of the manipulation of semantic and symbolic tokens, the cultural frames (narratives, discourses, and myths) necessary to activate these tokens, and the political opportunities to deploy these tokens to create images of security that enable mobilization. *Securitization theory* identifies a useful range of political contestation with three phases: non-politicized, politicized, and securitized (Buzan, Waever, and de Wilde 1998, 23–33). The work of Tarrow, Tilly, and McAdam in the area of *Contentious Politics* posits that groups use political opportunities, the appropriation of signs and discourses, appropriation of social organizations, and brokerage to mobilize large groups of people (Tarrow 1998; McAdam 2004; Tilly 2001; Tarrow and Tilly 2007). *Symbolic Politics*, the work of Stuart Kaufman (2001; 2006; 2015), describes the role of political elites who invoke myth-symbol complexes to stoke emotions in order to mobilize the masses. These theories are compatible; Kaufman's most recent work (2015) integrates them into a unified framework that enables a clearer model of mobilization and contributes significantly to social scientific and strategic understandings.

Securitization theory is based on the insights of Buzan, Wæver, and de Wilde of the Copenhagen School (CS), who in 1998 placed the discursive foundations of security at the center of attention. For the CS, security is defined as taking politics to emergency status, thereby enabling behavior outside of established rules (Buzan, Waever, and de Wilde 1998, 23). Securitization can be effectively understood as a spectrum. At the low end (the apolitical realm), an issue is not politicized at all, meaning the state is not involved in influencing policies or outcomes. In the middle of the spectrum, political characterization of contending parties is used to mobilize constituencies and prioritize problems. Securitization, at the high end, is a process by which political issues become separated from the established rules of conduct. *Securitization* is a "self-referential practice, because it is in this practice that the issue becomes a security issue—not necessarily because a genuine existential threat exists, but because the issue is presented as such a threat" (Buzan, Waever, and de Wilde 1998, 24). This resonates strongly with the idea of "perceptions of insecurity" in that it is actor frameworks that create these perceptions. The essential aspect of the theory is that the process of securitization is grounded in discourse and speech acts, where the utterance itself is the act (Buzan, Waever, and de Wilde 1998, 177–179; D'andrade 1985). But a speech act alone is insufficient to create securitization; its referent must have salience. Security is intersubjective and socially constructed and, as such, the referent to be securitized (i.e., the object to be defended) must "hold general legitimacy as something that *should* survive" (Buzan, Waever, and de Wilde 1998, 24). If the referent does not have the necessary level of legitimacy (including public salience) it cannot be securitized. This implies three interactive entities: the securitizing actor(s), the referent of interest, and the audience that decides and acts to securitize the issue.

The work of Tarrow, Tilly, and McAdam—Contentious Politics—identifies more specific mechanisms that groups use to mobilize. They are: political opportunities and threat attribution, the appropriation of signs and discourses, appropriation of social organizations, and brokerage (McAdam 2004; Tarrow 1998). Attribution creates opportunities for certain actions that would otherwise not exist. Reinforcing the securitization literature, the authors' state, "Threat-opportunity attribution often emerges from competition among advocates of differing interpretations, one of which finally prevails" (Tilly 2001). At times, the desire for the action predates the opportunity; at other times, the political desire arises with the opportunity. Social appropriation and brokerage work together. Brokers can unite disparate groups in unique ways because of their particular connection to the group and/or through the appropriation of a dominant narrative. Both social invocation and brokerage necessitate standing, although the types of standing required will differ. For both securitization and contentious politics, the cultural frames at work in shaping these dynamics are critically important but are not clearly theorized.

Tarrow's earlier work emphasized that social movements emerge when political opportunity structures change. The most important changes that he lists include: "1) the opening of access to participation for new actors; 2) the evidence of political realignment within the polity; 3) the appearance of influential allies; 4) emerging splits within the elite; and 5) a decline in the state's capacity or will to repress dissent" (Tarrow 1998, 76). The other two major components for successful social movement, according to Tarrow, are issue framing and mobilization structures.[1] That is, once the political opportunity structure allows for the emergence of a social movement, the movement must be able to capture or frame debates through the use of cultural signs and symbols. Related to this is the mobilization structure itself. Therefore, "The coordination of collective action depends on the trust and cooperation that are generated among participants' shared understandings and identities—or, to use a broader category, on the collective action *frames* that justify, dignify, and animate collective action" (Tarrow 1998, 21).

Reliance on group identity, for example, is essential to motivate individual members. "Although it is individuals who decide whether or not to take up collective action, it is in their face-to-face groups, their social networks, and the connective structures between them that is most activated and sustained" (Tarrow 1998, 22). Yet, identity alone is not a guarantee of mobilization. "It is no simple matter to convince timid people that the indignities of everyday life . . . can be attributed to some agent and that the action they take collectively can change that condition" (Tarrow 1998, 111). This is often done through religious language and symbolism, which can be extremely powerful in mobilization. "Because it is so reliable a source of emotion, religion is a recurring source of social movement framing" (Tarrow 1998, 112). The ready-made cultural symbols and myths that are provided by religions also exist in ethnic, tribal, national, and other sociopolitical groupings found throughout social systems of analysis.

Stuart Kaufman's work (2001; 2006; 2015) builds on the insights of securitization theory and mobilization theory, which focus primarily on how leaders lead by offering an explanation of why masses may follow mobilizing elites. Along with securitization theory, he emphasizes the importance of perceived threats: the key motive for mass mobilization, he suggests, is the belief that the group is in danger. In agreement with the contentious politics approach, Kaufman also emphasizes the importance of leadership and organization (i.e., threat attribution, social appropriation, and brokerage). Kaufman recasts these concepts by focusing on framing, which does the work of threat attribution and appropriation of symbols, along with organizing tasks such as brokerage.

Kaufman's main contribution is to fuse these insights with findings from social psychology and anthropology to create a unified framework that enables a clearer understanding of mobilization and contributes significantly to social scientific and strategic understandings. He asserts that "the only way to do [this] is to jettison the usual assumption made by most political scientists and economists that political behavior is 'rational' and instead to focus on the fact that people make decisions primarily on the basis of their biases, prejudices, values, and emotions. The theoretical approach I use to put these ideas together is symbolic politics theory" (Kaufman 2015). One key concept in this synthesis is the myth-symbol complex, which defines "a group history full of heroes, villains, and holy symbols" for ethnic, national, and religious groups (Kaufman 2015). The other key concept is symbolic predispositions, which are "durable inclinations people have to feel positively or negatively about an object. When people are confronted with anything that symbolizes the liked or disliked object, they tend to feel the corresponding emotion" (Kaufman 2015). Symbolic predispositions are created in part by socialization into the values of the group's myth-symbol complex. Together, these concepts illuminate when followers follow mobilizing elites: when elite frames resonate with the popular myth-symbol complex, evoke perceptions of threat, and activate symbolic predispositions so people are emotionally engaged to defend their group. With the population so motivated, mobilizing efforts can succeed.

Strategic influence, then, is about social mobilization. That is, since the goal of Strategic Influence is, in part, to capture the narrative in order to persuade local and regional audiences and erode the will of the enemy, it is useful to think of narrative, audiences, and will in terms of these robust theories. In what follows, I discuss in more detail what Iran's myth-symbol/cultural narrative looks like. In chapter 5, I give a near historical example to demonstrate how Iran conducted a successful influence strategy using social mobilization in Lebanon in the early- to mid-1980s. That model deployed in Lebanon that created Hizb'allah is the primary model of Strategic Influence that Iran is currently attempting to deploy in Iraq and Syria.

*Chapter 5*

# How Iran Does Influence

In the first place, it is important to keep in mind that the distinctions between soft power, hard power, and smart power rely on a separation between act and information that is unwarranted. It is also important to keep in mind that any individual piece of information can be connected with preexisting assembled pieces of information. These preexisting assembled pieces of information are what I refer to as myths, discourses, frames, beliefs, and so on. The act of connecting any individual piece of information with preexisting assembled pieces of information is what I mean by framing. Further, the reader should also keep in mind that the tendency to isolate bits of information in order to understand does not just happen in academic analysis of things such as soft, hard, and smart power, but it also happens in how strategists and practitioners analyze Iranian Strategic Influence. As Kagan puts it, "The pattern of Iranian economic, social, political, and diplomatic activity seemed to possess a unity that U.S. policy—stove-piped into separate U.S. concerns such as the war in Iraq, the Israel-Palestinian peace process, the Iranian nuclear program, and, subsequently, the Arab Spring—often seemed to miss. . . . The most important conclusion this study can offer is the growing importance of evaluating Iranian strategy in any one area within the context of Iranian strategy as a whole" (2012, 10).

It is the analytic lens, or frame, that favors the particular over the whole that produces correct, but insufficient analysis such as this. "The IRI has traditionally pursued a mixed soft/hard power national security strategy that prioritized soft power over hard power. This is because its leaders believe in the primacy of the moral, spiritual, and psychological dimensions of statecraft and strategy, and not because it is a failed hard power 'wannabe'" (Eisenstadt 2015, 12). The IRI may very well see themselves as morally, spiritually, and psychologically superior to the United States and the West. However, it is also clear that they believe the use of military power is also quite useful and they have not shied away from using it. That they prefer low footprint asymmetric approaches to large-scale military buildups is a practical concession to the overwhelming force that the United States can bring to bear in any confrontation.

Throughout the U.S. invasion and occupation of Iraq, Iran used asymmetric military power through proxies to achieve the erosion of the U.S. will to fight. This belies the view that "Iran's apparent decision to eschew a large, balanced conventional force structure may reflect an approach to national security that places greater emphasis on guile than on brute force, and on soft power than on hard power" (Eisenstadt 2015, 12). The broader view offered by a Strategic Influence approach that recognizes each kinetic action in terms of its information value helps us to better understand Iran's use of force. It clarifies the assumption that Iran prefers soft power over hard power; rather it uses all elements of national power at its disposal in a manner consistent with its long-term Strategic Influence goals and its twin characteristics—adaptive resistance and designed redundancy.

Eisenstadt's analysis, however, is correct in two key points. "The IRI's leaders believe that U.S. 'soft warfare' (in effect, the 'weaponization' of American soft power) has the potential to alienate Iran's youth from the ideology of the revolution, undermine popular support for the regime, and sap the social cohesion of the IRI" (Eisenstadt 2015, 12). Indeed, I will take this point up in the conclusion as a central theme for U.S. Strategic Influence. What the Iranian elite fear most is losing the generation that does not remember the Shah, the 1979 Revolution, or the Iran-Iraq war, seeing the West, especially the United States in a positive light, a role model. Given that it is particularly troubling that "U.S. officials tend to be wedded to a hard power approach to strategy and statecraft that underplays the importance of soft power. During the final phases of the U.S. occupation of Iraq, U.S. officials fretted that the Iraqi military would be unprepared to secure the country's airspace and waters against Iranian military incursions after U.S. forces left, while it was Iran's political influence, its influence over Iraqi militias, and its economic, religious, and informational activities that posed, and continued to pose, the greater long-term threat to Iraqi sovereignty and independence" (Eisenstadt 2015, 12). This theme will be examined with care in the chapter below on Iran's influence operations in Iraq.

There is an interesting, related point to be made here. Iran does not fear full-scale invasion by the United States or any regional power because of the way it has organized its homeland defense through the use of IRGC and Basij forces. It does fear an erosion of support from the populace, put another way the erosion of will in support of the regime. It therefore builds defensive and offensive capability in the spiritual, psychological, and social domains, coupled with asymmetric military capability. The United States, conversely, mostly underplays the importance of these factors and builds overwhelming military and economic force and leverages that power to achieve strategic ends. Eisenstadt and Kagan both point to this weakness in U.S. responses and I address this in the conclusion of this work.

To project Strategic Influence "Tehran presents itself as a dependable partner, a formidable adversary, as well as a moral force in the world, and it pushes a *triumphalist narrative* that asserts that it is a rising power that has God and history on its side. Its recent successes in extending its influence in Syria, Iraq, and Yemen have enhanced its image and standing in the region among its supporters, while unnerving its adversaries" [Emphasis added] (Eisenstadt 2015, 15). Iran can do a bit more, as it can claim that its support of Hizb'allah drove both Israel and the United States out of Lebanon. In fact, as I will show in chapter 6, Lebanese Hizb'allah is a model for Strategic Influence projection. It is the combination of political, social, spiritual, and military power that Iran sees as its own identity and strength that it attempts to replicate in its near abroad. The "triumphalist narrative" that Iran deploys is rooted deeply in its history of overcoming "oppression" through "resistance." Again, this notion of resistance permeates its influence campaigns.

This triumphalist narrative that Iran deploys motivates and mobilizes Shi'a and other "oppressed peoples" into participating in resistance. They do so by providing material goods, but also using narratives and symbolic grammar. "It is impossible for nations engaged in communication with each other not to engage in the use of tropes and figures of speech to characterize themselves and others. . . . The codes may differ significantly depending on the audience. Such differences in codes can also imply a difference in the key of the message—the manner in which the statement is to be taken" (Beeman 2008, 40). Iran is careful to project its image, to replicate its revolutionary Islamic culture and values, and to root these in its own struggle against oppression, its own Islamic revolution, and its own model of success. It deploys these narratives based on its historical, ideological, and structural influences and deploys them based on two major themes: (1) Islamic resistance culture and (2) non-aligned resistance culture. In the following sections, I unpack these themes.

## HISTORICAL, IDEOLOGICAL, AND STRUCTURAL INFLUENCES

Iran, like many nations of the world and the Middle East, has a long history of being invaded and occupied. This includes early invasions by Greeks, Arabs, and Mongols. In the early nineteenth century, it was forced to give up land to Russia. In the early twentieth century, the British deposed the Shah and gave his son Mohammed Reza the throne. During World War II, it was occupied by the United Kingdom and USSR. In 1953, Mossadeq, Iran's prime minister, was overthrown in a coup led by the United States and Britain. They certainly had reason to fear U.S. invasion in 1980 due to the hostage crisis, a fear that was only partially erased by the failed rescue attempt by the United States. This led to the creation of a sophisticated homeland defense network. "In April 1980, the IRI created the Basij, a popular militia auxiliary intended to be a '20 million man army' (the actual number is believed to be perhaps 4-5 million) which is controlled by the IRGC. The primary mission of the Basij is internal security, and waging a "popular war" against an invader" (Eisenstadt 2015, 12).

Iran's history gave rise to an ideology of resistance, a resistance carried out in pragmatic terms—adaptive resistance. It also gave rise to a complex system meant to prevent external interference and maintain internal cohesion—designed redundancy. It is no surprise then that these twin pillars of the Islamic Republic of Iran's became the twin pillars of its influence strategies. But self-replication is not the goal, per se. Although Iran's Islamic Revolutionary goals are meant to be exported, this was so before the *velayat-e faqih system*. "When, in 1972 in Tehran, Ali Shariati gave his first lectures on Islamology, he described the object of ideologising Islam as being to excite the intellectual and social energy that would awaken and mobilise people, and lead to the creation of a liberation movement. . . . He was in effect insisting on a re-assembly of past cultural values to underpin an overturning of the existing order" (Crooke 2009, 129). Khomeini agreed with and incorporated these views into the *nizam* (system), and this became a central tenet of their Strategic Influence campaigns. The goals they seek to achieve through Strategic Influence are the subject of the next section.

**Emergent Goals**

The goals of Iranian Strategic Influence can be summed up in a single word—*hegemony*. Although, it would be a mistake to think of their regional ambitions as hegemony in the typical sense. It is clear that Iran seeks to expand its economic, political, and social power throughout the Middle East, and beyond. It is clear that where there is a large Shi'a presence it also seeks to expand its *Velayat* system, and elsewhere it speaks to a unified and fortified Islam with Iran leading the *umma*. What is not so clear is whether these elements of national power also include military power projection, although Syria presents an interesting challenge to this question. Iran seeks to replicate its success in Lebanon in Iraq and Syria—the Hizb'allah model.

The term *hegemony*, of course, is broad. But as we will see in the Iraq case, Iran is busily building networks of influence among the militias, political parties, economic actors, and religious actors, and making Iraqi critical infrastructure dependent on Iran. Further, Iran seeks a deterrent capability against Israel and Saudi Arabia, to lead an Islamist resistance against the United States that drives it out of the region, and to be a cultural, scientific, and economic exemplar. Therefore, "one of the greatest mistakes the United States can make is to imagine that Iran's activities in one arena—the nuclear program, for example—are isolated from its undertakings in another" (Kagan, 2012, 10).

## APPROACHES

To achieve these goals Iran pursues influence strategies in keeping with its capability to project power and its rhetoric. Eisenstadt, highlights five principles "that together comprise the IRI's 'way of war.' These include: 1) the use of indirection (proxies), ambiguity (deniability and standoff), and strategic patience, in order to manage risk; 2) reciprocity, proportionality, and the calibrated use of violence; 3) emphasis on the moral, spiritual, and psychological dimensions of statecraft and strategy; 4) tactical flexibility, and; 5) efforts to disaggregate hostile coalitions by driving wedges between adversaries" (2015, 15). To these I would add (6) consistent, unified, and flexible strategic communication that presents both a soft face to those they wish to win over and the hard face of resistance against the United States, Saudi Arabia, and Israel.

Indirection and ambiguity are, indeed, efforts to manage risk. These are features of what I highlight above in the ideology section as adaptive resistance. Resistance is a central feature of the IRI, but resistance is not to be equated with fanaticism. The IRI seeks to resist U.S. and Western influences in the Middle East but they are careful to avoid any redlines for the following reasons. First, while Iran does not believe the United States will invade and find itself in a long quagmire of Basij and IRGC resistance, it knows it is susceptible to U.S. air and sea power. Second, lacking overwhelming force, it must rely on asymmetric force. Yes, this is guile; but it is guile borne of necessity. And third, the goal of indirection and ambiguity is more than just deniability. The goal is to erode the will of the enemy. The goal is to convince the enemy that they will never be able to govern, be safe and occupy territory where the "resistance" is active. In other words, indirection and ambiguity, particularly through the use of proxies, are borne of necessity, but have become strengths in Strategic Influence. And this, too, emerges from Iran's history and ideology.

But the notion of strategic patience should really be considered separately as it is a subject unto itself. It is here, perhaps more than anywhere else, that we see the history, ideology, and structure of the IRI playing the strongest role in informing strategy. Iran recalls, keeps alive, its long history. And from that long history there is a sense of *triumphalism*. They communicate that they have not only survived but thrived despite the many invasions, foreign interventions, and sanctions. They demonstrate that they have learned that patience, preparedness, and time will produce opportunities and that they are ready to exploit those opportunities when they arise. Coupled with an ideology of *resistance*, this strategic patience plays a long game of attrition that may not be discernible given the high turnover of strategists, planners, and practitioners among their adversaries. Iran must be patient and careful not to appear to be dominating its neighbors militarily while simultaneously pillorying the United States as "arrogant" and "hegemonistic." Iran's leadership also knows it will not be successful against the United States if it provokes America in extremis.

However, the Iranian leadership, particularly the clerical old guard, believes that their will cannot be broken because their *resistance* is based on spiritual values and their government is of God, where the United States is not. "According to Supreme Leader Khamenei's representative to the IRGC, Hojjat al-Eslam Ali Saidi, 'Our war with the dominant system [the U.S.] is an asymmetrical war. What makes [it an even struggle] is the element of spirituality, motivation, and will. Spirituality is an effective element that alters the equations of the combat field'" (Eisenstadt 2015, 20–21). Note well the claim that "spirituality is an effective element that alters the equations of the combat field." In that one thought the history, ideology, structure, goals, and approaches of Iran's influence strategies are captured. If the goal of Strategic Influence is to reduce the will of the adversary, spiritual fervor is a powerful weapon. During the Iran-Iraq war, Saddam's more professional and trained army was shocked by the human waves of Iranian believers (Murray 2014, 80).

Iran uses culture, dialogue, and diplomacy to pursue strategic goals, including resistance to the West. This is consistent with my definition of Strategic Influence—the deployment of the elements of national power with and through information to erode the will of the enemy by shoring up domestic audiences and degrading the support of the adversary among their population in order to shape the operational and informational environment. Iran practices this through necessity, but also because these approaches play to their strengths. A history that is replete with overcoming adversity, an ideology of adaptive resistance, and a decisionmaking structure that is designed to prevent interference and maintain balance is designed to favor a prudent, influence-based, strategic policy approach. Thus, information, from the Iranian point of view, is the most important element of national power.

## Islamic Resistance Cultural Approaches

For the IRI, Islam and Resistance are inseparable; Khomeini saw resistance as an Islamic duty. Simply put, the culture of Islamic resistance that the IRI promotes is built on their history, ideology, and structure, it is the fruit of their revolution, and it is the sum and summit of the Islamic Revolutionary Guard Corp's raison d'etre. "In order to achieve ideological, political, security and economic self-reliance we have no other choice but to mobilize all forces loyal to the Islamic Revolution, and through this mobilization, plant such a terror in the hearts of the enemies that they abandon the thought of an offensive and annihilation of our revolution . . . . If our revolution does not have an offensive and internationalist dimension, the enemies of Islam will again enslave us culturally, politically, and the like, and they will not abstain from plunder and looting" (Ostovar 2016, 102). This is the justification for the Islamic Republic, for the IRGC (Pasdaran), and for Strategic Influence.

Please note that the notion of planting terror in the hearts of the enemies[1] is precisely on point in the proposed definition of Strategic Influence, because to sow terror is to destroy the will of the enemy. This indicates how deeply ingrained it is in the IRGC and IRI's culture of Islamic resistance. It is also important to note that Islamic resistance, thusly conceived, cannot be entirely defensive but requires an offensive and internationalist component. As Eisenstadt puts it, "The 'resistance doctrine' exhorts its adherents to stand fast in the face of enemy threats, to push boundaries, and eschew compromise on matters of principle in the belief that in a zero-sum struggle, compromise is a sign of weakness that will be exploited by the enemies of Islam. It posits that victory is achieved by imposing costs and by *demoralizing the enemy*— through relentless psychological warfare, through terrorizing and bleeding its people and military, and by denying it battlefield victories" [Emphasis added] (Eisenstadt 2015, 21). In mobilization terms, then, the IRI creates and exploits a myth-symbol complex that is *triumphalist* by recalling and recasting their history of overcoming overwhelming odds and emerging victorious. Triumph is a product of faithful adherence to Islamic *resistance*.

For Iran to increase its Strategic Influence its target audiences must "find consistency with deeply held cultural values" (Wiktorowicz 2004, 15). Islam of course contains all of these elements. The Islamic Revolution, furthermore, put action to the words that resistance and Islamic duty are one. However, the type of system that is in place in Iran—the governance of the jurisprudent—is not attractive to the majority of Shi'a, let alone the majority of Muslims. Thus, Iran often draws on Persian culture, Islamic culture, and/or resistance culture to attract support (Wastnidge 2015, 364). In mobilization terms, here we see the adaptive resistance I described above. To mobilize on cultural frames/myths the IRI must adapt its message based on the audience.

Where adherence to the *Velayat* system is at play, authority, obedience, and loyalty are called upon to sustain and expand the range of influence, mobilize audiences, and erode the will of the enemy. Where adherence to the *Velayat* system is not at play, but the audience is Muslim, it is to cultural frames/myths of Islamic triumph over Western hegemony and imperialism, with the Islamic Revolution of 1979 being the primary example and model to which Iran appeals. Where Islam is not at play, resistance is used in a broader non-aligned way to appeal to a widely held sense of victimization and exploitation. It is worth noting Khomeini's rhetoric about imperialism dividing Iranians into two classes—oppressors and oppressed—is written into the constitution as a mandate to stand with all oppressed people worldwide, regardless of faith.

There is, though, another important reason for Iran's various cultural frames. Given the various ideological commitments of the factions and the key governance bodies they control and given the structure of the IRI, various messages emerge. "Thus, we can see how the President performs one role in terms of representing Iran on the world stage, while the Supreme Leader maintains control over some important soft power tools, such as the Islamic Republic's international media operations and its cultural attaches and related cultural outreach centres through the ICRO [Islamic Culture and Relations Office]" (Wastnidge 2015, 367). Wastnidge's article highlights key initiatives from the presidencies of Rafsanjani (1989–1997), Khatami (1997–2005), Ahmadinejad (2005–2013), and a brief foray into Rouhani's (2013–present). With the exception of Ahmadinejad, whose bellicosity earned him scorn at home and abroad, the presidents of Iran have favored openness to the West, trade, and discourse. The highlight of this was Khatami's "Dialogue Among Civilizations." Khatami himself sees the concept as forming a "new paradigm" in international relations, thus evidencing its efficacy as a foreign policy tool. This was an idea that came from a perception of Iranian civilizational weight and importance in the world (Wastnidge 2015, 368). That Iran is a great civilization—a great Islamic civilization—is the central idea for this theme of Strategic Influence. It certainly resonates with their long history and many accomplishments in math, science, art, military prowess, and so on. It also works well with the fact that Iran is disadvantaged in other areas—military and economic. By relying on culture, Iran can speak to great powers as equals rather than from a position of weakness.

It is this reality that ultimately makes former President Mahmoud Ahmadinejad such an anomaly. His rhetoric against Israel and the United States recalled early revolutionary fervor and was a dramatic departure from the presidencies of Rafsanjani, Khatami, and now Rouhani. While many hardliners in Iran and elsewhere appreciated Ahmadinejad's hard stance against Israel, the cost to Iran's prestige around the world was significant. The ratcheting up of sanctions against Iran's nuclear program was made easier by his bellicose style, which drew ire from the international community as well as other factions in Iran (Rivera 2016).

Nevertheless, cultural outreach was still an active part of statecraft during the Ahmadinejad years. In the aftermath of war in Afghanistan and Iraq, Iran saw opportunity to further its cultural reach among Shi'a and Farsi speakers. For example, "Iran regularly draws on cultural commonalities such as the celebration of the Persian new year Nowrooz across the region, and invited regional heads to the first international celebration of Nowrooz in Iran in 2010;" and in Central Asia, "Under Ahmadinejad, Iran sought to establish a 'Union of Persian Speaking Nations' between the three Persian-speaking states, which drew on cultural linkages as a means of furthering cooperation and making use of the common Persian bonds amongst them" (Wastnidge 2015, 370).

The continuity in cultural outreach, particularly Islamic cultural outreach, occurred primarily because of the designed redundancy of the IRI's system. While the president of Iran appoints the foreign minister, for example, the Supreme Leader uses key advisers, such as Ali Velayati, as envoys. But the arena of cultural affairs is so important to Iran's leaders that they have created an organization charged with carrying out Islamic cultural diplomacy. The Islamic Culture and Relations Organization (ICRO) was founded in 1995 to unify Iran's Islamic cultural diplomacy and coordinating bilateral cultural initiatives with other states (Wastnidge 2015, 370). As is common in the IRI, given the designed redundancy of the system, the ICRO is affiliated with the Ministry of Culture and Islamic Guidance but works "under the guidance of the Supreme Leader who directly appoints members of the ICRO's ruling council" (Wastnidge 2015, 371).

According to its website, the ICRO's aims are:

As per its constitution, the ICRO is to pursue the following aims and objectives: 1. Revival and dissemination of Islamic tenets and thoughts with a view to reaching the true message of Islam to the people of the world; 2. Creating awareness among the people of the world as regards the principles, the objectives, and the stance of the Islamic Revolution of Iran as well as the role it plays in the international arena; 3. Expansion of cultural relations with various nations and communities in general; and the Muslims and the oppressed, in particular; 4. Strengthening and regulating the existing cultural relations between the Islamic Republic of Iran and other countries of the world as well as global cultural organizations; 5. Appropriate presentation of the Iranian culture and civilization as well as its cultural, geographical, and historical characteristics; 6. Preparation of the necessary grounds for the unity among Muslims and the establishment of a united front among world Muslims on the basis of the indisputable principles of Islam; 7. Scholarly debates and confrontations with anti-religion, anti-Islam, and anti-Revolutionary cultures with a view to awakening the Muslims of the world regarding the divisive conspiracies of the enemies as well as protecting the rights of the Muslims; 8. Growth, development, and the improvement of the cultural, political, economic, and social conditions of the Muslims. (ICRO 2019)

These aims clearly demonstrate a commitment to revolutionary Islamic ideals. Its primary mission is to disseminate Islamic principles, but its second point clearly states that it is also about the IRI and its international relations. The first two points flow seamlessly into the third—outreach to Muslims and the oppressed of the world. Current news articles on the ICRO website report on inter-university cooperation with Iraq; cultural exchanges with Azerbaijan and the Autonomous Republic of Nakhchivan, among others; and much in the way of promoting Farsi and Islamic cultural values. However, in keeping with the other objectives listed above there is also a great deal of outreach to non-Muslim countries. For example, in a show of continuity with the Khatami administration, there was an event featuring the Dialogue Among Civilizations between Iran and China. Also, the head of the Islamic Culture and Relations Organization Abuzar Ebrahimi Torkman and Polish Deputy Culture Minister Monica Smullen met to explore avenues for reinvigorating and bolstering mutual cooperation in different cultural areas.

This presentation of a soft face is important to mitigate much of America's rhetoric about Iran being the world's largest state sponsor of terrorism and statements about Iran's intention to weaponize its nuclear program. Cultural exchanges are one way to mitigate the damage done to its image from these statements. Cultural exchanges also pave the way for economic cooperation, particularly since the lifting of sanctions. The message is consistent to a large degree, as Iran focuses on the greatness of their civilization, long cultural ties with various countries and cultures around the world, and the deeply abiding values of Islam. However, they are also clear that resistance against oppression is a key part of Islam, to include oppression against non-Muslims as well.

## Islamic Resistance Militant Approaches

Naturally, Iran's activities can be seen to have a nefarious intent, particularly from the Western point of view. "Call it destiny, entitlement, or even manifest destiny: what's critical to understand is that Iran today has an unshakable belief in its right to empire. It means to achieve this through proxy warfare and control over oil supplies" (Baer 2008, 110). Baer may be correct and certainly cultural outreach, economic trade, and other means could be added to proxy warfare and control over oil supplies as means to achieve "empire." However, the term *hegemony* here seems more on point. Empire maintains historical trappings of territorial expansion and control. Rather, what it seems Iran is doing is more in line with seeking hegemony through Strategic Influence. Where I agree with Baer is in the assessment of Iran's use of proxies and other asymmetric means to achieve their strategic goals. But this is in keeping with their stated mission to liberate the oppressed and resist the "hegemonistic" and "arrogant" West.

The use of proxies should be understood as part of Iran's deliberate strategy to spread their influence throughout the Arab world. This is evident when one considers their use of framing. "Concurrent to the intensive use of proxies, Iran is deliberately trying to weaken regimes through information framing. Iran's addresses to the Arab world are framed to a specific audience and with the tone of animosity towards the West and non-Muslims" (Alrumaithi 2010, 1). Based on their own and the region's experience with imperialism and colonialism and their more recent manifestations, Iran is able to portray itself and its allies, such as Hizb'allah, as examples of successful resistance against the West. It is certainly true that "the use of allies and proxies is generally cheap, reduces risk, and acts as a force multiplier. It also provides some degree of deniability—plausible or implausible" (A. Cordesman and Kleiber 2007, 203). But it is much more than that. The use of proxies in this way demonstrates the ideological message that resistance against the most powerful forces in the world and in the region, that is, the United States and Israel, can be successful. It serves Iran's *triumphalist* message that emerges from its history, is encapsulated in its ideology, and is embodied in its complex governmental structure. Therefore, while the focus on proxies is important, again, Strategic Influence demands that the messaging import cannot be overlooked, indeed, should be the focus. "Iran's support for [Hizb'allah] . . . could deliver two important foreign policy goals: the capacity to fight Israel through a proxy . . . and the expansion of Shiite Islam's influence in Lebanon through Hezbollah's developing role there" (Harik 2004, 39–40). It is precisely this intimate, intricate mingling of force and meaning that is the stuff of Strategic Influence.

It is with this understanding that I reinterpret this approach, "Iran's conventional military readiness, effectiveness, and capabilities have declined since the end of the Iran-Iraq War, and Iran has not been able to find a meaningful way to restore its conventional edge in the region" (A. Cordesman and Kleiber 2007, 29). To mean this: Iran would be foolish to rely on a large conventional force that could not survive a direct confrontation with either the United States or Israel. Rather, through the use of proxies and messaging, it uses asymmetric tools to achieve strategic goals with deniability, reduced risk, and at significantly reduced cost.

Through Islamic Resistance, Iran's Strategic Influence goals are to make the Middle East a hostile operating environment for the United States. "In characterizing the United States [as the Great Satan], Iranian revolutionaries were trying to emphasize the fact that America led Iran astray from its correct religious and spiritual path" (Beeman 2008, 43). However, by extension, Iran is saying that the United States has done so to other Muslim nations and, in fact, continues to do so. Again, because the United States is the Great Satan it is the duty of every able-bodied Muslim to resist it. The direct challenge to Saudi Arabia should be clear. Saudi Arabia cannot be a keeper of the holiest sites of Islam, a defender of the faith, and an ally to the Great Satan at the same time. But Iran is careful not to directly attack Israel or Saudi Arabia, instead even against a near-power-rival such as the Saudis, Iran prefers asymmetrical and rhetorical approaches.

The danger is to misunderstand the asymmetric/proxy approach as a weakness. The other danger is to misunderstand groups such as Hizb'allah as strictly a proxy group, militia, or terror group. Since the Iranian revolution, the IRGC and Quds force have been active in establishing *resistance* forces, such as Hizb'allah, throughout their near abroad. "Iran has tried to create militia proxies to expand its influence. And where these militias can be found, one can also find Iran's culture of resistance, jihad, and martyrdom being propagated as a first step toward institutionalizing Iranian influence in those societies, with participation in politics as the next step" (Eisenstadt 2015, 13). In other words, the material disposition of groups armed, trained, and funded by Iran is incomplete without manifestations of the *triumphalist* and *resistant* myth-symbol complexes.

Reinforcing Iran's role as the main defender of the Islamic Faith, Major General Qassem Soleimani, the former chief of the IRGC's Quds Force, spoke at an Iran-Iraq war veteran's ceremony and praised the Islamic Republic's decades-long effort to take the mantle of the Palestinian cause and boasted that Tehran's influence in the Middle East has expanded as a result of the Syrian war. He excoriated Saudi Arabia, as is often the case among Iranian elites, for being puppets of the United States, for betraying the Palestinian cause, and therefore betraying Islam. "If there's a lot of oil in a country . . . but mad logic rules, terrible events happen, and mad things like war with Yemen happen and these ignorant individuals are incapable of extinguishing this fire . . . Soleimani then chastised 'some Arab countries' that are 'surrounding' the 'oppressed' Palestinians. Tehran has accused Arab states of 'selling out' the Palestinian cause, because these same Arab nations have expanded ties with Israel over shared concerns about Iranian power" (Toumaj 2017).

The central point here is not that these speeches and messaging efforts produce massive defections from the West or conversions to Shi'a Islam in the Middle East. It is that Iranian influence has had some successes and demonstrable impact. The IRGC and Quds force have built Lebanese Hizb'allah into a successful model, and they are now busily deploying that model in Iraq and Syria. But their efforts transcend the Middle East and their near abroad. They also deploy their Strategic Influence techniques as far as Latin America. For all the bellicose rhetoric that certain elements in the U.S. policy-making world have against Iran, and much of it justified, there seems to be little understanding of what they are actually doing, how they are doing it, and why. In chapter 6, I explore this Hizb'allah model more in depth. In the following sections, In chapters 7–9, I demonstrate the exportation of this model to Iran's near abroad.

*Chapter 6*

# Resistance in Iran's Near Abroad

If the Islamic Republic of Iran is ever to emerge as a regional hegemon, two key steps toward that outcome will be (1) greater control over the Persian Gulf and (2) securing a direct line of support to Lebanese Hizb'allah. Iraq is key to both those efforts. In addition to being the primary space for the Shi'a Revival, a social movement stretching from Lebanon to Bahrain, Iraq is also perched at the mouth of possibly the most important body of water in the world, the Persian Gulf. Whoever controls the millions of barrels of crude oil passing from the Persian Gulf through the Strait of Hormuz in effect has economic control over the entire region and holds access to the bulk of the world's current energy supply.[1] The strategic importance of the Persian Gulf to Iran's rivals in the Gulf Cooperation Council (GCC) is difficult to overstate. Iraq, under Saddam Hussein's reign, was known as the Shield of the Gulf and acted as an Arab-Sunni bastion against Iranian expansion into the Arab gulf states. Realizing the geopolitical significance of the location of Saddam's former buffer state since the Iran-Iraq war, Iran has sought to mirror its success with its Lebanese proxies by influencing Iraq from within, through religious, political, and military means—primarily proxy forces.

This model of influence through proxy forces became especially important in filling the void left by the 2003 invasion of Iraq. This downfall of Saddam Hussein and the ruling Ba'ath party led to Iranian-backed parties and militias rising to power during the U.S.-led occupation, a power that grew stronger following the U.S. withdrawal. This was done namely through the political success of the Islamic Da'wa party and the tactical employment of groups such as the Mahdi Army and Kata'ib Hezbollah, all Shi'a groups supported by the IRGC's Quds Force. In 2016, the Iranian-backed militias collectively known as the Popular Mobilization Front (PMF) were formalized into the Iraqi armed forces through legislation (Roggio 2016). This move in effect institutionalized Iranian influence in Iraq, creating a political-military organization with significant force, much like Hizb'allah in Lebanon.

Lebanese Hizb'allah is a social service, religious, political, military organization that maintains enough power to shut down the Lebanese government, veto measures it deems unfavorable, maintains its own armed militia despite UN resolutions to the contrary, and engages in war with Israel and Daesh. While much has been written about the success of the Quds Force's effective model of proxy warfare in Lebanon through Hezbollah, there is significantly less discourse on this model's application within Iraq. In fact, very little writing is available about the PMF. This section seeks, in part, to fill that void by addressing the influence of Iranian proxies within Iraq as well as the larger implications for the region and for Iran's Strategic Influence.

However, while the political-military force of Iranian proxies is critical to understanding Iranian influence in Iraq, it is also critically important to understand how Iran is trying to capitalize on shared religious identity as well. The cultural narratives of Islamism, as the Iranian Revolution interprets it, are imbued with signs and symbols of resistance. These signs and symbols are part of Iran's Strategic Influence playbook. They speak in pan-Islamic terms to fellow Muslims, in part to overcome the minority status of being Shi'a. They speak in resistance terms, in part to overcome the minority status of being Persian. They speak in terms of Islamic Resistance as the main myth/symbol complex of their influence strategies. That is, by evoking the narratives of the myth/symbol complex Iranian elite trigger collective memories rooted in Shi'a history, which is replete with oppression, offering Iran as a triumphant Shi'a path to power and dignity. However, given that Strategic Influence is the use of the elements of national power, diplomatic, military, economic, *with and through information*, to erode the will of the enemy by shaping the information and operational environment, it is important to have a better understanding of *how* that works. To that end the following section briefly unpacks the history, ideology, and praxis of Lebanese Hizb'allah. It reiterates some of the themes found in the background and Strategic Influence chapters and instantiates them with examples from the Lebanese case both to clarify key concepts and to demonstrate their efficacy as a model for Iraq and Syria case studies below.

*Chapter 7*

# Lebanon

## *The Hizb'allah Model*

What is Hizb'allah? It is a manifestation of suddenly empowered, formerly repressed national and religious identity. It is a social movement. It is an armed resistance movement. It is a social service and health care provider. It is an Islamic organization and an Islamist organization. It is a democratic party. It is a Shi'a Islamic party whose leader is among the most popular leaders in the predominantly Sunni Middle East. It is an amalgamation. It is, for some, a radical ideological terror group. It is, for the West, a conundrum.

In order to understand the complex nature of what Hizb'allah is, it is necessary to understand how it emerged as, and is rooted in, social mobilization. Tarrow's theory, key points of which are reiterated here for the reader's convenience, posits that social movements emerge when political opportunity structures change in certain ways. "Most important among them . . . 1) the opening of access to participation for new actors; 2) the evidence of political realignment within the polity; 3) the appearance of influential allies; 4) emerging splits within the elite; and 5) a decline in the state's capacity or will to repress dissent" (Tarrow 1998, 76). Broadly, four separate "events" can be clearly posited as political opportunity structure changes that were permissive causes for the emergence of Hizb'allah. The first three are well known and widely written about. They are the Lebanese Civil War (a decisive split among the political elite, an opportunity for new actors to emerge, and a decline in the state's capacity or will to repress dissent), the Iranian Revolution of 1979 (the appearance of influential allies), and the Israeli invasion of Lebanon in 1982 (an opportunity for new actors to emerge). The fourth, however, is much less clearly understood by Western scholars and practitioners. It is the Shi'a Revival. Part of the motivation of this project is to explain in greater detail what this Shi'a Revival means generally, what it meant for Hizb'allah's emergence and what it means for its continued existence and mission, and what it means in terms of Iranian influence.

The other two major components for successful social movement, according to Tarrow, are issue framing and mobilization structures. That is, once the political opportunity structure allows for the emergence of a social movement, the movement must be able to capture or frame debates through the use of cultural signs and symbols. Related to this is the mobilization structure itself. Therefore, "the coordination of collective action depends on the trust and cooperation that are generated among participants shared understandings and identities—or, to use a broader category, on the collective action *frames* that justify, dignify, and animate collective action" (Tarrow 1998, 21). Thus identity, in this case Shi'a identity, is the sine qua non of social movement. Without this common identity and meaning political opportunity structures cannot be used to great effect. The reliance on group identity is essential to motivate the individual members. Here it is beneficial to remember the history of resistance in Iran and the power of the clergy to effect change through activating identity in face-to-face groups—Friday prayers at Mosques. "Although it is individuals who decide whether or not to take up collective action, it is in their face-to-face groups, their social networks, and the connective structures between them that is most activated and sustained" (Tarrow 1998, 22).

Kaufman's unifying frame relies on two theoretical interventions (Kaufman 2015). First, there is the myth-symbol complex. Where political opportunities can be productive of mobilization, they are only realized opportunities when elites can cast them in terms that are recognizable to the masses. Second, there is the symbolic predisposition. These predispositions exist both in individuals and in communities. These two theoretical interventions help us better understand how framing, brokerage, and other key mechanisms of mobilization work, because they foreground the structure of frames and what it is they awaken in the masses. Thus, the Shi'a Revival is not an Iranian story, but a broader myth-symbol complex with recognizable signs and symbols to which the masses have predispositions—positive toward the symbols of their faith and their endurance in long-suffering, as we have seen and negative toward their oppressors and oppressors generally.

While the Lebanese Civil War and Israeli invasion triggered greater suffering for the already downtrodden Shi'a in the south of Lebanon, these were local events. The Shi'a Revival, on the other hand, was an international phenomenon that had diverse causes and wide-ranging implications, most notably in the Islamic Revolution in Iran in 1979. Therefore, Hizb'allah elites were able to cast their efforts in the myth-symbol complex of Shi'a Revival, point to the symbols of Iran's revolution and Shi'a Islamic culture as their own, and activate identities through the symbolic predisposition of hope in the deliverance from oppression.

However, the emergence and immediate successes of any social movement does not mean long-term success. Hizb'allah was able to move from militia to powerful domestic political actor by engaging in the democratic process and creating a space for itself in the political landscape through its vast social networks, its social services, and its Islamic message. The first step was to mobilize the oppressed Shi'a population through Islamic language and demonstrated prowess against Israel. In this way, Hizb'allah was able to overcome a key mobilization problem particularly salient among the Shi'a of Southern Lebanon. "It is no simple matter to convince timid people that the indignities of everyday life . . . can be attributed to some agent and that the action they take collectively can change that condition" (Tarrow 1998, 111). This overcoming of timidity is a major payoff of the *Triumphalist* narrative that Iran deploys; it had immediate and powerful effects in Lebanon. Achieving these effects was done largely through religious language and symbolism, inherent in the Shi'a Revival narrative, which proved to be extremely powerful in social mobilization. "Because it is so reliable a source of emotion, religion is a recurring source of social movement framing. Religion provides ready-made symbols, rituals, and solidarities that can be accessed and appropriated by movement leaders" (Tarrow 1998, 112).

While it is certainly true that a shared religious experience set the framework for Hizb'allah's rise in Southern Lebanon, it is dangerous to see it as strictly this and not to be able to recognize the commonality with movements in the world over. "Despite the mobilizational value of the Shi'ite cultural heritage of oppression and suffering, which accorded Shi'ite politicization a distinctly communal character, the chief determinants of Shi'ite activism in Lebanon have been the same social, economic and political conditions which have spurred Third World radical and populist movements to action" (Saad-Ghorayeb 2002, 7). As Saad-Ghorayeb goes on to explain, the initial Shi'a reaction was to ally themselves with nationalist and even socialist movements (2002, 8). However, these movements in Lebanon, as in the broader Middle East failed to coalesce or last very long because the secular nationalists were mostly seen as corrupt and as fronts for the West (Harik 2004, 11–12). Sadat in Egypt, Hussein in Iraq, and even the Royal Saudis, though not secular, were seen as pawns of the West. The socialist and communist movements faced as deep a problem because they had to defend not only secular but in some cases atheistic ideologies and in places such as Egypt and Syria where the ruling parties were nationalist and socialist, respectively, the result was not empowerment and equality for the masses. Thus, frustration with other ideologies, constant misery, and oppression added to the political opportunity structures that Hizb'allah was readily able to seize (Harik 2004, 19).

Concerning the two other major political structure changes: the Lebanese Civil War and the Israeli invasion of Lebanon, both can be said to have had a disproportionate impact on the Shi'a of the south (Rostami-Povey 2010, 105). According to Saad-Ghorayeb, the Shi'a in the south suffered the most fatalities of any other group in the fifteen-year civil war. And there were the other indignities of the poor during war; over 100,000 Shi'as were evicted from Nab'a in August 1976 (2002, 9). But it is the Israeli invasion of Southern Lebanon in 1982 that is the most direct cause of Hizb'allah's rise. Not only did they inflict massive damage to 80 percent of Shi'a villages, including the almost total destruction of seven, they also killed over 19,000 people and left 32,000 injured (Saad-Ghorayeb 2002, 11). Not only did the civil war render the central government impotent to protect the Shi'a, the Israeli invasion had a religious and imperialist connotation that made the rise of a Shi'a religious resistance all but inevitable. "Expressed more explicitly by Nasru'llah, 'had the enemy not taken this step [the invasion], I do not know whether something called Hizb'allah would have been born. I doubt it'" (Saad-Ghorayeb 2002, 11).

All of the above demonstrates, to some degree, why Hizb'allah has had such success as a social movement and political actor. In addition, Hizb'allah publishes two newspapers and owns Al-Manar (Lighthouse) a television station, which "is the most popular in the region after Al Jazeera" (Rostami-Povey 2010, 108). In this way they fulfill another important function described by Tarrow, "by communicating information about what they do, once formed, movements *create* opportunities.... Challengers who seize political opportunities in response to openings in the polity are the catalysts for social movements and cycles of contention—and occasionally for revolutions and for democratic breakthroughs" (Tarrow 1998, 72). Victories against enemies and successes in political organization and social services would be "meaningless," if that meaning were not shaped and managed by Hizb'allah, with support from Iran. In other words, the principles of Strategic Influence were at play from the foundation of Hizb'allah. Each victory had to be communicated effectively—that is, each victory had to be shown to be a *triumph* of the resistance against the forces of the imperialists. Without this framing Hizb'allah would have been unable to control the narrative in order to persuade audiences and ultimately erode the will of the occupying Israelis. Like the IRGC that sponsored and trained them, Hizb'allah is an embodiment of Strategic Influence.

Another factor that bears careful consideration is the type of governance that Hizb'allah favors. It is one thing to gain political leverage; it is another to use it effectively. Hizb'allah as an organization and Nasrallah as its leader are advocates and believers in the *velayat-e faqih* system—that is, they are loyal to the Supreme Leader of Iran. Consequently, they believe that Sharia Law is just and necessary. But it is important to note that for both the Iranians and Hizb'allah, neither *velayat-e faqih* nor Sharia is incompatible with democracy. In fact, in pluralist societies like Lebanon, democracy is seen as advantageous to both Iran and Hizb'allah. In what follows I delve into the concepts of pluralist and Islamic democracy theory to help readers understand how Hizb'allah gained such power and prominence, but also to shed light later on what is currently going on in Iraq. That is, Strategic Influence seeks to mobilize audiences and in democracies that can often mean effective control of the organs of state.

## SHI'A AS DEMOS, HIZB'ALLAH AS PARTY

This, then, raises another major question: What is the relationship between a Shi'a Islamic party and the democratic process? Again, this is not just important for understanding Hizb'allah in Lebanon. It is important to understand Iran's influence strategies in Iraq and potentially Syria and beyond. To answer this question, I will explore the standard definitions of democracy and Islamic democracy. To do so I will first seek to compare standard definitions of democratic pluralism in the West with Islamic political philosophy and then look at Hizb'allah's practices to see how they adhere to these principles. Indeed, if Hizb'allah had taken sides in the Lebanese Civil War or had failed against Israel, or had not been a champion of the Shi'a, it would not have had such a large platform from which to run and win parliamentary seats and become an important and influential part of the government at the ministerial level. However, it could have accomplished all these things and used its position, and support from Iran and Syria, to call for revolution instead of democratic participation. For those who question whether Islam and democracy are compatible, as well as for those who think outright domination, rather than Strategic Influence is the goal of Iran, this presents quite a puzzle.

For Hizb'allah, democratic action *is* a religious obligation. "Central to Hizb'allah's notion of political action is the division of the world, formulated by Imam Khumayni, into 'oppressors' (*mustakbirin*) and 'oppressed' (*mustad'afin*). So pivotal is this conceptual dichotomy to Hizb'allah's political thought that it is invoked in almost every official's speech" (Saad-Ghorayeb 2002, 16). The pre-Taif government in Lebanon was an oppressive and unjust regime as seen by Hizb'allah and as such had to be replaced, through force if necessary. This was mandated by the rule that participation in oppression was sinful. However, the post-Taif government permitted representation to the oppressed and legal mechanisms for unheard voices to be heard. As such Hizb'allah participated and encouraged participation in the democratic process (Saad-Ghorayeb 2002, 26). For Hizb'allah there is no dichotomy between religious duty and democratic action. This will be unpacked later in greater detail, for the moment it is important to keep in mind that according to Hizb'allah it participates in the democratic process because it feels it must represent the underrepresented and oppressed. It has gained this ability through a sustained social movement predicated on Shi'a identity, its base. Given the significance of the Shi'a identity for both its domestic social mobilization and political success, as well as its ties to Iran and Iraq, I will explain in some detail the Shi'a Revival that, in part, enabled Hizb'allah's rise and success.

## THE SHI'A REVIVAL

Shi'as make up the second largest denomination of Muslims. The Shi'a emerged in the earliest days of Islam over a dispute concerning the succession of the Prophet Muhammad. Shi'as believe that Ali ibn Abi Talib (who would become the fourth Caliph) should have had the succession instead of Abu Bakr, who was succeeded by Umar, Uthman, and then, at last, Ali. This dispute over succession reveals very deep, important and lasting differences between the two major sects of Islam (Shanahan 2005, 9; Gleave 2007, 65). Shi'as believe that Ali should have had succession because of his familial ties to the Prophet and because of his deep spirituality and other personal qualities (Gleave 2007, 65). Meanwhile, the Sunni majority elected the Caliph following tribal customs (Nasr 2006, 34–36). This, as we shall see, will have very pronounced importance on Shi'a theology and political theory. For instance, the implication for interpreting rightful authority is still important, where the Shi'a imamate structure offers a hierarchical cohesion not present in Sunni Islam.

The second formative event in Shi'a history was the death of Ali's son Husayn and seventy-two of his companions at the hands of Yazid I, the second Ummayad Caliph. Husayn had refused to recognize the hereditary line of the Ummayad dynasty holding to the Shi'a line that only those who descended from the Prophet Muhammad's bloodline could rule over Muslims. The massacre of Husayn and his companions is celebrated every year by Shi'as the world over in the festival of Ashura and he is held up as an example of Shi'a strength and honor under oppressive conditions (Norton 1985, 114). "Military defeat paved the way for a deeper appeal to Muslim consciousness. Shi'ism thus evolved not as a political sedition against Umayyad authority but as a moral and religious resistance to what that authority based itself upon and represented" (Nasr 2006, 40). These theological and power differences would continue to manifest themselves. For example, "Shi'as believe that faith has an outer (*zahir*) manifestation and an inner (*batttin*) meaning . . . The inner meaning of religion, its esoteric dimension, can be accessed only through interpretation (*ta'wil*), and that is the domain of the imams and those who are privy to esoteric knowledge" (Nasr 2006, 52).

These theological differences were accompanied by long periods of persecution. "By the middle of the eleventh century, persecuting the Shi'a of al-Karkh had become a custom; every Saturday, Sunni mobs would show up at Shi'a mosques and shrines before looting the town, saying, 'You blasphemers! Convert to Islam!'" (Nasr 2006, 53) It is no surprise, then, that "the Shi'a grew insular, often hiding their true faith through dissimulation (taqqiya)" (Nasr 2006, 54). It would not be until the Safavid dynasty gained power in Iran in the sixteenth century that Shi'as would be in a position of power (Nasr 2006, 64). Interestingly, "the Safavids brought Shi'a ulama from Lebanon's Jabal Amel mountains, the Qatif region of the Arabian peninsula, and Bahrain—the backwaters of the Muslim world—to build new centers of Shi'a learning" (Nasr 2006, 66). There is no exact date available as to when the Shi'a came to Lebanon (Shanahan 2005, 13).

The modern world brought European domination of the Muslim Middle East, in particular, the West's insatiable desire for the region's vast oil reserves needed to fuel their economies and navies, is still struggling with the history and remnants of colonialism and imposed modernity. "Modernization also led to a secularist trend that was particularly visible among middle- and upper-class Shi'as in Lebanon, Iraq, Iran, and Pakistan" (Nasr 2006, 83). In Lebanon, as in other places, the Shi'as were represented in power centers by their elites (Norton 1985, 110). "These notables (*za'im* in Arabic or *zamindar* in Urdu) cut deals with the Sunni ruling classes, and it was through these elite-level bargains that rank and file Shi'as found their mostly humble places in the new states" (Nasr 2006, 84). After the Second World War, Shi'a in the Middle East faced a new challenge—Arab nationalism. Shi'a communities were seen by the Arab nationalists as Iranian proxies. "Many Arab regimes warn of the hidden Shi'a 'agenda' and have depicted the Shi'a as the Iranian fifth column" (Nasr 2006, 109). Naturally, this would only be exacerbated by the Iranian Revolution in 1979.

As we saw in chapter 2, the Ideology of Resistance, Khomeini was able to forge a power base on religious faith and a long history of *oppression*, which produced among the Shi'a a symbolic predisposition toward *resistance* and *triumphalism*. The suffering Shi'a majority of Iran and elsewhere would have hope and a model of just governance in his government. His governing philosophy had been articulated years before in Najaf as *velayat-e faqih* (*wilayat al-faqih* in Arabic), the guardianship of the jurist (Nasr 2006, 125). Shi'a theology, unlike Sunni theology calls for a special clerical role in the interpretation of the sacred texts of the Qur'an and the Hadith. This has led to a clerical hierarchy featuring Ayatallahs and *marjas* (those clerics worthy of emulation)—and the great dividing line with Sunnis—the concept of the Imamate. The majority of Shi'a believe that there are twelve imams and that the twelfth imam, went into hiding in the Occultation (Shanahan 2005, 10).

Shi'a eschatology holds that the twelfth Imam will return and upon his return, along with the return of Jesus, the end of times will come. Another concept of Shi'a theology is the *marja'al-taqlid* (Nasr 2006, 70). Through *marjas* Shi'as follow clerics and model their lives through their teachings and seek their guidance. The supreme *marjas* have the largest direct followings and have subordinate *marjas* that represent them. While none of these theological concepts are explicitly about governing a state, they intimate a clerical hierarchy and officialdom foreign to Sunni Islam.

The Iranian Revolution was one of the changes in the political opportunity structure that allowed Hizb'allah to emerge and later to coalesce. Khomeini's leadership was essential to the group's early organization and mission. It is true that many in Lebanon welcomed the Israeli invasion in 1982 because of the hope that they would settle the south and help bring the civil war to an end (Nasr 2006, 114). However, the Shi'a, already suffering from a lack of services from the fractured government, now had to suffer under the yoke of Israeli occupation (Nasr 2006, 142; Norton 1985, 115). Further, large migrations from the south to Southern Beirut into the "Belt of Misery" exacerbated the already bad economic conditions there (Norton 1985, 112). And so out of poverty, disenfranchised and disempowered, the Shi'a in the south of Lebanon turned to Hizb'allah and Hizb'allah's brand of resistance. "In Hizbullah's view, resistance is a mission and a responsibility for every Shi'a in his or her everyday life. Thus resistance is military, but it is foremost political and social: it is a choice of life, or a 'methodology,' as recently emphasised by Nasrallah. The resistance society is the product that Hizbullah's holistic network aims to achieve" (Harb 2005, 189).

This familiar mixture of spiritual and martial jihad had particular resonance among a Shi'a population long accustomed to repression. However, given the recent example of fellow Shi'as in Iran, there was reason for hope. For not only had the Iranian Revolution, in this view, overturned a corrupt pro-Western government, it openly and successfully defied the Western powers. If centuries of oppression and *taqiyya* were reversed in Iran through spiritual and militant resistance, it could have similar results in Southern Lebanon. Note well, "According to Hizb'allah, the power of resistance is that it is a righteous combat, supported by God, which inevitably leads to victory. The greatest evidence is the liberation of the South of Lebanon in May 2000 and the defeat of the Israeli army by the resistance" (Harb 2005, 189). As Khomeini had stood up to the Shah, and the Shah's benefactor the United States, so Hizb'allah had stood up to Israel and defeated it, the first such defeat ever handed to Israel. Interestingly, this was not achieved by a Sunni Arab state or combination of states, but by a Shi'a resistance movement. And thus this "resistance society modifies the perception of the Shi'a individuals as 'disinherited' (*mahrumin*) to one of being 'disempowered' (*mustada'afin*).

The nuance is essential, as the latter invokes an opportunity for transformation and change, whereas the former involves stagnation" (Harb 2005, 189).

In this way Shi'a identity became a source of strength and unity. And Hizb'allah worked to strengthen this identity through a vast social network that delivered such basic services as education and health care. "For instance, the educational policies of the Islamic Institute for Teaching and Education aim at 'redefining the structure of society' (*i'adat siyaghat tarkibat al-mujtama'*) and at erasing the victimisation approach inherent to Shi'a constituencies" (Harb 2005, 190). Further, "by providing Shi'a groups with meaning to their lives, Hizbullah's power is hence strongly and durably entrenched. In short, Hizbullah is a dominant and accepted authority today because it has succeeded in building a solid legitimacy among a majority of Shi'a. The commitment (*iltizam*) to Hizb'allah's *hala islamiyya* has become, in many ways, the norm for a majority of the community" (Harb 2005, 192). It is a natural progression, then, to transform this *iltizam* to Hizb'allah's *hala islamiyya* into political power.

## ISLAMIC DEMOCRACY

"Islamism is not compatible with democracy, for Islamism's sine qua non is the notion of *din-wa-dawla* (the organic unity of state and religion)" (Tibi 2008, 47). For Tibi this is so for two basic reasons. First, Islamists are essentially totalitarian—that is, Islamism is not compatible with pluralism. "In the religionized ideology of Islamism, difference appears as heresy and politics is placed within the ambit of that which is sacred and hence nonnegotiable (consider the charter of Hamas). Pluralism, diversity, and the culture of disagreement and debate are condemned as 'divisive'" (Tibi 2008, 45). Second, Islamists are essentially committed to violence as a means to achieving their ends. "Some Islamist movements that embrace ballots, moreover, do not at the same time give up bullets. Hamas in Palestine, Hezbollah in Lebanon, and the Supreme Council for the Islamic Revolution in Iraq, for instance, all retain armed wings and want to have it both ways: they field candidates and have seats in parliament, but at the same time they keep their jihadist wings and commit acts of terror" (Tibi 2008, 45). This view of Islamism, as distinct from Islam, as incompatible with democracy is controversial but if one reads Tibi as saying that Islamism is not an exhortation to religious duty but a political ideology, his meaning is clear. Islamism as a political ideology is distinct from and in competition with, if not hostile to, other forms of political ideology.

According to Tibi, "Islam itself is basically a faith, a cultural system, and an ethics. . . . But Islamism is a political ideology, albeit one based on a religion. Islam and Islamism are not just different words, but different things" (Tibi 2008, 43–44). And what of democracy? "Democracy is above all a political culture of pluralism and disagreement, based on core values combined with the acceptance of diversity" (Tibi 2008, 44). This precludes Islamists because of their insistence on establishing Shari'a law, which by definition, one must conclude, is inherently non-pluralistic. "All Islamists seek to '*shari'a*-tize' Islam. . . . Their aim in doing so is to establish an 'Islamic state' or 'Islamic order.' Neither the term *dawla* (state) nor the term *nizam* (system or order) occurs in the Koran. Islamism is a modern political ideology (albeit a religionized one) whose project is to remake the world in accord with an invented tradition" (Tibi 2008, 44–45).

For many political theorists the above is highly controversial, even for an ideological reading of Islamism, political Islam, and Islamic democracy. This is because, as described in depth below, Islamism need not be defined as narrowly as Tibi sees it. Rather, some argue that Islamism is carrying into practice the tenets of the Islamic faith in the political and social world. Since so much time and treasure is expended on encouraging democracy in the Middle East and elsewhere in the Muslim world and given current efforts in Iraq, it is particularly important to understand what the West means by these terms and what Iran and Hizb'allah mean by them. Because, as I will show, Khomeini believed Islam to be the purest and best democratic system possible and democracy provides opportunities important to Iranian Strategic Influence.

## Sachedina

In 2001 the Center for Strategic and International Studies published "The Islamic Roots of Democratic Pluralism" with the stated, "hope to contribute to the closing of the psychological gap between Islam and the West, thereby offering a measure of preventive diplomacy in the service of peace in the Middle East and everywhere Muslims and non-Muslims meet" (Sachedina 2001, ix). This psychological gap revolves around two core issues. The first is the recognition that individualism is not a universally accepted norm. The second is that secularism is not a universally accepted norm. Therefore, it may be entirely possible to find a religiously informed, communally based pluralist democracy.

For Islamists, the *umma* is determinant. The *umma* is the collective body of Muslim believers, united in their faith and origin in God, the Creator. This faith in God through the Prophet's mediation "constructed the umma on the principle of equality among believers, who through their personal commitment to Islamic faith undertook to realize interpersonal justice" (Sachedina 2001, 78). Therefore, we should consider an answer to Tibi in terms of Islamism and not Islamic democracy. For, we should recall, Tibi differentiates the Islamists as those who would impose Shari'a law. But given that the *umma* is a body of believers joined in faith toward a common end mediated by interpersonal justice, how could it not be based on a common conception of law—religious law, at that?

Thus, we can theorize Shari'a in this way. "The new religion brought by the Prophet Muhammad in the seventh century in Arabia laid the foundation of its universal community, the umma, as a religious-political society governed by the dictates of the divinely inspired law, the Shari'a" (Sachedina 2001, 135). If Islamists are seeking to impose Shari'a law, it is not automatically given that this is somehow an evil that must be prevented. The question must be posed, what is Shari'a and what are the implications of its imposition. For Sachedina, Shari'a is the founding principle of Islamic justice. "Public order must be maintained in worship, in the marketplace, and in all other arenas of human interaction. The *umur hisbiyya*—social transactions based on an ethical standard of conduct in the Shari'a—deal with enforcing the law by taking into account only what appears in the public sphere of human interaction. Though the injunctions of Shari'a cover even the most private acts, the judiciary in Islamic courts may rule only regarding what is brought to its attention without prying, unless the rights of an innocent party are being infringed" (Sachedina 2001, 25).

The problem that Tibi attributes to Islamism, that ideologically driven states may be more prone to violence than other states, is not ignored by Sachedina (2001, 109). However, it is crucial to be able to distinguish that which belongs to the essence of Islam and that which can be appropriated from Islam by those who seek other ends. Sachedina and others would argue that Islam lends itself to pluralism (the overall theme of his work) and nonviolence. "The Prophet and his immediate successors, the caliphs, were aware of the fact that concentration of power in the hands of powerful military leaders and governors in distant provinces was open to abuse. Consequently, to forestall the unnecessary use of force against their subjects, they provided these officials with detailed guidelines in statecraft founded on concern for justice and fairness" (Sachedina 2001, 109). In other words, per this view, the Qur'an and the Hadith literature must be manipulated to support violence and intolerance.

Tibi's objections rely too heavily, according to this interpretation, on observations of certain fundamentalists' practice and preaching. The errant practice of certain parties does not implicate the project of applying Shari'a law, per se. This holds true particularly if your understanding of Shari'a is based on a *tolerant* reading of the Qur'an. As Sachedina points out the history of Islamic rule has been largely tolerant of religious minorities (2001, 26–62). Further, it is safe to say that the Shari'a practiced by the Taliban, for instance, was widely recognized as an aberration of Islamic law and based primarily on particular cultural understandings. Nevertheless, the deeper issues raised by democratic theorists remain to be dealt with before these concepts can be used to understand Hizb'allah. Toward that end, the following section will look at the particular application of Shari'a law that directly influences Hizb'allah, that which has been in effect for nearly thirty years in the Islamic Republic of Iran.

## Khomeini

For Khomeini, like Muslims generally, the focal point of justice and order is the *umma*. In fact, according to Khomeini, one of the principal reasons for the revolution was to ensure freedom for the *umma*. "In order to assure the unity of the Islamic umma, in order to liberate the Islamic homeland from occupation and penetration by the imperialists and their puppet governments, it is imperative that we establish a government" (Algar 1981, 49). This is to be understood in two ways. First, this is to be understood as a deep commitment to collective identity, transcending individual identity, for the sake of establishing a moral underpinning for true democratic governance. Second, we should see this in light of Sachedina's Qur'anic exegesis, which posited that the role of the Shari'a was to protect each individual as part of the *umma*. Clearly, Khomeini, Sachedina, and millions of others believe that the Shari'a encourages moral commitment, love, and a clear understanding of what one's moral obligations are regardless of the size or dispersion of the community.

Further, "The nature and character of Islamic law and the divine ordinances of the Shari'a furnish additional proof of the necessity for establishing government, for they indicate that the laws were laid down for the purpose of creating a state and administering the political, economic, and cultural affairs of society . . . [T]he laws of the Shari'a embrace a diverse body of laws and regulations, which amounts to a complete social system" (Algar 1981, 49). In this view, the establishment of a government is a necessary outcome of Shari'a law. In other words, either the Shari'a is nonsense, and as such Islam is disproved, or, the Shari'a as expression of the Divine Will, as given through the Prophet, must be enforced. For Khomeini, rejecting Shari'a law is the same as rejecting Islam.

And to address objectives regarding the civic virtues needed for the well-ordered society, Khomeini writes, "Islam provides laws and instructions for all of these matters, aiming as it does, to produce integrated and virtuous human beings who are walking embodiments of the law, or to put it differently, the law's voluntary and instinctive executors" (Algar 1981, 44). In this way, individual civic virtue, moral civic virtue, and organic civic virtue have a common source and a common end. For Khomeini, then, individualism is not lost to the *umma*, but that the individual will is fulfilled in the *umma* through practicing good and rejecting evil.

Khomeini came to prominence first as a spiritual teacher and mystic. However, unlike other Shi'a religious leaders, he was not a Quietist. That is, he believed that the wealth of spiritual power that comes from mysticism and aestheticism provides an intellectual vigor with clear dictates for sociopolitical relations (Algar 1981, 14). The expression of these tenets came at the expense of the Shah, whose alliance with the United States, friendship with Israel, and modernization of Iran, which included secularization, made him the natural enemy of the clerical class. The Shah and the modernization forces in Iran felt the pressure from Khomeini and others and responded by raiding a Madrasa in 1963 with the use of paratroopers. As often happens, this resulted in a reaction from the faithful and in particular from Khomeini. The Shah had Khomeini arrested but popular protest resulted in his release. He was later arrested again and then eventually exiled to Turkey and then to Najaf, Iraq.

The hope of the Shah was to silence Khomeini through exile. However, while in Najaf, Khomeini developed his vision of an Islamic state. He laid out the justification for the establishment of an Islamic state, made necessary because of the Shi'a belief that only the returning twelfth Imam could restore order and establish a perfectly just state. Khomeini made no claims to being the twelfth Imam, but reasoned that the law had to be fulfilled and that if in a position to do so, it was the moral duty of all Muslims to contribute to Islamic rule for the good of the *umma*. More, that only those with deep knowledge of *fiqh* should govern. This is the foundation of Khomeini's system—the *velayat-e faqih* (*Wilayat al-faqih* in Arabic) the guardianship of the jurisprudent.

For Khomeini, "Islamic government is a government of law, not the arbitrary rule of an individual over the people or the domination of a group of individuals over the whole people. . . . If the ruler adheres to Islam, he must necessarily submit to the *faqih,* asking him about the laws and ordinances of Islam in order to implement them. This being the case, the true rulers are the *fuqaha* themselves, and rulership ought officially be theirs, to apply to them, not to those who are obliged to follow the guidance of the *fuqaha* on account of their own ignorance of the law" (Algar 1981, 60). Here, then, is the central tenet of *velayat-e faqih.* Since the goal of the Islamic state is justice and justice is defined by Islamic law, only he who is sufficiently well versed in the law should rule. Clearly the best able to understand Islamic law is the clerical class, whose sole job is to interpret the law. Again, among Shi'a who follow their *marja* because they believe them worthy of emulation, and whose wise opinion and good example set standards for moral and ethical behavior, this is not a foreign concept.

Khomeini was aware that neither the arbitrary rule of an individual nor the dominance of a group over the whole people can lead to true justice. The guardianship of the republic rests on the prudence and wisdom of the clerics because only the clerics have the necessary experience and knowledge sufficient to interpret and apply the sacred law in society. It is also important that technical skills not be lost and so particular roles are left to those with particular knowledge. The administration of the government, particularly provincial governments, may be left to non-clerics. It is sufficient that the *fuqaha* have the full authority of the state. And this is because "truly the scholars are the heirs of the prophets; the prophets bequeathed not a single dinar or dirham; instead they bequeathed knowledge, and whoever acquires it has indeed acquired a generous portion of their legacy" (Algar 1981, 99). This continuity of knowledge, to Khomeini, is the best guarantor against corruption and injustice. It is only through these means that Islam can return to peace and justice. According to Khomeini for far too long Islam had been following the ways of the West and had forgotten its own values and laws. And only the *ulama* (the learned) could bring about the necessary rule. "According to the tradition, then, the *ulama* of Islam have been appointed by the Imam (upon whom be peace) to the positions of ruler and judge, and those positions belong to them in perpetuity" (Algar 1981, 98).

These theories, derived and elaborated during Khomeini's exile in Najaf before the Iranian Revolution of 1979, became, in large part, the law of the land. A brief look at their implementation and Khomeini's view of them after their implementation is revealing. The following is from an interview given by Khomeini in January 1980. "The most valuable part of the entire Constitution is that which relates to the governance of the *faqih;* those who oppose it are acting out of either ignorance or self-interest" (Algar 1981, 342). Further, "the religious scholars do not wish to become Prime Minister or President, and indeed it is not in their interest to do so. They do, however, have a role to play . . . one of supervision, not of assuming executive positions without the proper expertise. . . . In addition, we are bound to follow the expressed wishes of the people" (Algar 1981, 342–343). It is the duty of the religious scholars to keep the revolution on the straight path of Islam. This is their particular duty, because only they have the power and knowledge to do so. The religious scholars are the true representatives of the people, according to Khomeini and without them there would have been no revolution. "If the religious scholars were eliminated from this movement, there would not have been a movement. The people do not listen to anyone else" (Algar 1981, 339).

It should also be noted that the Islamic Republic of Iran does not have the word democracy in its name. On these points, Khomeini is explicit. The term Islam does not need to be qualified by the term democratic, since Islam is the perfect implementation of democracy. "When you place the word 'democratic' in front of 'Islamic,' it means that Islam is lacking in the alleged virtues of democracy, although Islam is, in fact, superior to all forms of democracy. To speak of a 'democratic Islamic republic' is like speaking of a 'justice-oriented Islamic republic.' This is an insult to Islam because it suggests that justice is something extrinsic to Islam, whereas it is the very substance of Islam" (Algar 1981, 337–338). To Khomeini, then, democracy is intrinsic to Islam. Indeed, it should be noted that the *umma* chooses the *marja* they wish to emulate. In other words, unlike other hierarchies in other religions, "congregations" are not geographically determined and people are not bound to follow any one particular leader. The *umma* is free to choose the *marja* they wish to follow and follow his teachings only. In this sense, it is true that democracy, self-determination, selecting leadership, and so on are present in Islam.

But, there is more. According to the Imam, democracy has a vague meaning or, better, several meanings. And this only leads to confusion. Iran, for Khomeini, is a republic. This implies an important role for the populace. Here, we should remember that former president Khatami, a known reformer, won the presidency even though the Supreme Leader Grand Ayatallah Khamenei endorsed his opponent. It should also be noted that when Khatami was defeated by Ahmadinejad, Khatami retired from politics to teach and pursue his interests in dialogues among civilizations. In other words, a peaceful transition of power.

It is not my intention here to make the claim that the *velayat-e faqih* system is in fact the best and most proper expression of democratic pluralism as Khomeini and adherents to that system hold. Rather, I mean to demonstrate two major points. First, the articulation of the *Velayat* system maintains an interior logic that gives it resonance to those who are familiar with Islamic political discourse and those who are seeking guidance in political matters from the Islamic faith. It may still be wrong that judgment I leave to others, but it is a coherent system. Second, it also appears to have a logic that sustains criticism from external systems of thought such as Tibi's. More importantly, perhaps, for the case at hand, it gives a strength and logic to democratic participation.

## Competing Voices of Shi'ism

Contrarily, Nasr tells us that this experiment in Islamist governance was anything but pluralist and liberating. "The Islamic Republic of Iran relied for its ability to govern on the religious enthusiasm and economic frustrations of the poor. It was built on the religious values that Khomeini defined, but it functioned as a domineering Third World state, with a centralized authoritarian government, a large public sector, and left-populist economic policies. It fused Plato's rarified notion of government by an elite with a certain street-smart, play-to-the-galleries authoritarianism" (Nasr 2006, 134). Yet, Nasr acknowledges that the election of Khatami as president was a mark of genuine political participation and reform. One might say the same of the election of Rouhani. In 1997 Khatami ran on a platform of reform and won the presidency despite the endorsement of the Supreme Leader, Ayatallah Khamenei, of his opponent. "Iran is the only country in the Middle East where a former head of state has stepped down from power at the end of his constitutionally mandated term of office and continues to live peacefully in his own home" (Nasr 2006, 180).

Nasr also tells us that "no other country in the Muslim world is so rife with intellectual fervor and cultural experimentations at all levels of society" as Iran (2006, 213). There have been more translations of Immanuel Kant into Persian in the past decade than into any other language (and these have gone into multiple printings); one of them is by the current conservative speaker of the Iranian parliament (Nasr 2006, 213). This complex picture of Iranian society only serves to demonstrate that the temptation to paint with a broad brush must be avoided, for fear of losing the intricacy and inevitable complication of political life. Clearly Iran is neither a liberal democracy nor can we simply write it off as a repressive theocracy. There are shades of meaning in the political and societal structures that allow for information flows and movements of reform.

Before concluding this discussion on Shari'a and democracy, we should look at an Iraqi-born cleric of great importance. Sayyid Muhammad Hussein Fadlallah, who died in 2010, was born in 1935 in the city of Najaf, Iraq. He rose to prominence as the student of Ayatallah Koi, a prominent rival of Khomeini's, and achieved the status of *mujathid*. He returned to his ancestral home of Lebanon and in the late 1970s was appointed Koie's *wakil*—representative—which enabled him "to collect religious taxes, to disseminate his juridical rulings and opinions, answer queries of religious laypersons in the light of al-Koie's legal extrapolations, stipulate guidelines and precepts, and forward the more difficult or unprecedented issues to be tacked by the *marja* himself" (Sankari 2005, 161).

Even though his authority originated in Ayatallah Koi's *marja'iyya* Sayyid Fadlallah was from his earliest days in seminary an Islamist. He saw the secularization of Iraq and Western Imperialism as the same force and both as inherently anti-Islamic. He saw the defeat of the Arab states in the 1967 war with Israel as another manifestation of Western imperialism and further humiliation of the Arab and Muslim people. And he associated himself deeply with the plight of the Palestinians. Therefore, "despite his capacity as the official representative of al-Koie, and despite the latter's overtly quietest and generally apolitical leadership, Fadlallah had no hesitation—as a committed political activist and a *mujtahid* in his own right—in espousing the radical theory of *wilayat al-Faqih,* and recognizing Khomeini's revolutionary leadership. For Fadlallah, this parallel relationship did not necessarily pose a contradiction in allegiance, for each represented separate spheres of supreme authority: Sayyid al-Koie in religious-judicial matters, Khomeini in political leadership and organization" (Sankari 2005, 177). Sayyid Fadlallah agreed with prominent Iraqi Marja Sayyid Baqer al-Sadr's principle of *al-Marja'iyya al-Rashidah* (the rightly guarded *marja'iyya)*. This entailed a collegial view of the *marja'iyya* that enabled specialist departments to emerge and advise the *Marja*. If the analogy to the papacy remains valid, we might think of this concept as analogous to the Congregation of the Faith. The point was to ensure the timeliness and pertinence of the teachings of the *Marja* to the lives of everyday Muslims (Sankari 2005, 257).

Sayyid Fadlallah himself would be raised to the status *al-marja* amid some controversy. Ayatallah Khamenei, Khomeini's successor, and Sayyid Fadlallah endorsed competing candidates to replace Grand Ayatallah Sayyid Khoei. Interestingly, Sayyid Fadlallah endorsed the Quietist scholar Ayatallah Ali al-Sistani of Iraq. The Islamist Sayyid Fadlallah, a student of the Quietist Grand Ayatallah Sayyid Khoei, defied the supreme leader and the *wilayat al-faqih*, to support a Quietist successor. Further, this support of al-Sistani resulted in a cooling of relations with Hizb'allah's leadership, who supported the *wilayat al-faqih* in Tehran and their candidate in Najaf.

This is further evidence of the difficulty of creating all-inclusive categories. Sayyid Fadlallah is indeed an Islamist, but that does not mean that he is not mindful of particular historical circumstances and conditions. During the reform movement in Iran led by President Khatami there were many student protests. While meeting with Khatami, Sayyid Fadlallah opined that "if we want the new generation to be receptive to an Islam characterized by openness, than *(sic)* a genuine effort must be made to answer satisfactorily all of their concerns and fulfill their aspirations" (Sankari 2005, 263).

Indeed, "it is not surprising to find Fadlallah—a modernist and progressive Islamic thinker himself—sharing many of the key views espoused by Khatami. It was his succession to the *marja'iyya* in 1995 that provided Fadlallah with the institutional framework and juridical authority to develop a new body of religious-legal judgments based on rational interpretation of the canonical texts" (Sankari 2005, 263). This new body of religious-legal judgments was known as *Dawlat al-Insan* (the state of man.) He proposed this theory, not as a replacement of, but, rather, as a precursor to the Islamic state. "Fadlallah conceived the proposed polity as a state that fostered the humane attributes of all Lebanese citizens—one that was founded on common human values such as dignity, social justice, economic equity, political empowerment, and freedom from foreign subjugation and influence" (Sankari 2005, 229). Toward this end Sayyid Fadlallah has been a proponent of Islamic Liberation and has been an advocate for interreligious dialogue. "Invoking shared religious and moral values, Fadlallah appealed to Christian activists in Lebanon to forge a united front with their Muslim compatriots to combat their common enemy: Western imperialism" (Sankari 2005, 229). It would be the same modernizing Islamist thinking of *Dawlat al-Insan* that enabled him to encourage Hizb'allah to participate in elections. Sayyid Fadlallah believed that the path of revolution for the implementation of Islamic rule and Shari'a would be wrong for Lebanon given its multi-confessional demographics. He proposed, then, a gradual preparing of the ground for the Islamic state, through dialogue with Christian scholars with an emphasis on common problems and goals. For example, both religions are particularly sensitive to the needs of the poor and suspicious of the wealthy and powerful (Sankari 2005, 225).

But it would not be until the Taif Accords brought an end to the Gemayel (pro-Israeli) government that Hizb'allah would contest elections and participate in government. "In theorizing the integration of the Islamist movement into parliamentary democracy, Fadlallah contended that 'the means by which to transform society, politically, is by no means confined to revolution, but rather it may be possible to effect that metamorphosis through the existing institutions in political reality'" (Sankari 2005, 243). Sayyid Fadlallah's influence on Hizb'allah and his standing allowed them to participate in the parliamentary elections where they won 12 seats of the 128 member body. They were the single most cohesive voting bloc in the parliament.

## Hizb'allah and Wilayat al-Faqih

According to Sayyid Hassan Nasrallah, Secretary General of Hizb'allah, Hizb'allah is Islamic and Lebanese, but loyal to the Supreme Leader of Iran. "Its relationship is with the supreme leader, who draws general policy lines not only for Hizb'allah but for the nation as a whole, of which Hizb'allah is only a part. Since this fundamental relationship is with the *wilayat al-Faqih*, it is only natural for the Islamic Republic to feel comfortable in its relationship with us, and to be especially interested in mentoring and assisting us in certain cases" (Noe 2007, 135).

To be an Islamic party is, in part, to recognize the needs of the broader *umma* that extends beyond the confines of any particular state (Saad-Ghorayeb 2002, 74). This is certainly the case with Hizb'allah when they identify so readily with the Palestinian cause and resistance (Noe 2007, 10; Saad-Ghorayeb 2002, 72–73). Yet, they see themselves, simultaneously as Lebanese. This is an acknowledgment of the particular historical circumstances through which Islamic parties must work in order to bring Shari'a law into practice. And finally, the statement above is unequivocal in its support for the concept of *wilayat al-faqih*.

This inherent conflict between Islamism and Lebanese nationalism is not something to which Sayyid Nasrallah is oblivious. "From the point of view of ideology and Shari'a, we are required to establish God's rule over any part of this earth, regardless of particularities and details; this can only happen, however, if the nation adopts this ideology and safeguards it. We would like to allay the fears of those who think that Hizb'allah intends to impose Islamic rule by force, and to tell them that we shall not impose Islam; for us, this is a matter of general principle" (Noe 2007, 32; Saad-Ghorayeb 2002, 36).

This is consistent with the teachings of Sayyid Fadlallah, as we have seen. And it is also consistent with the general ethos of a party of resistance. It would be inconsistent, albeit not unusual, to reject someone's imposition of ideology on a party only to have that party impose its ideology on another. Here, Sayyid Nasrallah is consciously attempting to avoid this trap. He believes in pan-Islamic rule governed by the *wilayat al-faqih* and he believes that Hizb'allah should work to have Shari'a law adopted in Lebanon (Saad-Ghorayeb 2002, 35). But he wants this selection of Shari'a to be achieved through political and educational means. Since, as we have seen, Islam is understood to be synonymous with justice, the forceful imposition of Shari'a law would be irrational (Saad-Ghorayeb 2002, 36). This is in stark contrast to Tibi's interpretation of Hizb'allah and Islamist parties more generally. Further, Nasrallah endorses the language of resistance and thereby justifies being a militant party as well. Toward this end, he says, "we are now intent on removing colonialism from this region, doing away with colonial means of information and culture, and making the people understand Islam as it should be understood; a lot of Muslim political terminology has been distorted by colonial interpretations" (Noe 2007, 32). Note well the Strategic Influence implications.

Nor does Sayyid Nasrallah see the eventual rise of a pan-Islamic state headed by the *wilayat al-faqih* as an end to pluralism. "We do not believe in multiple Islamic republics; we do believe, however, in a single Islamic world governed by a central government, because we consider all borders throughout the Muslim world as fake and colonialist, and therefore doomed to disappear. We do not believe in a nation whose borders are 10,452 square kilometers in Lebanon; our project foresees Lebanon as part of the political map of an Islamic world in which specificities cease to exist, but in which the rights, freedom, and dignity of minorities within it are guaranteed" (Noe 2007, 32).

The particular history of Lebanon, however, calls for particular sets of policies and political arrangements. As stated above, this is the prior move to accommodating Islamic principles in the Lebanese framework. The long-term goal of accepting Islamic rule in Lebanon may be a long time in coming or may never come. In the meantime, Sayyid Nasrallah sees Hizb'allah as a primary actor seeking justice and an end to tyranny. In a letter to Chirac of France, Sayyid Nasrallah writes,

I therefore seize this opportunity to renew my call to all Lebanese political groups to come together and engage in a serious dialogue regarding all fundamental issues that concern the future well-being of the next generations of Lebanese citizens. These issues are: the vital importance of national unity; peaceful coexistence between Christians and Muslims; rejection of the notion of winners and losers; rejection of the use of arms and a return to civil war; commitment to freedom and democracy; adoption of a just and representative electoral system; [the] building [of] a modern state based on the rule of law; and the rejection of all foreign intervention in Lebanon's internal affairs. (Noe 2007, 333)

That Hizb'allah is a political party in a democratic system is obvious. What is a matter of debate is what it seeks to impose. As we have seen, Western ego-centric political theories fail to capture Islamic pluralist discourse as democratic because Islamic democratic theories focus on the *umma* and not the individual. But there is another problem. Western political theories on democracy are state-centric as well. This defense of the Westphalian system, a political sovereignty of a particular geographic unit, is foreign to Islamists in general and to Shi'a Islamists as well, particularly those who adhere to the *wilayat al-faqih*.

It is improper, and potentially chauvinistic, to hold Islam to these Western standards when the fundamental units are so different. Nevertheless, both systems seek an elaboration of justice and empowerment of the suppressed, at least in theory. Here, Hizb'allah's ideology sees three major weaknesses with the West's conception of democracy: (1) The tyranny of the majority was not only a theoretical possibility pointed out by John Stuart Mill, but a factual lived experience in most democratic countries and certainly in the United States. It is only convenient memory lapses that permit broad defense of majority rule. (2) They see the problem of powerful minorities stealing the public agenda. And (3) "is the defectiveness and injustice of a system that only claims to represent the current generation of voting age and completely disregards the rights and interests of those who are currently under age and of future generations" (Saad-Ghorayeb 2002, 39). The present generation of leaders elected to serve the interests of the present demos cannot claim to speak for future generations, and it cannot be assumed that future generations can simply change things by majority rule, particularly if resources are depleted (Saad-Ghorayeb 2002, 39).

Genuine pluralism can exist in an Islamic state; indeed, under the Ottomans the well-known Dhimmi system is such an example. But note that Principle 26 of the Iranian constitution holds that religious minorities should be able to contest elections and represent the interests of their faithful (Saad-Ghorayeb 2002, 41). Therefore, "Islam does accord people the right to choose, but this does not mean unlimited choice. The political options available to people must fall within the ideological parameters of Islam and the framework of the *wilayat al-Faqih*" (Saad-Ghorayeb 2002, 41). Here it should be noted that non-religious parties are ignored. This is presumably because no non-religious party would accept the concept of *wilayat al-faqih*. Direct political participation in voting and contesting elections for non-Muslim candidates is a departure from the Dhimmi model. Another major difference is the *jizya* or poll tax that was imposed on non-Muslims under Ottoman rule in order to avoid conscription into the armed services. Article 144 of the Iranian constitution holds that the army should be guided by Islamic principles and says nothing about the religious makeup of its members and no *jizya* is imposed on religious minorities.

We should recall that Hizb'allah is committed to several ideas. It is true that they want a pan-Islamic state and as such adhere to the principle of *wilayat al-faqih*. But they recognize that Lebanon, being multi-confessional, is not ready to adopt Islamic rule. Therefore, they are willing to work within this system to slowly bring about recognition of the great value of Islam and bring other parties to the conclusion that a Lebanese Islamic state would be good for all. Toward this end, Hizb'allah works tirelessly among the poor and disenfranchised. This fuels its political power, but it also serves as a reminder to others that Islam should be equated with justice and that an Islamic state would mean justice for all. In these senses, we can ask the following. Is democratic participation the new *taqiyya* for Shi'a Muslims?

"Precisely because Hizb'allah's decision to participate in the democratic system was motivated in part by rational considerations related to the party's survival, it could be argued that Hizb'allah is only using democracy to preserve its political status and is therefore not genuinely committed to it as an ideological principle. . . . However, it does not necessarily follow that the party does not genuinely endorse democracy as a 'system of government,' but merely advocates its use as a 'a procedure of transition to power'" (Saad-Ghorayeb 2002, 55). It would be disingenuous for any Islamist party to hold that democracy was the best form of government, unless it is with the understanding of those terms described by Khomeini, or something along those lines. Not only for the problems identified with democracy listed above, but because, and more importantly, Islam is a total system of ethics, governance, and jurisprudence. In other words, as stated previously, the Shari'a is the best system of government for Islamists and all democracy can be is a measure of how ready a society is to embrace it.

Given this discussion it is difficult to summarily dismiss Hizb'allah as a terrorist organization or militia or Islamic fundamentalist movement. Its commitment to democracy may be secondary, as only Islam can be primary, it nevertheless remains true to its commitment to the Lebanese political structure. It is a staunch supporter of interreligious dialogue and tolerance and wants Lebanon to heal old wounds, primarily as a social justice issue. The wars and strife of Lebanese politics affect the poor and the disempowered disproportionately. If all of this is true, then why does Hizb'allah not give up its arms?

We have seen this objection raised before by Tibi (2008, 46). He describes a struggle that emerged when the Lebanese government attempted to fire the security chief of the airport and to bring down Hizb'allah's communication infrastructure. Hizb'allah responded by securing the airport and showed that they were better trained, equipped, and capable than the government forces. What is missing from Tibi's analysis is that the primary reason for Hizb'allah's militancy is resistance to the state of Israel. Israel was and remains the number one enemy of the Party of God. Israel is still in possession of the Sheba Farms and its possession of other Arab land means, from their perspective, that Hizb'allah must remain armed and ready to resist the enemy.

Calls to disarm Hizb'allah must be seen in the light of the United States and, in the eyes of Hizb'allah, Israeli interference in Lebanese politics. The Lebanese people do not want Hizb'allah disarmed argues the movement; it is only the U.S. acting at the behest of its regional proxy Israel that wants to disarm and weaken Hizb'allah. In this regard, the objective observer must be very careful. Insofar as the Lebanese government is sovereign, as that term is understood in the West, it should have a monopoly on the use of force. However, in its long history the armed forces of Lebanon have not been effective against Israel and as such leave Lebanon, and the south of Lebanon in particular, vulnerable to Israeli attack and intimidation. It is in this light that Hizb'allah justifies maintaining its arms and continues its resistance against the colonial powers, as they see it. This lack of nuance in the understanding of Hizb'allah and Hamas, both local forces intent on liberation, from their point of view, of illegally occupied lands, mars the debate around international terrorism. This is one of the central points of Harb and Lendeers piece, "Know thy enemy: Hizbullah, 'terrorism' and the politics of perception" (Harb 2005). The production of knowledge surrounding Hizb'allah in the West poorly serves the interest of scholars and policymakers alike; because they attempt to use labels too broadly, they fail to mean anything at all.

## SUMMARY

We have seen that Hizb'allah is a democratic party with Islamic ideals and a vast social service network within Lebanon. We have also seen that it is a pan-Islamic party. As such, it should be keenly interested in the Shi'a

Revival broadly and in the Shi'a Crescent as warned about by King Abdullah of Jordan in 2004 (Blanford 2006). This Shi'a Crescent was envisioned to be a Tehran, Baghdad, Damascus, Beirut nexus. And the Summer 2006 war between Hizb'allah and Israel was perceived as an Iranian supported endeavor to show the weakness of Israel and the United States again, what Sunni Arab armies could not accomplish, this Shi'a resistance movement could. Israeli's called for a ceasefire after Hizb'allah's rockets hit Haifa. The myth of Israeli invincibility was shattered. Instead the world saw a poorly organized attack with poor intelligence supporting it. At the end of the day, Israel appeared disoriented and weak and Hizb'allah, once again victorious. Sayyid Nasrallah became ever more popular among the Arab men and women of the Middle East, particularly in Palestine, for obvious reasons. These events raise the following questions: What is this Shi'a crescent King Abdullah warned about? How extensive is it? And what role will a resurgent, unified, Shi'a Iraq play in it? And what role, if any, will Hizb'allah play in it?

Hizb'allah has cemented a position for itself in regional politics, through its electoral success and social service network within Lebanon and its triumphant defiance of Israel. Its allegiance to Tehran and the theory of *wilayat al-faqih* has been treated at length here. However, this should not be read as an automatic and perpetual allegiance between the movement and the Iranian clerics. In fact, as early as 1993 Sayyid Nasrallah, speaking of the guardianship of the jurist, said, "This person does not have to be from a particular nationality or tribe: he could be the first or the second [of the] Lebanese martyrs; he could be Sayyed Mohsen al-Hakim, who is an Iraqi; Sayyed Al-Khoeie; or Imam al-Khomeini, who is an Iranian; or, one day, maybe even a Pakistani or a Bahraini. You will therefore notice the Constitution of the Islamic Republic says the president of the Republic has to be an Iranian, but not necessarily the *wilayat al-Faqih*" (Noe 2007, 133). In fact, there are two preeminent Shi'a leaders: Grand Ayatallah Ali al-Sistani in Iraq and Ayatallah Khamenei in Iran.

However, there is little doubt that the premier *Marja al-taqlid* is the erudite, semi-cloistered Grand Ayatallah Ali al-Sistani. It is not only that he surpasses the others in scholarly credentials, but it is also because he has struck a chord that has resonated across borders and raised Shi'a hopes in a new way with potentially profound impact. "Shi'as in Lebanon, Bahrain and Saudi Arabia have all watched developments in Iraq with great interest. They all embraced Sistani's pragmatic approach to politics and were quick to echo his call for 'one man, one vote' Amal and Hizb'allah leaders and preachers praised Sistani, hinting that once again Lebanon would look to Najaf rather than Qom for religious direction" (Nasr 2006, 231). Much should be made about the Quietist leanings of al-Sistani; he has called for all clerics not to hold elected office. For Hizb'allah, though, the one man one vote mantra which forced the United States to concede to Shi'a power in Iraq, could prove greatly beneficial in Lebanon.

Hizb'allah has adopted a democratic approach as have Shi'a in Bahrain and Saudi Arabia and in Iran as well. In Bahrain, unlike Saudi Arabia, Shi'a make up 70 percent of the population and they have been agitating against the Sunni Monarchy for some time. Politically, the Shi'a have two very different approaches to follow, that of Iran or that of Iraq. They seem to be coming out onto the streets demanding one man, one vote. The West, fearful of angering its erstwhile Sunni Arab allies in Jordan, Saudi Arabia, and Egypt cannot support these democratic movements, even if they are the direct result of the "democratization" of Iraq. Yet why would anyone expect a "democratic" Iraq not to lead to a similar situation as Lebanon? That is, why would armed Shi'a groups not compete for political power and maintain a strong constituency based on providing social services, and so on. Spiritually, too, the Shi'a have two models in Iran and Iraq. However, Ayatallah Khamenei was the Supreme Leader of Iran for years before issuing a single Fatwa. Both Sistani and Khamenei are aging and in poor health; the future of their respective positions remains unclear. In fact, it is interesting how little is discussed concerning Sistani's succession, despite the fact that so much hinges on it. I discuss the Sistani succession and the Popular Mobilization Front at length in chapter 8 on Iraq using the U.S. invasion of Iraq as an opportunity structure for Iranian Strategic Influence.

## Chapter 8

# Iraq

This section, on Iraq, builds on the discussion above concerning democratic governance and Iranian Strategic Influence in the context of two opportunity structures, the U.S. invasion of Iraq in 2003 and the war against Daesh. It does so by examining two institutions that are or can be major conduits for Iran's influence. These are the Marja'iyya network and the role of the Popular Mobilization Forces. Armed with the understanding of Iran's own history, ideology, and structure, and the understanding of how influence works, and with an understanding of what opportunity structures are and how democracy is seen as an opportunity for Strategic Influence, the following will bring to light the Iranian long game in Iraq.

### THE SUCCESSION OF SISTANI: THE MARJA'IYYA AS INFLUENCE NETWORK

Shi'a clerics are divided, roughly, into two camps. There are those who accept the notion of *velayat-e faqih* that undergirds the clerical rule of Iran and the quietist school that does not see such a direct role for clerics in governance. The primary opponent to Khomeini's theory was Grand Ayatallah Abol-Qasem al-Khoei. Khoei was of equal rank as Khomeini; both had vast networks of scholars and writings that consolidated the quietist and *velayat-e faqih* schools of thought. For Khoei, *velayat-e Faqih* was "an innovation with no support in Shi'a theology or law" (Nasr, 2006, 125). For a clerical establishment steeped in tradition, the charge of innovation approximated heresy. Khoei was born in Iran, was of Azeri ethnicity, and was a religious conservative (Nasr, 2006, 145). He considered the proper role of clerics to be spiritual guides for their people and that therefore clerics should shun direct political participation. This "Quietest" school of thought in Shi'a theology is prominent in Iraq today primarily due to Khoei and his student and successor Grand Ayatallah Ali al-Sistani. The Iraqi constitution, while influenced by Shi'a theology, bears the stamp of Khoei and not of the theocratic style of his rival Khomeini.

While the focus of this chapter is on Iraqi Shi'a and what that means for potential Iranian influence, the difference in these two schools of thought has deeper implications that cut across state lines in forming Shi'a identity and allegiances. For instance, Nasr tells us, "In a village in northern Pakistan in 1989, I asked Shi'as which ayatallah they followed. The answer came back 'In religious matters Ayatallah Khoei, and in political matters Ayatallah Khomeini'" (Nasr, 2006, 144). I have described the way in which Shi'as choose their religious leader and emulate him by following his teachings and obeying his edicts. In this way we see a theoretical divide among Shi'a between the religious doctrine of *marja'iyya* and the political doctrine of *velayat-e Faqih*. One of the key questions this chapter examines is what does this tension mean for Iranian influence in Iraq. The primary vehicle for examining this question is the succession of Grand Ayatallah Ali al-Sistani.

## Theology and Politics: A Primer

The central theater for the Shi'a Revival is now Iraq. Not only are there more Shi'a holy sites in Iraq than anywhere else in the world, the holy city of Najaf is the second busiest center of learning in the Shi'a world. It is second only to Qom in Iran. Yet with the rise of a Shi'a government (or pro-Shi'a government, at least) in Iraq, replacing the secular anti-Shi'a regime of Saddam Hussein, Najaf has already returned to its former position as the center of Shi'a (especially quietist) theology. As such, the debates within the Iraqi seminaries could shape the future of Shi'a theology and identity for decades to come with profound implications for the Middle East generally and for Iraq very directly. The implications, therefore, for U.S. policy are enormous. How will the United States adjust its policies and effectively counter Iranian Strategic Influence without understanding, acknowledging, and potentially shaping religious and theological discussions?

The rise to prominence of Sistani and the Shi'a clerics in Iraq more generally was a direct consequence of the chaos that followed the U.S. invasion of Iraq. "The authority of the Shi'ite *ulama* became clear after the 2003 invasion of Iraq, when scholars emerged as the major Shi'ite power brokers" (Gleave, 2007, 63). Major policy decisions concerning how the Iraqi constitution would be written, how governance would be instituted, and how national security and defense would be executed could not be made or implemented without input from the *ulama*. Just as in Lebanon where the civil war and the invasion by Israel created the opportunity structures that gave rise to Hizb'allah, so the U.S. invasion of Iraq created a divide among the elite, opportunities to activate identities and mobilize communities, and organize political and militant action arms. The clergy, the Mosque system, provided a means to communicate a single message efficiently across large parts of the country, and this helped make the *ulama* a powerful force in post-invasion Iraq. However, the senior clerics had important theological disagreements that shaped policy outcomes.

Gleave examines the authority and theological positions of three of the Iraqi *ulama*: Ayatallah Kazim al-Ha'iri is the heir to Ayatallah Muhammad Sadiq al-Sadr, father of Moqtada al-Sadr; Ayatallah Muhammad Baqir al-Hakim, the leader of the Supreme Council of the Islamic Revolution in Iraq (SCIRI); and the aforementioned Ayatallah Ali al-Sistani. His work is an exposition of the theories of *ijtihad, taqlid,* and *marja'iyya,* particularly as it involves *ijtihad* and *taqlid.* A major tenet of Shi'a eschatological theology holds that the Twelfth Imam went into hiding in the Occultation (*ghayba*) only to return at the end times to restore justice. Since the Imam is the only source of certainty in knowledge (*ilm, yaqin*), during the *ghayba* Shi'a faithful and lower clerics could only rely on considered scholarly opinion (*zann*). To render *zann* a scholar had to be of a certain status, *mujtahid,* which means one qualified to practice *ijtihad*—independent juristic reasoning. All other Shi'as were required, then, to practice *taqlid*—imitating or following the *mujtahid* (Gleave, 2007, 65–66).

Between the writings of al-Sistani and al-Hakim there emerged a dispute regarding how the *umma* can recognize the *mujtahid*. For al-Sistani, the *ulama*—the body of scholars—confers this status and the *umma* accepts it and chooses which recognized *mujtahid* to follow. For al-Hakim, the ultimate authority is the conscience of the individual who must investigate the credentials and teachings of the scholar before accepting him as *mujtahid*. Without pursuing the theological question in great depth, as that is outside the scope of this work, the issue of genuine authority matters significantly for a hierarchical religion. In practice, however, the distinction here is minor. While mid-ranking clerics, such as Muqtada al-Sadr, have loyal followers, they lack recognition from the *ulama* and therefore lack legitimacy in religious matters. In other words, for certain matters a lesser-ranked cleric can have his own following, following al-Hakim's principle of *mujtahid*, but in practice it remains the case that only the *ulama* can confer higher status. Those few in the competition for succeeding al-Sistani are recognized by the *ulama* as having sufficient rank.

The next contested issue is which of the learned scholars to follow. Here the dispute is between al Ha'iri and al-Sistani. Al-Hairi says that the most learned scholar (*a'lam*) must be followed, but that recognizing him is all but impossible and that the individual must choose whom to follow conscientiously. For al-Sistani the disagreement is on how the *a'lam* is recognized, for this, too, is a matter for the *ulama* to settle. The scholar who has the respect and following of the *ulama* is clearly the *a'lam* (Gleave, 2007, 68). Here, too, the theological niceties, beyond our scope, may be quite intricate, but in practical matters the people have followed Sistani largely as they followed his predecessor. That is, the *ulama* and the *umma* have been in sync as to who the *a'lam* is. Nevertheless, this does not mean that minor clerics as well as other high-ranking clerics do not have their own following. The question here concerns ultimate authority, but since each Shi'a must follow the teachings of his Marja, there is little practical results from theological disputes between the Marjas, in most cases.

While these disputes involving the structure and authority of Shi'a Islam are important, the key element of dispute for the purposes of this work is to understand how these scholars interpret and teach regarding the *vilayet-e faqih*. Not surprisingly, both al-Ha'iri and al-Hakim are followers of the *vilayet-e faqih*. Their political participation in Iraq is overt and both men head political parties and have control or influence over Shi'a militia. Al-Sistani, as we have seen, is the leader of the "Quietist" school and is not a part of any established political party. It would be wrong to assume from this that al-Sistani was not active in the political developments in Iraq since the U.S. invasion (Gleave, 2007, 70).

Al-Ha'iri teaches, "There is no difference in *taqlid* between political and other matters. In every issue, on which you know the opinion of the one you follow, you should follow his opinion" (Gleave, 2007, 70). Al-Ha'iri's point here is that the learned are best able to discern how Islam should inform the current political landscape—the issues of the day—and how the *umma* should live their lives as faithful Muslims cannot preclude the political sphere. Al-Hakim makes a similar point, but with a caveat. "Baqir al-Hakim is . . . mak[ing] a distinction between what he called *marja'iyya diniyya fiqhiyya* (legal religious leadership) and *marja'iyya diniyya siyasiyya* (political religious leadership)" (Gleave, 2007, 71). This gives legal authority to those who would follow Sistani for religious guidance and Khamenei for the political. Once again, however, in a political climate like that of Iraq, where security is tenuous, where decisions being made at present can have long-term effects, it has proved impossible for even a quietest like Sistani not to involve himself in political affairs.

A difference of opinion emerges between al-Ha'iri and al-Hakim. Al-Ha'iri believes the *wali* (the jurist who leads the Muslims) does not have to be a *marja al-taqlid*, he need only have sufficient knowledge to govern well (Gleave, 2007, 72). This is interesting insofar as a reading of the *vilayat-e faqih* doctrine seems to support this interpretation. Neither accepts the *vilayet-e faqih* as an article of faith. If one's *Marja* does not support the *vilayet-e faqih*, then the believer must follow his *Marja* (Gleave, 2007, 74). These considerations increase in importance as Ayatallah Sistani is in his early nineties and of ill health. To put it simply, the succession battle has begun and if this most revered cleric is replaced by someone who supports the *velayat-e faqih* system, then Iran will get a great boon in its influence in Iraq.

## Why Sistani's Succession Matters

Grand Ayatallah Ali Hussaini al-Sistani is the most prominent Shi'a cleric in the world. As the successor to Grand Ayatallah Khoei, Sistani inherited a network that extends from Pakistan to Iran, Iraq, Lebanon, through to London and New York. As such, his word is law to millions of the Shi'a faithful and his income from the various foundations, educational centers, and religious taxes are in the tens of millions. Sistani, like Khoei before him, is of the quietest school, as discussed above. The fundamental disagreement Sistani had with Khomeini and has with his successor Khamenei is what comprises *fiqh*, or jurisprudence, and where *fiqh* fits into society. Sistani believes that the authority of the Islamic Jurist is limited to religious affairs only and should not extend to the political realm. While Khomeini understood the Guardianship of the Islamic Jurist as a necessity and the obligation to oversee governance part of the privilege assigned by God to jurists, Sistani, on the other hand, believes that "popularity and social acceptability" is a major requirement of any single Marjas' authority (Khalaji, 2006).

Theological differences can have great worldly impact where religious authority heavily influences social, economic, and political factors. Mobilization at various points in Iran's history, and more recently in Lebanon as well, is facilitated by an information and influence network that runs throughout these countries—the Marja'iyya and their respective mosques, charities, and educational centers. This is especially true in Iraq today. "Since the war, to procure any public goods, Iraqis have needed to collectively act in a wide range of new situations. Locally, they need to devise new social norms and enforcement strategies to dispose of trash and protect neighborhoods. Nationally, they are better off if they can coordinate their votes and bargaining positions with a sufficient number of other Iraqis" (Patel, 2005, 1). That is, being able to mobilize communities enables effective capitalization of opportunity structures.

Patel, as if speaking to the mobilization and Strategic Influence theories defined above, goes on to say, "Islam also provides a shared symbolic system that helps Muslims know how other Muslims, at least those with the same theological interpretations, understand sermons' messages. . . . Sermons coordinate beliefs about the behavior expected of individuals in various circumstances, helping Iraqis form shared understandings of the new, postwar world around them and what to expect from others" (Patel, 2005, 6).[1] Further, in post-invasion Iraq, much like in Civil War Lebanon, the failure of the state apparatus to provide essential services gave impetus to local responses often led by religious or militant organizations. "Locally, Iraqis need to collectively act to provide public goods previously supplied by the state, such as trash collection and security. Trash and sewage piled in streets when municipal collection stopped, drains clogged without maintenance, and dumpsters were looted for scrap metal" (Patel, 2005, 7). The structure of the Marja'iyya system enables a senior cleric like Sistani to train and dispatch clerics throughout Iraq sending a unified message; these clerics mention the name of their Marja, reinforcing the authority and authenticity of the message (Patel, 2005, 13–14). These networks create "imagined communities" through common knowledge generation (Patel, 2005, 14). This unified message has significant effects on organizing public life in Iraq.

A well-known example of this power concerns the Coalition Provisional Authority's plan for postwar constitutional and governmental formation. The initial plan called for a confessional system, similar to what is emplaced in Lebanon, where each branch of government "belongs to" either the Sunni, Shi'a, or Christian groups. Sistani opposed this plan and called for direct elections for the constitution drafting council (Rostami-Povey 2010, 138). Sistani activated his influence network and before the CPA could effectively communicate its version, Sistani had shaped the information environment in his favor. "Immediately after Sistani's statement was released, however, Shiite opinion became firmly entrenched against the idea of unelected caucuses and for direct national elections for the entire assembly" (Patel, 2005, 15). Please note, the CPA was keenly aware of Sistani's information and influence network. "Larry Diamond, a CPA official at the time, states, *'We understood that Sistani could reach the Iraqi people more rapidly and effectively than could the CPA, with its cumbersome communications machine.'* He continues by quoting a top CPA governance official, *'Our ability to communicate with the Iraqi people is much less than his* [Sistani's]*, and he has the simpler message: 'we want elections'"* (Emphasis in original) (Patel, 2005, 15). The CPA ultimately had to agree to Sistani's terms, after several large protests across Iraq showed Sistani's influence. "After mid-January's demonstration, all Shiites in Iraq recognized Sistani's ability to coordinate public opinion on key issues and effectively control mobilization initiated by his network" (Patel, 2005, 16).

The range of Sistani's influence is partly due to his own authority as a religious leader who has remained above the fray of politics. He is seen as an authentic voice for the Iraqi people, his hermitical and humble lifestyle adds to his appeal. He also sits atop a pyramid of clerics that spreads across Iraq, and beyond, giving him significant religious and economic power. Should Iran succeed in replacing Sistani, their influence in Iraq and throughout the Shi'a world would increase appreciably, assuming Sistani's successor had the authority and legitimacy to sustain the network, of course. Since religious authority and legitimacy are key factors in the succession question, before delving into the Sistani succession question directly, the next section gives some background on Sistani and the scope of his network.

**Sistani and His Vast Network**

Sistani was born in the Iranian city of Mashhad on August 4, 1930. His lineage traces back to the Prophet Mohammed himself, allowing him to use the honorific of Seyyed, a major source of religious authority and prestige (Rahimi 2007). Sistani's father, Seyyed Mohammed Hussaini was also a prominent Shi'a cleric who was closely associated with Mohammed Hussain Na'ini, the mentor and teacher of Sistani's religious instructor, Ayatallah Abdul Qassim al-Khoei. It is from Na'ini and al-Khoei that Sistani inherited the practice of quietism (Rahimi 2007).

Sistani began his religious education at the tender age of five in a hometown Mosque. In 1949, Sistani relocated to the Shi'a holy city of Qom, where he studied under Ayatallah Mohammed Mahdi Burujirdi, another prominent practitioner of quietism. After completing his basic studies and his abilities and talent recognized, Sistani moved to Najaf in 1951 where he began his education under one of the most important clerics of the time, his mentor and predecessor, Grand Ayatallah al-Khoei (Rahimi 2007). In 1960 Sistani earned the title of mujtahid, which secured his recognition among the Shi'a clerical community as being a clerical jurist and religious authority for Shi'a Islam. One of only three at the time, Sistani was only thirty years old when he received this title (Rahimi 2007).

In 1961, Sistani permanently relocated to the city of Najaf, has seldom left since, and lives in relative seclusion. Little is known about Sistani's activities in the immediate aftermath of the Iranian Revolution and during the Iran-Iraq War from 1980 to 1988 due to the intense oppression of the Shi'a community under Saddam Hussein during those years. Under the Ba'athist regime's rule Sistani faced a considerable number of challenges and threats. He survived multiple assassination attempts and was under constant monitoring. In 1993 Hussein closed the al-Khaza Mosque, which Sistani presided over, inhibiting his ability to communicate directly with his followers. When Ayatallah Mohammed Sadeq al-Sadr was assassinated in 1998, Sistani virtually ceased all activities rarely leaving his home. It was not until the fall of the Iraqi regime in 2003 that Sistani reemerged as a publicly influential figure in Iraqi society. Among the Shi'a, including the political elite, Sistani is a figure of

Iraqi national unity, despite his being born in Iran. In fact, Sistani has refused to return to Iran because "he does not want the Iranian government to take political advantage of his travel to his homeland" (Rahimi 2007, 4).

Sistani is the leading Cleric of Najaf's "Hawza al-Illmiya" which is a network of various religious institutions and seminaries to which many different high-ranking clerics belong (Rahimi 2007, 5). Najaf, a sacred city to Shi'a Muslims, is the burial site of the Prophet's cousin and the first Imam, Ali, who was assassinated after he became Caliph during a time of civil war and unrest. As the leading Ayatallah there, Sistani and his organization receive the bulk of Islamic taxes, known as Khoms, paid by Shi'as to their Marja, their source of emulation. Khoms, literally meaning a fifth in Arabic, are dues that comprise one-fifth of excess end-of-the-year income of Shi'a Muslims. This money goes toward supporting the many different projects of the Marjas who receive them, such as their various seminaries, schools, orphanages, and other social institutions. Without a significant collection of religious taxes a Marja cannot properly support his own network and thus loses influence. Sistani's network is vast, ranging from Pakistan, through the Middle East, and even as far away as London and New York. With such a massive financial network Sistani is also able to provide significant amounts of charitable donations in the form of money, medicine, clothing, food, and other alms. Along with this charitable network, of course, comes a network for disseminating information.

Sistani's large financial strength allows him to fund a large network of lower-ranking clerics that interacts directly with local Shi'a populations around the world in his name. He is also able to pay his seminary students well, including providing health care to his students' families during their studies. Sistani's network continues to grow because "the bigger a senior cleric's purse, the wider patronage network he can build in the clerical ranks below him" (Nasr 2006, 72). And the larger the network the greater the purse. Further, Sistani's organization is international in scope, with offices in Iraq, Afghanistan, Azerbaijan, Bahrain, Britain, Georgia, India, Iran, Kuwait, Lebanon, Pakistan, Saudi Arabia, Syria, Turkey, and the United States. In addition to the brick-and-mortar offices Sistani maintains, he was one of the first Marjas to use the Internet as a significant medium to project his teachings. His websites allow for followers to engage with his office directly by asking questions seeking political and religious guidance as well as offering direct portals to pay religious taxes. Through his websites Sistani receives nearly 1,000 questions a day from his followers (Rahimi 2007, 7). The most recent estimation I could find of the number of Sistani's followers is around twenty million faithful (Schiavenza 2014).

Because of Sistani's large network of followers, he is able to directly influence and shape political events in the region. In addition to the example given above consider this. In the aftermath of the overthrow of Saddam Hussein by American forces in 2003, the Coalition Provisional Government was charged with coordinating with elected officials to draft a constitution. "Kurdish leaders at the last moment insisted on a clause, 61(c), in the TAL [Transitional Administrative Law] giving any three provinces the power to veto a final constitution if 2/3 of voters rejected it in a planned national referendum" (Patel 2005, 17). As in the example above, Sistani objected to this and let it be known through his emissaries. "Dramatically, the TAL signing ceremony scheduled for the following day was postponed when five prominent Shiites on the GC [Governing Council] did not show up. These Shiite leaders, including the leaders of Da'wa and SCIRI, knew that their credibility among the Shiite public would be destroyed if they openly endorsed the TAL after Sistani's mosques subsequently condemned it. Instead, they demanded the revisions that Sistani requested, despite having agreed to the text two days earlier" (Patel 2005, 17).

This is just one of many examples where Sistani has used his influence to shape political events. A more recent and impactful example is the Spring 2014 fatwa Sistani issued to the young and able-bodied male population of Iraq in response to the threat of the Daesh (unfortunately called IS, ISIS, or ISIL elsewhere). As a result, thousands of young men took up arms against Daesh, joining the multitude of Shi'a militias that are fighting in Iraq today. Sistani, through representatives in his Friday sermons, pressured Prime Minister Haider al-Abadi to "hold corrupt officials accountable, to reform the judiciary and to support the national security forces instead of Iran-backed militias" (Arango 2015). It has not gone unnoticed that for a self-proclaimed quietist, Sistani has indeed been active in Iraqi politics. Arango goes so far as to question whether these efforts to aid a fledgling democratic government in Iraq are actually paving the way for clerical rule, demonstrating Khomeini's point that the most learned Jurist is needed to guide politicians toward just rule (2015). Indeed, it is worth considering whether the distance between the Quietist and *Velayat* schools has closed significantly.

Nevertheless, Sistani's vast patronage network among the clerical establishment and his vast information network, make him, arguably, the single most influential person in Iraq. It is reasonable to question whether Sistani's vast network may disperse upon his death. However, since to a large degree it is held together by patronage, infrastructure (both brick and mortar and virtual), and information; in other words, it has become institutionalized, it could be held together by someone who also has the resources and sufficient religious credentials. These are certainly among the necessary factors for selecting a successor. Iran's Supreme Leader, recognizing the immense value of capturing this network, has been busily securing patronage networks in anticipation of the passing of Grand Ayatallah Ali al-Sistani. The succession question, however, remains very open.

## What the Succession Battle Looks Like

While there is no formal succession protocol or set of qualifications, any successor must possess significant religious credentials and following. This is both because of the prestige needed to be considered and the financial resources needed to maintain the patronage network required to be a Marja. "The succession, a lengthy and opaque process in which the outcome is by no means assured, could shape the interplay of Islam and democracy not only in Iraq, where Shiites are the majority, but also across a Shiite Muslim world that stretches from India to Iran, Lebanon and beyond" (Arango 2012). Further, as we will see, there is a preference that the successor for this position should be a Marja from Najaf. It is safe to assume that what motivates this is, in part, a desire for Iraqi national unity and to maintain the independence of the Hawzas of Najaf, from governmental or foreign, particularly Iranian, interference. Given these general guidelines, there are four major contenders for Sistani's exalted position.

One potential successor to Grand Ayatallah Sistani is Grand Ayatallah Muhammed Ishaq al-Fayyad. Ayatallah al-Fayyad is one of the four most senior-ranking clerics in the Hawza of Najaf, the same Hawza to which Sistani belongs. Fayyad was born in a small village in Afghanistan in 1930. At ten years old, he and his family moved to Najaf, Iraq where he would continue his religious studies. Fayyad came under the guidance and mentorship of Grand Ayatallah al-Khoei. When al-Khoei died in 1992 al-Fayyad elected not to compete for his position, but rather to support Sistani, who succeeded al-Khoei. After the 2003 U.S. invasion of Iraq, Fayyad was the most willing of all other Ayatallahs to engage with American forces. However, Fayyad rejected the notion that Iraq's system of governance should be purely secular and that there is no way to have absolute separation of religion and state. Nonetheless, Fayyad does not support the *wilayat al-faqih* system of government practiced in Iran. Although he believes that the Marja should play a role in Iraqi society he rejects the notion of clerical rule there (Anzalone 2009; Cole 2004). At ninety years old if he is chosen it would clearly be in a caretaker position because no suitable candidate had been found.

Another contender is Grand Ayatallah Bashir al-Najafi. Al-Najafi was born in Jalandhar, India in 1942. In 1947 his family moved to Gujranwalla, Pakistan, where he began his religious education. In the 1960s he relocated to Iraq and later resumed his religious studies in Najaf. Al-Najafi has a broad base of popularity and reverence based on the many social services projects he has organized and undertaken. Some of these projects include providing electricity to Shi'a neighborhoods where electrical power was limited, orphanages for children whose parents were killed either in war or by oppression, as well as stepping in on several occasions as head of the Hawza when Ayatallah al-Khoei was ill (Anzalone 2009; Cole 2004).

Grand Ayatallah Sayyid Muhammad Saeed al-Tabataba'i al-Hakim is among the four Grand Marjas of the Hawza of Najaf, along with al-Najafi, Fayyad, and, of course, Sistani. He was born in February 1934 in Najaf, Iraq, to the prominent Hakim family. His father was Ayatallah Saeed Mohammed Ali al-Hakim, who was a top scholar of *fiqh* and the principles of *fiqh*, an expert in the fields of Islamic spirituality, ethics, Islamic inheritance law, and high-level mathematics. Al-Hakim is the grandnephew of Grand Ayatallah Muhsin al-Hakim who preceded Grand Ayatallah al-Khoei. Ayatallah Saeed al-Hakim received his religious education early on in his life from both his father and granduncle. He would later go on to study under Grand Ayatallah al-Khoei in the Hawza of Najaf where he would rise to become one of the highest Shi'a religious authority. In 1983 Ayatallah al-Hakim along with his father and many other members of his family were detained and imprisoned by Saddam Hussein due to the dictator's fear of the Hakim family starting a Shi'a rebellion against his regime. During his internment Ayatallah al-Hakim gave religious guidance and educational services to the detainees of Iraq's infamous Abu Ghraib prison. It is noteworthy that Grand Ayatallah al-Hakim is related to the founder of the Islamic Supreme Council of Iraq (ISCI), Ayatallah Sayyed Mohammed Baqir al-Hakim, whose current leader is Seyyed Ammar al-Hakim. The ISCI, at that time, was a Shi'a Islamist political party within Iraq that adhered to the Iranian concept of *velayat-e faqih*.

For some time, it appeared that the only succession candidate who was not of the Hawza but was being groomed by Khamenei to succeed Sistani was Ayatallah Mahmoud Hashemi Shahroudi. Ayatallah Shahroudi was born on September 1, 1948. Although he was born in Iraq he held both Iranian and Iraqi citizenship (Bordbar 2014; Arango 2012). Little is known about his early life; Shahroudi's biography "contains the details of a life of activism, exile and rise to political power, with deep sympathies toward militant Islam" (Arango 2012). Ayatallah Shahroudi received his religious education under the highly respected and extremely prominent late Shi'a cleric Ayatallah Bakr al-Sadr, father-in-law of Moqtada al-Sadr. He also studied under Iran's Revolutionary Leader Ayatallah Khomeini. In 1999 Iran's Supreme Leader Ali Khamenei appointed Shahroudi to the head of the Iranian Judiciary; he remained in that position until 2009. Shahroudi at one point also temporarily held the important position of Chairman of the Assembly of Experts after its previous chairman, Mahdavi Kani, suffered a heart attack (Bordbar 2014). As a religious authority, he has presided over the education of other important figures including Iran's Supreme Leader, Khamenei, and Hassan Nasrallah, the leader of Hizb'allah (AP 2012). Iran-backed Shahroudi and for a time his posters were seen all over Najaf and an extensive campaign of funding seminarians and minor clerics in his name was undertaken. His death in December 2018 left a void in Iranian-backed candidates for this important post. Although it is safe to assume that the efforts will continue to gain a significant "voting bloc" to influence the succession question.

The succession of Sistani is not a simple matter in another sense. The role he plays as Marja al-taqlid requires stature and many years of scholarship. Any of the men discussed above as well as other potential candidates possesses those qualification to varying degrees. However, the vast patronage network, the charities, the schools, the al-Khoi foundation, and other global institutions that Sistani currently controls are another matter. Those currently running these institutions, loyal to Sistani, some his family, could retain their positions no matter who replaces the Marja. If this happens some of the influence of the position will weaken. This is something that will need to be watched closely. Further, this could happen temporarily as the new Marja gains prominence he may assume more authority over the Sistani network. This is not just a matter of speculation but of critical importance if Iran has any leverage over Sistani's replacement.

Another important factor to consider is the age of the candidates being spoken about. It is not clear that the men discussed above, if any are selected, could be more than caretakers which would give a younger group of scholars time to burnish their credentials. This last point is important if one thinks of Moqtada al-Sadr as a potential candidate down the road. Currently he lacks the religious credentials and authority, but in ten years that could change. He has undergone more theological training in Qom and could continue developing his theological credentials. Lastly, it is not clear whether quietism could survive an Iraq in civil war, or an Iraq as a battle ground between the United States and Iran, or battleground for Iraqi Shi'a militias who have voted on the expulsion of U.S. troops but feel compelled to use force to effect that expulsion. All of these contextual factors will impact the importance and value of Sistani's successor and the role he will be able to play in Iraq and consequently Iran's potential influence through this office.

## Evaluation of Candidates

It should be noted that Sistani is unlikely to name a successor. If he did so it would be a significant break from practice. Generally, the Hawzas and the international Shi'a community choose among the most prominent Grand Ayatallahs who will be the preeminent Marja—*a'lam*. It is, normally, a slow and organic process. Second, Sistani could hurt his legacy by naming someone who is not ultimately selected by his contemporaries or become entangled with corruption, for example. Further, the ability to maintain a large patronage network requires standing and prestige among the clerical elite and financial resources. For these reasons, al-Hakim emerges as the most likely successor among the senior clerics of the Hawza, in my estimation.

Najafi is well known and liked among the clerics and seminarians in Najaf. He is closely associated with the three other senior Marjas, with special ties to Sistani. However, Najafi's connections outside of the Hawza of Najaf are limited. He does not have considerable influence outside this Iraqi city and his network of followers is nowhere near the size of Sistani's or the other Marjas under consideration. Also, Najafi is of Indian descent which, while not a disqualification, can be seen as a weakness as Iraqi Shi'a may be looking for a sign of national unity in its next Grand Marja. More importantly, Najafi is also regarded as less religiously educated than some of his competitors. Because of these factors, Grand Ayatallah Bashir al-Najafi has "very little political influence on the Shi'a community of Iraq" (Khalaji 2005).

Grand Ayatallah Fayyad is perhaps the most educated of the other clerics in the Hawza of Najaf. He studied under Sistani's predecessor Ayatallah al-Khoei where he was reported to be "one of his most trusted and loved students" (Rahimi 2007, 7). Fayyad, like Sistani, is a quietist and rejects Iran's *velayat-e faqih* system. However, Fayyad like Najafi has a limited network that barely extends outside of Najaf. Further, Fayyad, like Sistani, is quite elderly. The Shi'a may want long-term continuity and would likely, then, choose a relatively younger man. However, if no suitable candidate emerges, Fayyad may be chosen even if he "may only be an interim figure" (Hendawi 2011). Fayyad, like Najafi, is foreign-born; he is of Afghan descent which, as noted, could be a disadvantage among the almost exclusively Arab Shi'a population of Iraq, who may want a symbol of national unity in their Grand Marja. However, neither Najafi nor Fayyad should be discounted entirely because of their nationalities. Ayatallah al-Khoei was an ethnic Azeri and yet was still beloved by the Iraqi people (Rahimi 2007). And Sistani himself was born in Iran. This history, however, must be balanced with the contemporary context. Iraq is a divided, war-torn country, and the Shi'a may want a national leader to emerge, although admittedly that leader could be foreign-born, a native son could bring additional credibility, particularly against outside interference.

Ayatallah Hashemi Shahroudi was the candidate Iran, specifically Khamenei, was grooming to install in this position. He was a great choice for Iran in that he was an adamant believer of the *velayat-e faqih* system of government and was close to Ayatallah Khamenei. For a period of time Shahroudi served as the leader of the Supreme Islamic Council of Iraq which connects him closely to the Hakim family as well. Shahroudi, due to his position within the Iranian government, and his own extensive religious patronage network, was extremely wealthy. Additionally, in the competition to replace Sistani, Shahroudi brought a virtually unlimited supply of income from Iran. These funds were being used to sponsor a large network of clerics, seminaries, and institutions, all key components to becoming a high-ranking Marja (Arango 2012).

With Shahroudi's demise all that effort is not likely to go to waste. It means that Supreme Leader Ali Khamenei is ready to promote a candidate or back a candidate—play kingmaker. That is, Iran is ready to "influence" the outcome of the Sistani succession with hard cash, appointments, and other inducements. Nevertheless, all of that support cannot make a bad candidate a good candidate or make a good candidate appear from thin air. The candidate must still be a senior cleric, a Grand Ayatallah, have a significant following and economic means, which means he will enjoy a certain independence.

These key factors, in my opinion, favor Grand Ayatallah Seyyed Mohammed al-Hakim. Seyyed al-Hakim, a native of Iraq, is a member of the extremely prominent and politically active al-Hakim family. He is a Marja al-Taqlid, like the other men under consideration here, but al-Hakim maintains a significant following. A 2005 estimate put the total number of Hakim's followers around 5 percent of the entire Shi'a community (Arango 2012). With this following, his vast family connections, and his wealth al-Hakim is a strong contender.

However, his political connections both within and outside Iraq make him both more attractive and less attractive simultaneously. Hakim's uncle, Ayatallah Mohammed Baqir al-Hakim was the founder of the SCIRI, now known as the ISCI. The formerly known SCIRI was originally founded in Iran. The Shi'a Islamic party promotes the agenda of establishing a government similar to that of Iran. ISCI is heavily supported, both financially and militarily, by Iran (Nasr 2006, 186). Its armed wing, the Badr Brigade, which was one of the Shi'a militias leading the fight against the Islamic State, is led by a fiercely pro-Iranian Iraqi named Hadi al-Amiri and is closely advised by the Iranian Revolutionary Guard (George 2014). Grand Ayatallah al-Hakim's interconnectedness with Iraqi politics has slightly hurt his network of followers who adhere to the quietist school. However, after Sistani's 2014 fatwa, which called for every able-bodied Shi'a male to take arms against Daesh, al-Hakim's association with ISCI and the Badr brigade may not be as damaging as it might have been prior.

## Summary

It is important to note that while some speak of Sistani's succession as inevitable, it could be the case that his vast network dissipates upon his death. This is unlikely, however, since much of his network is formally institutionalized through the al-Khoei Foundation and other formal institutions. However, it is possible that the formal institutions continue to be run by the Sistani family and a handful of senior clerics, in effect a committee that prevents the rise of a single *a'lam*.² The difficulty with this line of thought is that it goes against many long years of tradition and against the need to unify Iraq, which argues for a strong *a'lam*. Therefore, it is likely that the network will remain largely intact.

However, the succession process itself could take time to resolve itself. Sami al-Askari, a Shi'a politician, states that "It will take Najaf two to three years before a strong marja emerges," following Sistani's death (Arango 2012). And, as noted, Marjas almost always avoid appointing their own successors because they carry "the responsibility for the successor's possible impieties or mistakes after the *marja's* own death," which further complicates the process of Sistani's succession (Rahimi 2007). Given Iranian influence and Iraq's fragile unity many may feel the need to immediately fill the leadership void left by Sistani's death. In other words, the fear of instability and vulnerability that Sistani's death could create might require quicker action than the normal slower pace of organic emergence of a leader. This is where a short-term caretaker such as Grand Ayatallah Ishaq al-Fayyad emerges as a strong possibility. This will allow for Fayyad to immediately assume the day-to-day operations of the Hawza of Najaf while Sistani's family will continue to run his organization and institutions. However, because of his advanced age, Fayyad will likely only be an interim replacement for Sistani. It is very unlikely that Fayyad will be able to maintain a network that makes him the leader of all Shi'a Muslims.

This would allow Grand Ayatallah Seyyed al-Hakim more time to consolidate his position as the leading contender to assume Sistani's role in the Hawza of Najaf. Hakim already commands a large following of pious Shi'as and his political connectedness in Iraq and with Iran will enable him to gain a significant amount of funding to sustain a large network. The succession of Sistani by Hakim is a development the United States should look upon with caution. His family connections by default tie him with the pro-Iranian ISCI. This makes him susceptible to subtle or overt Iranian influence. However, Hakim, at the age of eighty-five, is also quite elderly creating doubt as to how long he will be able to maintain this position. However, the consolidation of power for the Hakim family could prove difficult to reverse, given that he could use much of his family's position and wealth to begin securing his succession with another Hakim immediately upon accession.

Given all of these variables how this extremely important succession question will be resolved remains a mystery. Three strong possibilities emerge. The first is the rise of some Iranian-backed candidate, who can bring to bear very large coffers and positions to barter with for support, but this could lead to weakened legitimacy as Iraqi clergy and citizens fear Iranian dominance. The other is the decentralization of religious authority which would mean a greater number of prominent marjas with lesser influence throughout Iraq. This would make it difficult for any single Marja to exert significant power over Iraqi political affairs. The Hawza of Najaf has a relatively small number of Grand Ayatallahs (four), compared to other Hawzas such as the Hawza of Qom which has around ten (Al-Kifaee 2010). Yet none of the four can exert the kind of influence that Sistani can. Should decentralization occur, this could favor Iran's influence campaign significantly as it would be easier to overwhelm information coming from various sources with a unified single message and it would be very easy to outspend several and institutionally divided Marjas. The third possibility is that a weakened and divided Hawza leadership become a rubber stamp for a charismatic forceful younger cleric like Sayyed Moqtada al-Sadr. Sadr has a strong family pedigree, a large militia, a larger political following, decent relations with Iran, and growing religious credentials. He could keep the Sistani seat open, slowly position himself to succeed by managing some of the al-Khoi foundation (by hook or by crook) and gaining de facto preeminence. Of the three possibilities mentioned here the second is the most likely, the third the least.

Another critical point that bears consideration is whether the difference between the quietist school and the *velayat-e faqih* system has, in fact, shrunk. The chaos that has engulfed Iraq since 2003 till today has created a set of conditions that have both increased the need of Sistani's interference in politics and his power in doing so. This is a far cry from Sistani, or his successor, becoming the commander-in-chief of the Armed Forces, like Khamenei is in Iran. Yet, the idea that clerics should shy away from politics seems to have been abandoned, albeit by emergency conditions. There is uncertainty here as to how this will unfold. However inadvertently, Sistani's active participation in Iraqi politics, born of necessity, seems to set precedent for a more activist successor. If that successor is aligned with Iran and the Shi'a militias in Iraq, like Hakim is, then this could be the beginning of the end for the quietist school in Najaf, a great boon for Iran, and a major problem for the United States and its allies. What makes this more problematic from the U.S. perspective is that the United States seems to have made a high-level and long-term policy decision not to get involved in religious affairs. The United States does not appear to be leveraging any influence, even at the margins, to affect the Sistani question. Policy discussions in journals, think tanks, editorial pages, and other such outlets are relatively silent on this critical issue. Unlike the United States, Iran is well positioned to control or deeply influence Sistani's successor using the Strategic Influence mechanisms discussed in this work.

The primary driver seems to be a symbolic predisposition among the Shi'as in Iraq toward the *resistance* and *triumphalist* themes emanating from Iran. The symbolism of resistance taken up by the Shi'a militias, discussed in the next section, helps rally the masses around a myth-symbol complex of *resistance* and *triumph*. For decades under Saddam Hussein's rule, Iran supported groups loyal to the *Velayat* system. The raised fist clutching a Kalashnikov rifle on the IRGC logo is not just a symbol of *resistance* against oppressors but a symbol of *triumph* over oppressors based on adherence to religious principles given by the jurisprudent—the *Rahbar*—of the *Velayat* system. Ideologically, the Grand Marjas of Iraq may resist the symbolic representational force of *resistance* and *triumph* based on the religious ideology of the *Velayat* system, but these factors coupled with financial and institutional support coming from Iran may be hard to resist for the *ulama* and their faithful followers. This is evidenced by how the militias and their Iranian supporters have mobilized the masses, activating their symbolic predispositions, by successfully deploying myth-symbol complexes of *resistance* and *triumph* through Strategic Influence to gain hegemony over Iraq. Against this there is a strong Iraqi nationalist force. Many Iraqis, even many Iraqi Shi'a, do not want to see Iraq fall under Iranian dominance. If Iran can place a successor in Sistani's role, they will gain a great Strategic Influence advantage in Iraq. Further, they are also well-positioned given their relationship with the various Iraqi Shi'a militias that are part of the Popular Mobilization Forces, the subject of the next section.

## THE HIZB'ALLAH MODEL IN IRAQ: THE PMF

Shi'a militias in Iraq have a long history, predating the fall of Saddam Hussein in 2003. However, two major events created opportunity structures for their increase in power and consequently for Iranian influence. These are the U.S. invasion of Iraq in 2003 and the rise of Daesh in 2014. Both events, but particularly the latter, gave these militias a sense of sacred duty and popular support. Fighting Daesh, for some saving Iraq from Daesh, was a sacred duty, a response to Grand Ayatallah Ali al-Sistani's fatwa calling for the defense of holy shrines against Daesh. This Fatwa evoked the *resistance* to oppression narrative that already resonated with the militias but cloaked it in religious duty. The response to Sistani's call was swift and sure. From this response was born the Popular Mobilization Forces (PMF).

The PMF, which comprises a few major Shi'a militias and dozens of smaller forces, was formally instated as part of the Iraqi Armed Forces by parliament in November 2016 (Al-Qarawee 2017, 4, Hendawi 2016). A process that had begun in June 2014, when the then Iraqi prime minister Nouri al-Maliki, "signed an official decree to form the Commission for the PMF (Hay'at al-Hashd al-Shaabi)" (Mansour 2017, 6). Maliki's successor, Haider al-Abadi, passed "Executive Order 91," which states that "the PMF will be an independent military formation and a part of the Iraqi armed forces, and attached to the general commander of the armed forces" (Mansour 2017, 10). With the formal integration of the PMF into the armed forces comes not only salary, access to government resources, and authority, but a recognition of the legitimacy the PMF enjoys among the Iraqi people. As a force whose leadership has strong ties to Iran, this becomes a major source of Iranian influence in the military and security sphere, with important implications for social and political influence as the major militias also have social service and political wings (Hendawi 2016).

The seminal event that led to the founding of the PMF was a Fatwa issued by Grand Ayatallah Ali al-Sistani. As Daesh was sweeping through Northern Iraq, having captured nearly one-third of the country's territory (Mansour 2017), Sistani issued a decree that every able-bodied man should take up arms to defend holy sites from desecration. After the decree was issued the ranks of militias swelled with new members, some with limited experience, but fueled by faith and the edict of their Grand Marja. Others in these militias that make up the PMF are veterans of insurgencies against the U.S.-led occupation; some have been organized since their resistance to Saddam Hussein, while many of them retained deep ties to Iran and the IRGC.

The PMF has performed more effectively against Daesh than the standing Iraqi Army that was trained and armed by the United States. This is particularly true at the onset of that conflict, when the regular Iraqi Army collapsed, abandoning American supplied equipment on the roadside as they fled. The experienced fighters of the PMF, however, were able to halt the advance of Daesh outside the capital city of Baghdad. Although the religious Fatwa issued by Ayatallah Sistani, which is often credited as the impetus of the PMF's founding, called only for Iraqis to defend holy sites from destruction, the militias of the PMF have played active roles in nearly all campaigns retaking Iraqi territory from Daesh. This is a major source of their popularity and legitimacy among the Iraqi people.

The Iranian Quds Force has been quite active in supporting these Shi'a insurgent groups since their inception, and are now working closely with the PMF as an umbrella organization and formal organ of the Iraqi government. This strong link between Iranian Special Forces and Iraqi insurgents materializes through the branding of these militias, and through funding, the supply of weapons, and tactical and technical training. An overt example of this connection is the adoption of the Hizb'allah (party of God) name among Iraqi groups, for example, Kata'ib Hizb'allah. However, the more blatant symbolic evidence of the ties between the militias and the Quds Force is the adoption of the clenched Kalashnikov logo of the IRGC by most of the PMF-affiliated militias. Further, throughout the war against Daesh, there have been multiple pictures of then Quds Force Commander Major General Qasem Soleimani in

Iraq with various militia leaders. He is photographed often with Abu Mahdi al-Muhandis, the leader of Kata'ib Hizb'allah and simultaneously, a PMF commander, until his death by a U.S. airstrike in January 2020 that also killed Soleimani. But most importantly, there is the equipping and training of these groups with armor-penetrating explosive devices during the U.S.-led coalition that led to the death of hundreds of U.S. soldiers. The ties between the PMF and Iran are deep, and from the U.S. perspective, deeply troubling.

What does this linkage between these groups and the IRGC Quds Force mean for Iranian influence in Iraq? This chapter addresses this question by examining the PMF as an outgrowth of both the militant and political factions that have populated the landscape since the 1980s and their long-standing, and sometimes recent, affiliation with Iran. These groups have coalesced into a few larger groups and with the fight against Daesh unified even further until they were formally recognized by the very political factions from which some of them emerged. Given the close ties to the Iranian Quds Force it is fair to ask, is the PMF the Iraqi equivalent of Lebanese Hizb'allah? Or is it more like the IRGC, a parallel military organization? Further, what are the implications of the PMF status for Iranian influence in Iraq? To understand the founding of this organization, and before examining the background of the militias, the next section explores the seminal act of the creation of the PMF, the Fatwa issued by Sistani.

## Sistani's Fatwa

In the summer of 2014, seemingly uncontested, Daesh took over Iraq's second largest city. Mosul was defended by the Iraqi Army and police, which had been equipped and trained by the United States. "But during Monday night and early Tuesday morning, the 100,000 strong police and army forces left the city without local residents being aware of their withdrawal" (Hars 2015). What ensued was a three-year battle to retake Mosul made more difficult by the great treasure the retreating Iraqi forces left for Daesh. "A vast amounts of cash (*sic*) was in local banks when Mosul fell. On the first day, ISIS took over $2 billion in addition to 2,700 military vehicles, including U.S.-made Humvees, tanks and army trucks" (Hars 2015).

The following day, Daesh took over the city of Tikrit (Nabhan 2014). Tikrit, south of Mosul and north of Baghdad, is the birthplace of Saddam Hussein and on the road to Baghdad. And just as in Mosul, Iraqi forces in Tikrit were not able to defend against Daesh, raising serious questions about the defense of the capital. "U.S.-armed and trained Iraqi security forces put up almost no fight throughout the militants' daylong rout on Wednesday, witnesses said. The ease with which the fighters beat back the military raised questions about whether Iraqi troops would be able to defend the capital if challenged" (Nabhan 2014). Indeed, the Iraqi state itself seemed imperiled.

It was at this point that the reclusive and quietist Sistani issued his famous fatwa and changed the course of the war and Iraqi history. He rebuked then prime minister al-Maliki and called for the faithful to defend the holy sites against the invading Daesh forces. The latter call was quickly interpreted as a call to arms more generally and led to the swelling of ranks of local militias. The moves were alarming to the Maliki government but reassuring to Iran. Did the quietist Sistani prove Iran's *Velayat* system necessary and true and did he provide Iran with yet another window of opportunity to extend its influence in Iraq?

The Maliki government, seen as corrupt and incompetent, was a target of Sistani and Sadr. But the inability to defend against Daesh may have been the final turning point for Sistani. "From his spartan office in the holy city of Najaf, down an alleyway protected by armed guards, Sistani has asserted his dominance over public affairs, demanding politicians choose a new government without delay and potentially hastening the end of Prime Minister Nuri al-Maliki's eight-year tenure" (Dziadosz 2014). Further, Sistani "called on political blocs to choose a prime minister, president and speaker of parliament by July 1, meaning Maliki could be replaced within days" (Dziadosz 2014). Dziadosz and Salman wrote that insightful piece in June 2014; by September 2014 Abadi had become the prime minister of Iraq. Sistani's power, however, was not limited to political matters. "The cleric, a recluse who favors a behind-the-scenes role, kicked off his newly assertive stance on June 13 with a call for Iraqis to take up arms against a Sunni insurgency—the first fatwa of its kind in a century, clerics familiar with Sistani's thinking say, motivated by his fear the state faced collapse" (Dziadosz 2014).

This raised significant questions at the time concerning what role the Hawza would come to play in Iraqi national politics. As we have seen, those debates are central to Shi'a theological debates, fueled in no small part by the *velayat-e faqih* system in place in Iran. As we have also seen, attempts to position successors to replace the aging and ailing Sistani are motivated, in part, by precisely the kind of power being described here. With his words, Sistani brought down Maliki and inspired tens of thousands to take up arms against Daesh. "Nevertheless, critics say the fatwa has provided legitimacy to extra-legal Shi'ite militias" (Dziadosz 2014). Indeed, PM Abadi has publicly recognized Sistani's significant contribution to the defeat of Daesh and the capture of Mosul. "In a statement issued on Friday, Abadi offered his 'deep thanks' to Ayatallah Sistani for 'his great and continuing support to the heroic fighters.' He also stressed that the Shi'a cleric's 2014 call 'saved Iraq and paved the way for victory' over Daesh" (PressTV 2017). However, Sistani, through spokesmen, attempted to correct this image of him endorsing the PMF. "Just a few days after Sistani issued his fatwa, his representative in Karbala clarified that the fatwa was not intended to legitimize the formation of irregular paramilitary groups, but rather was promulgated to support Iraqi security forces. Sistani's statements and his representatives' avoided using the term PMF when this term became a reference to IRGC-backed groups, instead adopting the term 'volunteers'" (Al-Qarawee 2017, 4). Interestingly, the symbolic predisposition of the masses and the successful manipulation of symbols and narratives by Iran and its allies seem to have usurped the meaning of Sistani's fatwa, despite his attempts to clarify his intent.

I shall return to the implications for Iraqi politics and security in the chapter summary. But it is important to pause here to see what this looks like from Iran's perspective. For Iran, the establishment of the PMF, Abadi's recognition of it in 2014, and the Iraqi parliament's adoption of it as a formal institution in 2016 were steps toward consolidating its influence in Iraq. The leader of the PMF, Muhandis, was referred to as a "living martyr," by Major General Soleimani then head of Iran's Special Forces and point person for Iran's Iraq policy (Toumaj 2017a). Sistani's fatwa elicited praise from the Supreme Leader of Iran himself. "Khamenei described Sistani's fatwa as a 'divine inspiration,' which was unsurprising given that the fatwa provided IRGC-backed groups with an excuse to expand their role in Iraq" (Al-Qarawee 2017). And then Quds Force Commander Soleimani said, "The blood of Shiite youth spilled to save the Sunni youth, which is valuable and showed that none can divide this nation . . . all of these are owed to the effects of Ayatallah Sistani's *fatwa*" (Toumaj 2017a). With both the legitimization of clerical interference in the political life of Iraq and a hand in establishing the PMF, Sistani, presumably inadvertently, created the conditions for further Iranian influence in Iraq.

In the next two sections I discuss two models that Iran might be using for the PMF in Iraq. They are the Hizb'allah model and the IRGC model. These are not intended to be understood as formal models or as precise articulations of what one will observe empirically. Rather, they are a set of practices that determine relationships and the use of resources in somewhat identifiable and forecastable ways. They are also built on narratives and symbolic communication. The Hizb'allah and IRGC models are both inspired and empowered by the adaptive resistance culture of the Islamic Republic. However, the degree to which they are embodiments of the designed redundancy of the Iranian system differs. This and their relationship to the Supreme Leader and the *velayat-e faqih* system are key to understanding the role of the PMF in Iraq.

## The Hizb'allah Model

Lebanese Hizb'allah (LH) is a multifaceted organization; it is a terror network, social service provider, militia, and political party. It is also an extension of the adaptive resistance ideology of Iran, as it was founded through the support and training of the IRGC. But it is more than just that. It remains, up to this writing, a powerful symbol of successful resistance against more powerful forces. It is also a sort of modern-day phoenix, as it emerged from the consuming flames of a fifteen-year civil war strong enough to triumph over Israel and drive it and the United States out of Lebanon. For the myth-makers of the IRGC and their fellow travelers, this story writes itself.

Yet, LH claims not to want to impose Shari'a or the *velayat-e faqih* doctrine on Lebanon. From their perspective, they seek to educate and lead by example. By creating a just state within a state, by providing social services, by defending the weak, by resisting the oppressors, they are demonstrating the value of Shari'a and the *velayat-e* faqih system. What LH claims to do is prevent the United States and its allies from making Lebanon an oppressed colonial output or snuffing out the practice of Shari'a, where it is practiced. While Hizb'allah as militia is not formally recognized as a part of the Lebanese military, their political participation guarantees the power of veto. This practice of maintaining the power of veto is a key feature of the designed redundancy aspect of Iran. So, we see in LH, in a circumscribed way, the twin pillars of Iranian Strategic Influence I demonstrated at the beginning of this work—designed redundancy and adaptive resistance.

It is my contention that Iran is seeking, in part, to deploy a version of this model in Iraq. It does not seek outright control of Iraq. That is, it does not seek to fly its flag, so to speak, and overtly control the government in Baghdad. Rather it seeks a significant presence to influence decisionmaking, enough freedom of movement for its agents to pursue particular interests, and the ability to block events contrary to its interests—enhanced control of the northern Persian Gulf and a direct line of supply and support, a land bridge, to LH, the Mediterranean, and the border with Israel. Iran is seeking to establish an arm of adaptive resistance to function with designed redundancy within the Iraqi system. The formal status of the PMF, however, is significantly different from the Hizb'allah model. Hizb'allah remains a popular/populist movement and social mobilization influencer because of its myths of origin (much like the IRGC and the PMF, born out of conflict to serve the oppressed Shi'a) but also because it is "among" the people and of the people.

This is what Iran was able to achieve in Lebanon with Hizb'allah and it is reasonable to expect it to want to replicate that success in Iraq. This is their motivation for trying to weigh in on the succession of Sistani and why the PMF and its constituent militias as proxies are valuable to Iran. They are a highly cost-effective method of escalation control and plausible deniability, but primarily as an influence leverage point. In inciting and supporting Shi'a resistance in Lebanon, Iran has discovered a counter to the economic and military superiority of the West and its Middle Eastern allies through asymmetric political and military warfare. The same model of resistance via proxy forces has been implemented in Iraq to great effect. The PMF, as a conglomerate of various factions, is certainly a proven military force; however, it is also an opportunity to maintain unity of identity and effort among the various political wings as well. The ability to replicate the Hizb'allah model in Iraq requires deep connection with the populace through delivery of goods and services, trust, and a narrative of *resistance* and *triumph*. At this point, some of the militias that are part of the PMF (but also others outside of it, primarily that of Moqtada al-Sadr) resemble a newly formed Hizb'allah toward the end of the Lebanese Civil War. In this case, the "opportunity structure" is the chaos that began with the U.S. invasion in 2003 and continued through the recent battle against Daesh.

While Iraq is a Shi'a-majority country, it was not until the fall of Saddam Hussein that they gained the right of self-representation and only through the intervention of Grand Marja Sistani that they gained one person-one vote self-rule. The methods by which Hussein maintained control over a population that was over 60 percent Shi'a could fairly be described as brutal oppression. Of course, that oppression and dependence on them is probably what the British had in mind when they set up the Sunni Hashemite kingdom in Iraq and then supported the military coup that deposed the king. Hussein, recognizing that the main opposition to his rule was not force of arms but ideas, spent a great deal of time suppressing political dissent and disrupting religious organization. This included assassination of key religious figures, closing of mosques, and other tactics and techniques.

It is no surprise, then, that post-invasion Iraq was plunged into a brutal civil conflict with widespread retribution against former Ba'ath party members and brutality against Sunnis in what began to look like ethnic civil war. In the immediate aftermath of the invasion the United States was ill-prepared for the Sunni insurgency or the Shi'a retribution. The fall of Saddam Hussein was a great boon to Iran (Al-Qarawee 2017, 4). Then, just a few years after the U.S. withdrawal, Daesh emerged as an existential threat to the Shi'a population as well as to the Iraqi state. These events are opportunity structures; they come with ready-made myth-evoking symbols, such as the centuries of oppression the Shi'a have suffered at Sunni hands, the assassination of Hussein, and the Shi'a Revival in Iran and Lebanon to galvanize and fuel social mobilization in Iraq.

These opportunity structures are what the IRGC and its Special Forces wing, the Quds Force, prefer for their recruiting, training, and operating missions. Among the Shi'a there was a mixture of fear and potential triumph, but a strong desire for becoming masters of their own destiny. So, began the Shi'a resistance in Iraq. And with it came the various anti-Coalition insurgent groups, including Kata'ib Hizb'allah, the Jaysh al-Mahdi, and the Badr

Organization among others. Much of this was expressed in religious, quasi-messianic terms, revenge for the murder of Hussein, the son of the fourth Caliph Ali, a martyr to the Shi'a, was a common theme. The Shi'a Revival had come to Iraq, and the IRGC and Quds Force were leading the charge, just as they had done in Lebanon.

However, the connection between LH and Iraq is not merely metaphorical, but actual as well. On June 17, 2014, in response to Grand Marja Sistani's fatwa, LH Commander Sheikh Hassan Nasrallah said, "We are ready to sacrifice martyrs in Iraq five times more than what we sacrificed in Syria in order to protect shrines" (Levitt 2015). LH, of course, has had some presence in Iraq since the anti-coalition insurgency in the early 2000s when they established Unit 3800. "To this end, Hezbollah created Unit 3800, whose sole purpose was to support Iraqi Shiite militant groups targeting multinational forces there. According to U.S. intelligence, Unit 3800 sent a small number of personnel to Iraq to train hundreds of fighters in-country, while others were brought to Lebanon for more advanced training" (Levitt 2015) . Then Quds Commander Soleimani, credited Nasrallah for being a major factor in the PMF's success; he "praised Lebanese Hezbollah for 'transferring experience to' the PMF: 'I should kiss the hand of the great sayyid Hassan Nasrallah'" (Toumaj 2017a).

Just as in Lebanon in the late to mid-1980s, the IRGC and Quds Force were busy funding local and national politicians, militias, clerics, businessmen, and others (Al-Qarawee 2017, 4). They funded Christian militias, Sunni groups, and competing Shi'a groups. They funded new groups and groups that had been resisting since the rule of Saddam Hussein. Many of these groups changed names, leaders, some resisted arming themselves, while some other grew more powerful through training against U.S. and Coalition forces. The IRGC supplied the resistance fighters with relatively cheap, but fairly sophisticated weapons with which to harass and kill "occupying" forces.

There are two other points that should be noted. Like in Lebanon, the Shi'a movement now had another Arab face. Iran's Persian heritage, often a handicap in the Arab-dominated Middle East could be overcome through having strong Arab allies. In the early days of the resistance in Iraq there was reluctance by some in Iraq to fight alongside Iranians. LH was brought in to work alongside their Arab, Shi'a brothers. But Iraq is significantly different from Lebanon, offering a greater opportunity. Unlike Lebanon, Iraq is an Arab state with a large Shi'a majority. Second, the formal alliance, or deep influence model that Iran seems to be pursuing indicates a potential domination of the Northern Persian Gulf, a threatening posture to Kuwait and the other smaller Gulf States and a key building block to extending a direct supply line to Lebanon. While these considerations are serious, Iran does not control Iraq and it does not seem to appear that they are set to do so or even that it is their goal. As I argued above, their intent is Strategic Influence, not control.

The Lebonization of Iraq, as a model, would require an organization with a militant wing, a political wing, a social services wing, and a communications wing. In Lebanon, one such group emerged and became the focal point of Iranian strategy. In Iraq, no single group has yet to emerge, but given the size of Iraq that may never happen. Rather, there may be a few such organizations that get Iranian support, and indeed, playing these groups against each other might well be part of Iran's strategy. To understand this better the section after next provides a background and assessment of the larger Shi'a militias operating today. But it may also be the case that this model is neither the model that Iran is pursuing nor the only model it is pursuing. Another viable model at play is the IRGC model.

## The IRGC Model

The Iranian constitution describes the role of the IRGC in military terms, as one would expect, but also unsurprisingly, in ideological terms.

> In establishing and equipping the defense forces of the country, the focus shall be on maintaining ideology and faith as the foundation and the measure. . . . They will undertake the responsibility of not only guarding and protecting the borders, but also the weight of ideological mission, i.e. striving ( jehād) on the path of God and struggle on the path of expanding the sovereignty of the law of God in the world; in accordance with the Qur'anic verse: "Against them make ready your strength to the utmost of your power, including steeds of war, to strike terror into (the hearts of) the enemies, of Allah and your enemies." (8: 60) (The Constitution of the Islamic Republic of Iran 1989, Introduction)

Iran's Revolutionary Guard Corps (IRGC) was founded by Khomeini in the chaos and opportunity of the 1979 Islamic Revolution. It was created with a dual mission of maintaining the ideological and physical security of the regime and projecting "terror into the hearts of their enemy." While still charged with this responsibility, the IRGC today presides over a vast power structure with influence over almost every aspect of Iranian life with vast economic holdings and deep political power. And while their loyalty to the Supreme Leader and general support of hardline politicians are consistent, "it is far from a cohesive unit of like-minded conservatives" (Bruno 2013, 1).

Like its progeny in Lebanon and Iraq, the IRGC was born in revolution and warfare. They were built to support the new ruling principle of the *velayat-e faqih* with expressed support to the Supreme Leader, their commander-in-chief, as their guiding principle. The Islamic Revolution required consolidation through the elimination of enemies and the establishment of a force that could be relied upon by Khomeini and his coterie. "The Artesh [Iran's regular armed forces] was the shah's main prop; they were also trained and supplied by the United States, so were viewed with suspicion by the regime" (Nader 2015, 1). The IRGC were essential to the preservation of the regime in those early days of the revolution when it was far from clear that the new cleric elite could hold power (Bruno 2013). But they were also essential to the defense of Iran against the invading Iraqi Army.

The IRGC took the lead in resisting and ultimately repelling Iraq's invasion. Their role in Iran's "sacred defense," continues to earn them legitimacy and has propelled them to the forefront of Iran's security apparatus. The Iran-Iraq War in the 1980s helped transform the Guards into a modern, conventional fighting force. The "regular" fighting units of the IRGC consist of naval, air, and ground components, and total roughly 150,000 fighters (Bruno 2013, 2; Nader 2015). It is also responsible for developing and maintaining Iran's growing missile capability. However, their responsibility for maintaining internal domestic security is manifested through the Basij. Iran's Basij Resistance Force "is an all-volunteer paramilitary wing, which, according to a 2009 RAND study, consists of as many as one million conscripts" (Bruno 2013, 3). Their recruits range from students to retired military; they are organized by province, city, and town just as the IRGC are. They are trained in guerilla and urban warfare and are designed to resist in the case of major domestic upheavals, as in the 2009 "Green Revolution," where they took to the streets to disrupt protests, and in the case of foreign invasion.

The other major wing of the IRGC is the elite Quds Force led by Major General Qasem Soleimani from its inception until his assassination by the United States in 2020. Through the Quds Force Iran maintains an asymmetric warfare capability and deterrence strategy against U.S. or Israeli attack. The IRGC and Quds Force have trained and equipped proxy groups, including Hizb'allah, Hamas, and Iraqi Shi'a insurgents. Hizb'allah and Hamas have been perpetual threats against Israel and Iranian "surrogates have already been used to target U.S. and other Western forces in Lebanon, Iraq and Afghanistan" (Nader 2015, 2).

The IRGC is also one of Iran's most powerful economic players, with wide-ranging economic interests in such strategic industries as construction, oil and natural gas development, commercial services, and black-market activities. The IRGC "is perceived by some as a business empire, with an estimated quarter of the country's economy under its control" (Lob 2017). According to a 2007 *Los Angeles Times* report, the IRGC owns or is tied to over 100 businesses that control roughly $12 billion in construction and engineering capital (Murphy). Murphy goes on to report, "Across Iran, public works projects involving pipelines, roads, bridges and, increasingly, oil and gas are dominated by the Guard's engineering arm, the equivalent of the U.S. Army Corps of Engineers, or by companies with which the Guard has a close relationship" (2007). Council on Foreign Relations Senior Fellow Ray Takeyh "has linked the Guards to university laboratories, weapons manufacturers, and companies connected to nuclear technology" (Bruno 2013, 6).

The accumulation of economic and martial power has made the IRGC one of the most powerful actors in Iran. "Over time, the Guards have also been transformed into a leading economic and political actor. The IRGC and its associated companies are involved in many sectors of Iran's economy, allowing it to amass unprecedented power" (Nader 2015, 1). This has been exacerbated by the many IRGC officials who have entered directly into government service. The Guards' political influence began its ascendancy as a counterweight to former reformist president Mohammad Khatami. But analysts say the number of former Guards entering political life spiked during President Mahmoud Ahmadinejad's first term, beginning in 2005 (Bruno 2013, 4).

The vast economic and political power that the IRGC has amassed does not necessarily mean that they are a threat to the Supreme Leader or that they are a unitary actor with very specific goals. They are diverse politically, although the majority of the leadership remains loyal to the Supreme Leader and the most hardline of the Iranian political elite. Nevertheless, pragmatic leaders such as Iran's speaker of the Parliament and former guard member Ali Larijani are open to trading with the West and seeks many reforms. As does another prominent former Guardsmen, such as former Tehran Mayor Qalibaf. President Rouhani is attempting to reign in some of their economic power and contains their influence to mixed results.

Rouhani's administration and the IRGC recently signed a deal where the IRGC would go to Iranian border regions and engage in opening and expanding investment loan opportunities, economic development, and infrastructure projects, such as roads, bridges, and electricity. "In principle, such development could help subdue their marginalized and restless, ethnic populations and dissuade them, especially their youth, from joining the ranks of separatists and militants, such as the Kurdish Party of Free Life of Kurdistan (PJAK) and the Baluch God's Brigade (Jundallah). The agreement would also allow the IRGC, which already maintains an active military and security presence in these regions, to extend patronage and informant networks among the local residents who benefit from its economic initiatives" (Lob 2017).

In 2003, then commander of the IRGC major general Yahya Rahim Safavi wrote to the Majles. "The IRGC considers itself responsible for the defense of the Islamic Revolution, its achievements, and the ideology and values of Khomeini. Our main mission is to stop those who wish to destroy and overthrow the Islamic Revolution" (Murphy 2007). Their economic power, while seen as a threat by some, including perhaps President Rouhani himself, appears to be in line with Khamenei's vision of a resistance economy. "His continued call for a 'resistance economy' in the face of renewed and persistent U.S. sanctions has given an added justification to the IRGC to expand its economic role beyond construction and finance into rural development [the PDH program]. When announcing the creation of the PDH, Jafari invoked the Supreme Leader's call for a resistance economy as the main rationale for the new economic mission of the IRGC—a demonstration of its resolve to remain relevant to the domestic economy" (Lob 2017).

What is clear is that the IRGC is not a typical military organization. It maintains a regular army, navy, air force, ballistic missile program, cyber warfare capability, domestic militia, external special operations unit, a vast economic enterprise, and indirect political involvement. The Iranian regular armed forces—the Artesh—pale in comparison in terms of scope, reach, resources, and power. The IRGC's close ties to the Supreme Leader, who enjoys both the security that a powerful IRGC provides the regime, but also the wealth they create in doing so, create the condition for their continued expansion of power.

This is an example of the designed redundancy I mentioned above. By maintaining the IRGC as a parallel structure to the Artesh, the Supreme Leader enables a check on the traditional military, preventing a coup from its most likely source as he and his fellow revolutionaries well know; allows for direct intervention in the economy on ideological grounds; and creates a permissive environment for activities that would otherwise be illegal. No one in Iran is eager to take on the IRGC's power structure, not only because it is as vast as described here but because the Supreme Leader stands firmly with it.

If this is the model that the PMF is to follow in Iraq, we would expect to see certain things. We would expect a parallel command structure to Iraq's regular military with equal or greater firepower, maintenance of units outside the formal command structure to perform acts that could be deemed illegal or illicit by properly vested authority; maintain an ideological base of operations that promotes the *velayat-e faqih* doctrine and *resistance*; create and maintain an economic base; venture directly or indirectly into the political sphere. I should note that the formalization of the PMF already indicates a move toward the IRGC model rather than the Hizb'allah model, where the militant aspect of the group is separate from the command structure of government, but equally if not more powerful than the regular security forces.

Nevertheless, things are rarely what they seem and an examination of the groups that make up the PMF might reveal that they use aspects of both the IRGC and Hizb'allah models, which is not surprising since Hizb'allah itself is a near replica of the IRGC model. However, as of this writing the PMF is not anywhere nearly as entrenched in the Iraqi government as the IRGC is in Iran. For that matter, Hizb'allah is not nearly as entrenched in Lebanon as the IRGC is in Iran. Put simply, at present there is little empirical evidence suggesting the IRGC model is at play in Iraq aside from the adoption of the PMF as a formal security organ of the state, it does not have the ideological authority from the state, a large economic mandate, nor does it have a unified leadership structure in both its formal and informal operations. The PMF is an umbrella structure for a group of militias each following the Hizb'allah model. Each of these militias has their own social service, media, education, propaganda, political, and armed wings, like Hizb'allah. Further, there is competition and sometimes conflict between these groups. "These organisations are not simply a manipulated extension of Iran. They are diverse and independent of Iran. They are independent of Iran, and have been competing with each other for power according to their very different visions of state-building in Iraq" (Rostami-Povey 2010, 140–141). The next few sections examine their background and analysis as well as provide context on the major militias operating in Iraq today.

## The PMF and Iraqi Militias: Background and Analysis

The contemporary history of the Shi'as in Iraq has been one of long-suffering under Saddam Hussein, invasion by the United States, and facing down the existential threat of Daesh. In short, their collective memories of oppression, relived every year at the Festival Ashura, have been their day-to-day existence since the 1960s. The emergence of a fledgling democratic Shi'a state, the possibility of self-rule, came with risks of U.S. or Iranian domination, sectarian war, and, with the rise of Daesh, annihilation. What the Fatwa issued by Grand Marja Ali al-Sistani did was combine three primal forces of the Shi'a culture—faith, politics, and sacrifice—*resistance* and *triumph*. That these were necessary for the survival of Iraq facing down Daesh so soon after the American withdrawal is clear. That they are also the tenets of Iran's *velayat-e faqih* system, pillars of Iranian history and culture, and central themes of their influence campaigns may prove critical to the future of Iranian influence in Iraq. Can the belief in a modern state—nationalism—trump these more primal beliefs? Can a belief in an imagined "Iraq" supersede a regional if not global Islamism that informs and shapes politics, and demands sacrifice? Recall that much of Iran's modern history was a competition between modernization and nationalism versus conservativism and religion. It is for others to take up the question about how necessary this is for Muslim societies, in general, to face this dilemma once they are free of colonial control. In Iraq part of the resolution of this tension is found in the fate of the militias that make up the PMF and the fate of the PMF itself.

In their timely and insightful piece, "The Popular Mobilization Forces and Iraq's Future," Mansour and Jabar take up some of these central questions

(2017). For these authors the Shi'as in Iraq are caught up in a power struggle over the state, although the struggle, in my view, is about more than just political power. They posit the contest to be between Nouri al-Maliki, the former prime minister who they believe is trying to regain power. Abadi, who was prime minister at the time of their writing, and Muqtada al-Sadr, who in addition to gaining power and preventing the return of Maliki, also focused on maintaining independence from Iran. "A crucial factor that will help determine who gains an advantage in this struggle will be whether the PMF paramilitaries are integrated into the state's existing security apparatus and used to reinforce the country's political status quo, or if instead these paramilitary groups are retained as a separate parallel and independent military force that can be used to reshape Iraq's current political and security landscape" (Mansour 2017, 4). In truth, these alignments are deeper than political arrangements.

Maliki was a key agent of Iranian influence and he empowered other elements that were directly sympathetic to the *velayat-e faqih* and adherence to it in Iraq. He was a direct supporter of the PMF, and the PMF as a sort of IRGC for Iraq. In other words, Maliki represents the political wing of the *Velayat* system. Abadi, like on the other hand, seems to be trying to establish a modern, secular, nationalist state with strong ties to the West and Iraq's Arab neighbors—presumably to balance against Iranian influence. Abadi's efforts to control the PMF are predicated on modern ideas about how militaries and police function in a modern state. Muqtada al-Sadr remains a bit of an enigma, and the idea that his primary motivation is preventing Maliki's return to power is probably off point, his ambitions are greater. Sadr also seeks an independent Iraq. He, too, is a nationalist. However, he is also a cleric and a militant. At various points since the U.S. invasion of Iraq, Sadr has played each of these roles, sometimes overlapping roles, with deadly effect. His relationships with clerics in Qom and Najaf remain obscure, his religious credentials are far from remarkable, yet he is a voice to hundreds of thousands of Shi'a in Iraq's south. His relationship with Soleimani was strong, yet he rejects the notion of Iraq falling under Khamenei's guardianship.

Given this, one has to integrate Mansour's and Jabar's two points concerning the political and clerical allegiances of the various groups that make up the PMF. "The PMF has become part of a growing intra-Shi'a power contest. This pits Nouri al-Maliki, considered the 'godfather' of the PMF, against Sadr, who calls for disbanding the 'imprudent militias,' and Abadi, who advocates reducing and controlling the PMF" and "The PMF contains three distinct factions, based on various subgroups' respective allegiances to Ayatallah Ali Khamenei, Ayatallah Ali al-Sistani, and Muqtada al-Sadr" (Mansour 2017, 1). In other words, we have the *velayat-e faqih*, quietism, and a quasi-Hizb'allah model at work (I use the qualifier because Sadr does not overtly adopt the *velayat-e faqih* ideology as Hizb'allah does). Given that the PMF is so tied to the *velayat-e faqih* system and to the Quds Force/IRGC in particular, their critique of Abadi seems off point. Abadi seems to "struggle to control the PMF rather than integrate it into existing state military forces" (Mansour 2017, 1). So long as the PMF is active and tied to Iran, they are implementing a designed redundancy model—a distinctive feature of the *velayat-e faqih* system. Further integration into the armed forces could be useful in reducing Iranian influence, or, more likely, it could exacerbate it.

This misunderstanding is also captured in one of their other main points, "The PMF was central to early efforts to roll back the Islamic State; however, the state's security apparatus has since regrouped, reducing the PMF's role in subsequent battles, including the ongoing campaign in Mosul" (Mansour 2017, 1). The PMF and its component militias are busily at work expanding and perpetuating Iranian influence. One such example is the Shi'a Militia Nujaba, which "fights under the umbrella of the Popular Mobilization Forces" (Dehghanpisheh 2017). According to this Reuters special report, "Though made up of Iraqis, [Nujaba] is loyal to Iran and is helping Tehran create a supply route through Iraq to Damascus, according to Iraqi lawmaker Shakhwan Abdullah, retired Lebanese general Elias Farhat, and other current and former officials in Iraq. The route will run through a string of small cities including Qayrawan. To open it up, Iranian-backed militias are pushing into southeast Syria near the border with Iraq, where U.S. forces are based" (Dehghanpisheh 2017).

The importance of understanding and looking through ideological lenses—communities of meaning—is partly revealed here. As discussed at length above, the *nizam* is not solely concerned with how Iran should be governed. Rather, it speaks to the larger Islamic community, the *umma*, and how the guardianship of the jurist is essential to restore order and justice. But it is also an ideology of resistance. It is the duty of able-bodied Muslims to take up arms against the oppressors. This is why Sistani's Fatwa in 2014 was so celebrated by Khamenei. Further, resistance is strategic, that is, adaptive. For Iran and its proxies working within what is possible to extend their influence and expand their control is part and parcel of their asymmetric strategy. In other words, Iran is busy building infrastructure to support its influence campaign over Iraq and Syria and while the PMF may have played less of a role in the capture of Mosul, robbing them perhaps of a moment of glory, they remain very active in that area and others perpetuating Iranian influence.

The difficulty for Abadi, Sistani, Sadr, and others working to curtail Iranian influence in Iraq is the great legitimacy the PMF seems to enjoy among the Iraqi people. "For many Iraqis . . . the PMF is a set of religiously sanctioned paramilitaries—some refer to it as al-Hashd al-muqadis (the Sacred Mobilization Units). As one fighter from the city of Amarah stated, 'You can criticize any politician or even religious cleric, but you cannot speak against the Hashd and its martyrs.' To many, these martyrs have given up their lives in defense of their country. Iraqi society is now full of popular songs, commercials, and banners that honor the leaders and martyrs of various PMF military groups. For other Iraqis, however, the PMF is a group of problematic militias neither accountable to the state nor under the rule of law" (Mansour 2017, 3). While the PMF may have many detractors, here there is a clear effort to build the founding myth of the PMF as a "sacred defense force." The IRGC, as we have seen, was heralded as just such a force. The Iran-Iraq War is referred to as the "Sacred Defense," in Iran to this day. Here, the same myth-making is clearly at play. The PMF is a "Sacred Defense Force." They defended the Shi'a from the kafiri Daesh and saved Iraq. They are thusly celebrated. That kind of myth-making creates a political veneer that protects them from those who seek to weaken them.

This is a challenge to many, including Grand Ayatallah Ali al-Sistani, "who criticize the monopolistic conduct of certain PMF leaders, particularly Abu Mehdi al-Muhandis" (Mansour 2017, 4). This is also true of Abadi and other political leaders as well. "An August 2015 poll claims that 99 percent of Shi'a respondents support the use of the PMF to fight the Islamic State. Abadi's chief intelligence officer has stated that up to 75 percent of men between eighteen and thirty years old living in Shi'a-majority provinces had signed up to enlist in the PMF by the spring of 2016" (Mansour 2017, 10–11). While that number is high, the indications are that there are more volunteers ready to join, more than the militias can take on, train, and equip (Mansour 2017, 11). The poor performance of the Iraqi Army in the early days of the fight against Daesh is a major contributor to this trend, as is the good performance of the PMF. However, even given the exclusion of the PMF from retaking of Mosul and the Iraqi Army's good performance there, the framing of the PMF as a "Sacred Defense Force" seems to have taken hold. The line of thought here is much like in Iran. Should the regular army fail, the IRGC/PMF is there to protect the faithful. This is important to understand. The PMF as a "Sacred Defense Force" is more than a militia; it is a force born of centuries of resistance to oppression, finally delivering *triumph* over the enemies of the people. Every significant symbolic predisposition is activated and every tenet of the myth-symbol complex Iran uses to influence Iraq is verified in the PMF.

Before delving into the major militias and trying to understand their ideological claims, their loyalties, and determining the potential for Iranian influence, I think it is important to understand how the PMF is viewed from Tehran. "Iran's Supreme Leader Ayatallah Ali Khamenei warned the Iraqi prime Minister Haider al-Abadi on Tuesday [June 20, 2017] against any measures that could weaken the Tehran-backed Shi'ite paramilitary groups, saying such actions would endanger Baghdad's stability" (Staff 2017). Khamenei grounds his warning (threat?) in the PMF's foundational myth of Sacred Defense and distrust of the imperialist oppressive West. "'The Daesh is retreating from Iraq and that is thanks to the government's trust in these young devoted forces,' Khamenei told Abadi in Tehran. 'The Americans are against Popular Forces because they want Iraq to lose its main source of strength,' he added" (Staff 2017).

With this it is clear that there are various perspectives among key actors as to what the PMF is, what role it should play, and how it should be governed. In what follows I give the reader background and analysis on each of the major militias that are part of the PMF and wherever possible their leadership. I do this to help highlight their history, ideology, and structure, and how these three pillars (as with Iran itself) enable the mobilization of the masses through deploying myths and narratives—Iranian Strategic Influence.

**Badr Organization**

The Badr Organization of Reconstruction and Development (Badr Organization), also referred to as the Badr Brigade, or the Badr Corps was formed by Hadi al-Amiri in 1983 "as the armed wing of the largest Shiite political party in Iraq, the SCIRI. The Badr Organization is considered 'Iran's oldest proxy in Iraq' because of its close and lasting ties to Tehran" (Stanford 2016, 1). Their lineage, as part of SCIRI, goes back to the second Ba'athist coup in Iraq in the early 1980s and brings to sharp relief the long-suffering of the Shi'a in Iraq. Two incidents in particular highlight this history of oppression. "In 1977 there was a popular uprising when the regime prevented the people from visiting the Shrine of Imam Husain in the holy city of Karbala. Sayed Mohamad Baqir al-Hakim, the leader of SCIRI and the son of Grand Ayatallah Sayed Muhsin Al Hakim, was arrested, tortured and sentenced to life imprisonment without a trial" (GlobalSecurity 2014, 1). Bear in mind that this is the same al-Hakim family that is now contending to dominate the Hawza in Iraq. Their *resistance* credentials are well-established.

Moqtada al-Sadr is another cleric whose lineage suffered greatly at the hands of Saddam Hussein. "In 1980 Ayatallah Mohamad Baqir Al Sadr, who became the religious leader after the death of Sayed Muhsin Al Hakim, was executed with his sister Amina Al Sadr. Saddam's regime issued a decree to execute all the members of the Islamic Movement" (GlobalSecurity 2014, 1). The assassination of Ayatallah Sadr soon became an international focal point and rallying cry for Islamic *resistance* more broadly, albeit with a Shi'a tinge (Crooke 2009, 87). But these events are not just stories; these and many others like them are told and retold as discursive practices that keep alive the narrative of *oppression* that necessitates *resistance* which results in *triumph* when faithful allegiance is placed in the *velayat-e faqih* system.

Prior to the second Ba'athist coup in 1968 Shi'a Islamists worked within the law to gain political and legal traction. After the coup, however, the Islamic leadership came under heavy government repression. "Thousands of religious scholars and Islamic activists have been arrested and tortured. Hundreds of them have been killed while being tortured" (GlobalSecurity 2014, 3). Those who were able to flee, fled to neighboring Iran for refuge, among these groups was the large and well-organized SCIRI. From 1983 until the U.S. invasion of Iraq in 2003 SCIRI worked against the Saddam Hussein regime in Iraq, taking an active role alongside the IRGC during the 1980–1988 Iran-Iraq War (Stanford 2016, 1).

With the fall of Saddam Hussein and the U.S. occupation starting in 2003, SCIRI and its militia counterpart the Badr Brigade returned to Iraq. American occupation officials demanded that SCIRI disband the Badr Brigade, "instead, the SCIRI changed the name to the Badr Organization of Reconstruction and Development to appear less militant" (Stanford 2016, 1). Despite their claims of disarming and continued U.S. insistence on the matter, SCIRI maintained Badr as an armed wing. However, in keeping with the new order in Iraq and in deference to the Shi'a-majority government in Baghdad and to avoid appearing as an agent of Iran SCIRI removed the word "revolutionary" from its name to signify its acceptance of Iraq's new order" (GlobalSecurity 2014, 3; Juneau 2015, 109).

The newly branded ISCI was availing itself of the new conditions in Iraq to adapt to a new role. They moved from playing a revolutionary role to becoming an ally of the new Iraqi government, even going so far as to integrate some of their fighters with the Iraqi security apparatus. In yet another major role change ISCI changed the object of its religious emulation from Iranian Supreme Leader Ali al-Khamenei to Grand Ayatallah Ali al-Sistani (GlobalSecurity 2014, 3).

The move was significant as it signaled a change from supporting the *Velayat* ideology to supporting the quietist ideology. Further, it signaled a turn to Iraqi nationalism, over pan-Islamism. However, the leader of the Badr Organization, the armed wing of ISCI, Hadi Al-Amiri, was still an adherent of the *Velayat* ideology and he broke away from ISCI (Mansour 2017, 14; Stanford 2016, 5). Under Amiri's leadership the Badr Organization became an important player in the Iraqi political scene, including capturing twenty-two seats in Iraq's parliament in 2014 (Stanford 2016, 5). In the 2018 parliamentary election the Sadrist line won the largest block of seats followed closely by Amiri's Fateh Alliance. Also, "Under the new government of Haider al-Abadi, Ameri was able to get a member of his party, Mohammed

Salem al-Ghabban, confirmed as interior minister" (Sowell 2014). The interior minister is the de facto government official that supervises the PMF, although the PMF is technically directly tied to the prime minister's office (Mansour 2017, 19). This is because the Interior Ministry controls the federal police and intelligence agencies, and boasts a budget for arms procurement that rivals that of the Defense Ministry (George 2014, 2).

The Badr Organization split with ISCI over ISCI's move away from the *Velayat* ideology. To put it succinctly, "As a separate organization, the Badr Organization strives to obtain greater political influence, expand Shiite power in Iraq, and create an autonomous Shiite province in southern Iraq. The group is a strong supporter of Iran's Supreme Leader, Ayatallah Ali Khamenei; the leader of the Badr Organization, al-Amiri, described Khamenei as 'the leader not only for Iranians, but the Islamic nation'" (Stanford 2016, 3). That is, Amiri sees the pan-Islamist umma led by the Supreme Leader of Iran. Because their base of operations is in southern Iraq, and because Amiri is closely associated with Sadr rival Nouri al-Maliki, but primarily because of their adherence to the *velayat-e faqih* system, the Badr Organization and Sadr's Mahdi Army have come into open conflict on several occasions. "According to American military officials, the rivalry between the groups, called the 'Badr vs. Sadr' conflict, is so pronounced that it shapes politics and society in southern Iraq" (Stanford 2016, 6). However, the Badr Organization has good relations with pro-Iranian groups Asa'ib Ahl al-Haq and Kata'ib Hizb'allah, also rivals of the Sadrist camp.

The Badr Organization proclaims a long history of resistance against oppression and defense of the faithful. This is particularly true in contrast to much newer groups such as Asa'ib Ahl al-Haq and Kata'ib Hizb'allah. However, much of their current prominence is based on their leader Hadi al-Amiri. "In October 2014, Ameri was often described as the 'leader' of the militia-led offensive to subdue Jurf al-Sakhr, a mostly Sunni area south of Baghdad, and consolidate Shi'a control around the capital. By February 2015 Badr had secured Diyala, whose narrow Sunni Arab majority is nestled between Baghdad and Iran" (Sowell 2014). Amiri was also celebrated for his role in liberating Tikrit and Salahuddin. These victories shored up his credentials as defender of the faith, but also his close affiliation with Iran. "Iran, through Badr, initially played more of a role in the offensive than Iraqi leaders did, and photos of the infamous Quds Force commander Qassem Soleimani sometimes appeared alongside Ameri himself, dominating media coverage" (Sowell 2014). In Amiri's own words, "I worked for four years every day and people never recognized that. Now, just four months as a fighter and all the people are talking about is Amiri," he said. "It's because people love the one who defends them" (George 2014, 2). He goes on to say, "I would like to illuminate you with some information," he explained leaning back in his chair, "if there is anything I'm proud of in my life, it's being part of the resistance against Saddam Hussein." And, "Iran supported us then," Amiri said, referring to his time fighting against Saddam. "And Iran supports Iraq now. If Iran had not helped, IS would be in Baghdad" (George 2014, 3). Amiri explicitly mentions Iranian support in the context of the resistance against Saddam and the "Sacred Resistance" against Daesh. Note well, the implied call to the "Sacred Defense" and the role of protector of the faithful, these myth-symbol complexes that play directly to the symbolic predispositions of the masses are openly recognized and clearly articulated.

Unlike Sadr, who openly calls for rejecting Iranian influence in Iraq, Amiri openly praises Iran, publicly acknowledges his relationship with them, and explains how vital they are to Iraq's future. In his interview with George, "He described Suleimani as 'a friend, a good man and a good fighter,' and said that his organization is 'proud'" of its alliance with Tehran. "There's nothing to hide there," he said. "We have a 14,000-kilometer long border with Iran, we're neighbors, what are we going to do? We're not renting Iraq, we can't just move somewhere else" (George 2014, 4). Dhiya al-Asadi, who heads the Sadrist bloc in the Iraqi parliamentarian describes Iran's and Amiri's relationship in this way. "In terms of his political affiliation, [Amiri's loyalty] is to Iraq and the Iraqi government," Asadi said. "But Iran will continue to be his conscience and his moral leader" (George 2014, 7). Amiri appears to agree, saying, "I don't have a single bullet that comes from anywhere else besides the Iraqi government. . . . We don't receive any weapons directly from Iran, everything is from the state. . . . Besides, we don't need weapons—we have weapons. We're part of the Iraqi government now" (George 2014, 7).

Indeed, the PMF seems to be the leading organization in the PMF and Amiri its de facto head as his organization continues to increase its political capital and maintain their separate arms cache and militia activities. Here, we see a peculiar blend of both the IRGC model and the Hizb'allah model. The Badr Organization has long-standing ties to the lower-income Shi'a in the south of Iraq and in Baghdad; it is because of this operational area that the Badr Organization and Sadr's Mahdi Army often clash. They are competing for the same audience. However, as the PMF remains an independent but affiliated armed group it looks more like the designed redundancy of the IRGC. This organization appears, then, to either be a hybrid of the Hizb'allah and IRGC models or is in transition from one to the other. As groups like the Badr Organization attempt to gain political leverage their ability to compete at the ballot box means having to maintain political offices and the good will of the people through providing social services, they should also appear as defenders of the faith and have strong credentials as warriors, these are key elements of the Hizb'allah model which are all present in the Badr Organization. They are also the leaders of the PMF a separate, more popular (among the Shi'a faithful), and seemingly more powerful military than the Iraqi Army, with the ability through its constituent members to recruit, arm, and finance operations. What may be transpiring here is a hybrid model where each of the militias maintains their own autonomy and deploys the Hizb'allah model, while together through the PMF auspices, they deploy the IRGC model. It is typical of either Iranian model to have these layers of designed redundancy in service of their adaptive resistance.

## Kata'ib Hizb'allah

Little is known about Kata'ib Hizb'allah (KH); it is like Asa'ib Ahl al-Haq (AAH), a group that splintered off of Moqtada al-Sadr's Mahdi Army. The splintering was largely due to two factors. First, then prime minister Nouri al-Maliki and Sadr were bitter rivals. Maliki, known for being pro-Iranian, sought intervention from Tehran. Given Sadr's open calls for reducing Iranian influence in Iraq and his strong Iraqi nationalism, Maliki and Iran's interests coincided. KH and AAH were encouraged with money, arms, and training to splinter off of the Mahdi Army and form their own militias. Second, the leaders of Kata'ib and Asa'ib seem to be genuine believers of the *Velayat* system and ambitious men who wanted more power and prestige. Kata'ib Hizb'allah (Brigades of the Party of God) is a surrogate of Iran's Quds Force in Iraq. Its leader Jamal Ja'far Muhammad, better known as Abu Mahdi al-Muhandis "has been described as the 'right-hand man' of Qassem Suleimani" (Strouse 2010). In fact, Muhandis died alongside Soleimani in a U.S. attack in January 2020. Yet, despite the fact that Kata'ib is listed as a terror organization for its role in killing U.S. soldiers, "al-Muhandis has been a member of the Iraqi parliament since March 2006 as part of the main Shi'a block, the United Iraqi Alliance" (Strouse 2010). KH publicly avows allegiance to Iran's *velayat-e faqih* system, is designated as a terror organization by the United States, and even after the U.S. withdrawal from Iraq c. 2011, remained virulently anti-American (CEP 2017b).

During the U.S.-led war in Iraq that began in 2003, KH earned a reputation for planting deadly roadside bombs and using improvised rocket-assisted mortars (IRAMs) to attack U.S. and coalition forces. According to U.S. diplomat Ali Khedery, KH is responsible for "some of the most lethal attacks against U.S. and coalition forces" (CEP 2017b). They have made public statements stressing their anti-Americanism, even in the common fight against Daesh. "In September 2014, for example, KH released a statement saying, 'We will not fight alongside the American troops under any kind of conditions whatsoever. [Our only contact with Americans will be] if we fight each other'" This anti-Americanism is coupled with a public and private adherence to the *velayat-e faqih*. "Members of KH swear an oath of loyalty to Iran's

Supreme Leader, Ayatallah Ali Khamenei, and accept him as their own spiritual leader" (CEP 2017b).

KH appears to be a strong militia but do not appear to be very active politically or in the religious or social service sectors. KH may be an exclusively militant organization trained, armed, and financed by the Quds Force. As such it would appear to be following the IRGC model through its standing in the PMF. Along with the Badr Organization and AAH, KH, make up the largest group inside the PMF; they remain fiercely loyal to the Supreme Leader of Iran with strong ties to the Quds Force.

## Asaib Ahl al-Haq

Asa'ib Ahl al-Haq (AAH), also emerged after separating from the Mahdi Army in 2006 (Stanford 2017a; CEP 2017a). Prior to founding AAH, Khazali was a brigade commander under Muqtada al-Sadr. Like KH, Asa'ib Ahl al-Haq is anti-American and pro-*velayat-e faqih*. One of the reasons it split with the Mahdi Army was Sadr's call for a cease fire. "Khazali's brigade continued to fight U.S. troops in the summer of 2004 despite Sadr's orders that the Mahdi Army lay down its arms" (Stanford 2017a, 1). Khazali and Sadr would reconcile, but the tension between them was known by Maliki and Soleimani and they engineered a final break. "Khazali was recruited by the Iranian Revolutionary Guard Corps (IRGC) to lead AAH, a new militia that had begun receiving IRGC training in Iraq. Since its inception, AAH has relied heavily on Iranian funding, training, and logistical support, and in return has acted as an Iranian proxy in Iraq, carrying out its agenda and promoting its interests" (Stanford 2017a, 1). Khazali was also close to Soleimani who personally supervised their operations. AAH also has offices in Lebanon and a very close working relationship with LH (Stanford 2017a, 1; Wyer 2012, 7). AAH fought alongside LH against Israel in their 2006 War (Stanford 2017a, 2). And until the U.S. military withdrawal from Iraq in 2011, "AAH launched more than 6,000 attacks on American and Iraqi forces, including highly sophisticated operations and targeted kidnappings of Westerners" (CEP 2017a).

Between the American withdrawal from Iraq in 2011 and the rise of Daesh in 2014, AAH rebranded itself as a political and social service provider. Much like its Lebanese partner, AAH "opened a number of political offices and religious schools and offered social services to widows and orphans. According to a Reuters report, 'The model [AAH] uses is Hezbollah in Lebanon'" (CEP 2017a). AAH enjoyed the political patronage of Maliki, who invited them to join his political group. Its political career, like its militant one was marked by loyalty to Iran and the Supreme Leader. "In 2012, the group attempted to garner support for its pro-Iranian political agenda by launching a massive poster campaign, in which it distributed over 20,000 posters of Ayatallah Khamenei throughout Iraq" (Stanford 2017a, 2). In the 2014 parliamentary elections, AAH allied with Maliki's coalition and won a single seat in the parliament (Stanford 2017a, 2).

It is clear that AAH is an adherent to the *velayat-e faqih* system and their size and strength an important indicator of Iranian influence (CEP 2017a). "Despite attempting to portray itself as nationalist, AAH continues to promote Iranian interests in Iraq and pursue closer links between the two states. AAH also seeks to shore up the Assad Regime in Syria and to combat the Islamic State in both Syria and Iraq" (Stanford 2017a, 4). Further, the group does not follow Sistani, or the Sadrist line of clerics; rather they follow the revolutionary clerical line, "AAH overtly displays its commitment to figures of the 'tradition of the Iranian Revolution,' including Ruhollah Khomeini, Ali Khamenei, Kazim al-Haeri, and Mahmoud Hashemi Shahroudi. . . . Fundamentally, AAH is a Khomeinist organization that seeks to create a suitable environment for the return of Imam Mahdi" (Wyer 2012, 9).

AAH draws on the myth of the Sacred Defense, that is *resistance* that leads to *triumph*, to recruit new members. "One of the main ways AAH draws recruits is by advertising itself as a protector of the Shiite community within Iraq and abroad. AAH uses posters and issues calls for recruits on Iraqi television stations, often emphasizing its connection with Iran and Hezbollah" (CEP 2017a, 4). The myth-making is perpetuated through a system of schools and mosques "as hubs for recruitment. AAH leaders give sermons at these mosques, advocating social and religious reform in Iraq in an attempt to entice attendees into joining, financing, or otherwise contributing to AAH's mission." They have established a network of religious schools, the Seal of the Apostles. "These schools, spread throughout Iraq, serve as propaganda and recruitment facilities for the group. As with its military and political structures, AAH also appears to be emulating Hezbollah by launching social services programs for widows and orphans" (CEP 2017a, 5). The role of protector of the oppressed, also a key theme in the Shi'a myth-symbol complex, has been under competition for some time between AAH and the Sadrists (Wyer 2012, 6).

To be clear, religious proselytizing and education may be a genuine goal of the group, but these actions enhance their own influence and thereby force multiply Iranian influence in Iraq and beyond. Wyer noted in 2012 that they seek to "promote a Shi'a-controlled Iraqi state, replace the Sadrist Trend as the principal champion of Shi'a religious activism, be a proponent of the vilayat-e faqih system, and generally promote Iranian political and religious influence in Iraq in advance of Iranian Islamic Revolutionary goals, including facilitating Iranian lethal support to other regional allies and proxies and the expulsion of the remaining U.S. military and diplomatic presence from Iraq" (Wyer 2012, 10).

Asa'ib Ahl al-Haq is an extension of the Quds Force strategy of infiltrating the Iraqi security forces. They are a main pillar of the PMF and as such are recognized by the Iraqi government. As Wyer puts it, "AAH seems to have become an integral part of Iran's multi-pronged proxy strategy to project influence in the region" (Wyer 2012, 10). However, much like the Badr Organization, they maintain political offices and social services. They are present in Lebanon and boast of very strong ties to Hizb'allah. They, too, appear to be a hybrid organization. As part of the PMF they are following the IRGC model, but as a separate militia they are very much following the Hizb'allah model.

## Mahdi Army/Peace Brigade

As we have seen, each of the Shi'a militias in Iraq has an origin myth that is rooted in the notion of resisting oppression and defending the faithful. The group currently known as the Peace Brigades, which was originally known as the Mahdi Army or Jaysh al-Mahdi (JAM), was founded in 2003 in reaction to the U.S. invasion of Iraq, and it follows these general trends. And just as Asa'ib Ahl al-Haq, Kata'ib Hizb'allah, and the Badr Organization have charismatic leaders that draw the faithful and galvanize the loyal, so the Mahdi Army become the Peace Brigades has Moqtada al-Sadr. Sadr comes from a prominent family of clerics. His father was Grand Ayatallah Mohammed Sadiq al-Sadr, the namesake of the widely popular Sadrist movement, a vehemently nationalist and populist political movement representative of Iraq's Shi'a poor. Mohammad Sadiq was assassinated in 1999, most likely at the orders of Saddam Hussein (Stanford 2017b; BBC 2012). Moqtada succeeded his father as leader of the Sadrist movement and when the United States invaded Iraq, formed the Mahdi Army to expel Coalition forces and to form an Iraqi Shi'a government in Baghdad. Despite the nationalist ideological strain, fighters in the Mahdi Army "were sent to Hezbollah camps in Lebanon for training" (Stanford 2017b, 1). That is, from its very inception the Mahdi Army was both Iraqi nationalist and Iran dependent.

Much like Hizb'allah, Sadr shored up his populist credentials by providing care, both physical and spiritual, to the neediest. "In the first weeks following the U.S.-led invasion, Moqtada Sadr's followers patrolled the streets of Baghdad's Shi'a suburbs, distributing food, providing healthcare and taking on many of the functions of local government" (BBC 2012, 2). Sadr's populist credentials made him an important political partner and the network of religious charities founded by his father gave him a large conduit by which to convey his messages (BBC 2012). The Dawa Party and SCIRI reached out to Sadr to join their coalition. "The Sadrists' participation was crucial to the success of the coalition and ultimately resulted in the ascension of Nouri al-Maliki as prime minister. However, Sadr and Maliki were often at odds, and by 2006, Sadr and the Mahdi Army had begun to openly oppose the Iraqi government" (Stanford 2017b, 1).

This rupture was soon followed by a series of public relations problems as the Mahdi Army was accused of participating in sectarian conflicts, targeting and killing Sunni Iraqis. "Although Sadr has always denied running 'death squads' targeting Sunni civilians, the Mahdi Army, or at least rogue elements within it, was reportedly very active in the sectarian violence of 2006–2007" (Stanford 2017b, 2). It is, of course, highly counterproductive to a movement that seeks national unity and the exclusion of outside actors to engage in ethnic and/or sectarian violence. Further, violence directed at Sunni terrorist groups or Coalition forces are largely supported by the Shi'as who suffered at their hands, but internecine fighting was another matter, and this eventually forced Sadr's hand. This is, in part, a result of origin, resistance, and triumphalist myths that emphasize Shi'a identity. Yet, many Shi'as reject this sectarian violence. "The group's provocation of a series of bloody skirmishes in early 2007 tarnished the Mahdi Army's reputation among even its Shiite supporters, eventually forcing Sadr to re-orient the group. This turning point occurred in August 2007 following a violent clash in Karbala between the Mahdi Army and another Shiite militia, the Badr Brigades, in which 50 Shiite pilgrims were killed. The Mahdi Army was blamed for the casualties and in light of the group's already tainted reputation as an instigator of sectarian violence, Sadr ordered his supporters to lay down their arms" (Stanford 2017b, 2). In other words, Sadr was unable to control his group and focus their energies.

It was around this time that Sadr left Iraq for Iran for religious studies. Why a vociferous Iraqi nationalist would choose Qom over Najaf for religious studies makes sense only in the light of Sadr believing he had to leave Iraq or that he traveled there at the "invitation" of senior Iranian clerics. In 2008 the Maliki government, with U.S. support, mounted an offensive against the Mahdi Army. "Over 30,000 Iraqi Security Force troops were involved in the operation and over 600 civilians and combatants were killed within the first few days of hostilities alone. As the fighting ground to a stalemate, Sadr finally agreed to an Iran-brokered ceasefire agreement on March 31, 2008. By the time hostilities ceased, over 2,000 Mahdi Army fighters had been killed" (Stanford 2017b, 2).

It was at this point that Sadr rebranded his organization. Realizing, it appears, that he could neither maintain the discipline nor the size that was needed for his militia to be effective, Sadr moved his group's focus from military affairs to the realm of social services. Toward this end he created the

Mumahidoon, a non-violent social service organization. "Although the majority of the Mahdi Army was reassigned to the Mumahidoon, Sadr retained a small elite military branch called the Promised Day Brigades (PDB). The PDB was prohibited from attacking Iraqi citizens or Iraqi troops, but did continue to assail U.S. forces through 2011" (Stanford 2017b, 3). In what seems like another attempt to remain relevant Sadr reorganized his group once again in 2010 in preparation for elections. He moved resources and people from providing services to political positions. "Regardless, the elections were a relative success for the Sadrists, with the Iraqi National Alliance party winning 40 out of 325 seats in the Iraqi parliament. At the urging of Iran, Sadr and his Iraqi National Alliance party agreed to enter Maliki's coalition, even though they had violently opposed him from 2006–2008" (Stanford 2017b, 3). This, again, shows the influence Iran has on Sadr, even though he is an avowed nationalist.

"On August 6, 2013, Sadr shocked his supporters and critics alike when he announced that he would retire from political activity and dismantle the Mahdi Army. It remains unclear what precipitated this proclamation. . . . After the fall of Mosul to the Islamic State in June 2014, Sadr called upon his supporters once again, reforming the Mahdi Army under a new name, the Peace Brigades" (Stanford 2017b, 3). This was around the time of Sistani's fatwa and, like Sistani, Sadr had two goals in mind, the defeat of Daesh and the removal of Maliki from power. When Abadi succeeded Maliki to the premiership, Sadr supported him. However, in January 2016, Sadr confronted Abadi "demanding that the cabinet be comprised of skilled technocrats rather than career politicians, that the government absorb the Shiite militias—including the Peace Brigades—into the Iraqi Army and that it 'allocate a share for each Iraqi citizen from the oil revenues' collected by the Iraqi state" (Stanford 2017b, 4). Sadr himself marched into the Green Zone in Baghdad and set up a protest tent. He was there for five days until Abadi announced that he would form a new government (Stanford 2017b, 4). It remains unclear what lasting political effects came from this confrontation. However, according to Hayder al-Khoei, an Iraq analyst at the London-based Chatham House think tank, there was great potential for the Iranian-backed militias and Sadr to come into open conflict (Morris 2016).

As Sadr's followers stormed the Green Zone, his militiamen took position around its perimeter. In response, the Khorasani Brigades, an Iranian proxy militia, and others closer to Tehran, deployed heavily on the streets of Baghdad. Other militias close to Iran pulled fighters back from the country's conflict zones. "It's not outside the realms of possibility for them to turn their guns on each other, Khoei said" (Morris 2016). There was no fighting between the Shi'a militias on that day or notably since, but the notion that Sadr had a clear path to challenge the government of Abadi was refuted. And given how much better armed the PMF militias are and how well supported they are by Iran, one has to wonder, yet again, what Sadr was thinking. The Post article includes this very interesting and telling fact. "A day after his supporters packed up and left their short-lived sit-in, Sadr got on a plane and left for Iran. His office said it was a personal trip to visit an Iranian shrine, despite coming at a time when thousands of Shiites stream to a shrine in Baghdad to pay their respects on the anniversary of the death of an 8th-century imam, a pilgrimage he missed" (Morris 2016). Soon thereafter Sadr's office issued a directive that all protests should be held locally and not in Baghdad. Again, while the protest itself seemed ill-conceived, the turnaround after a visit to Tehran leaves this observer wondering just how independent Sadr really is.

These facts provide reasons to doubt the veracity of Sadr being "a counterweight against Iranian influence in Iraq" (Alaaldin 2017, 2). And the claim of the author that "due to his unparalleled capacity to mobilize the masses, his father's legacy, and growing discontent in Iraq, al-Sadr may indeed be the best hope the country has of reducing Iran's influence in Iraq and enhancing government accountability in the foreseeable future" (Alaaldin 2017, 2). It would seem that Sadr is still in the process of finding his footing. He has not been very successful as a militia leader, he is a very junior cleric, and his political authority, although enhanced by his support by the Shi'a populace, is undercut by his support from his poor relations with the clerical and political elite, and his lack of an important external sponsor such as Iran. All of which make his rivals in the Badr Organization a more likely long-term conduit of Iranian influence as opposed to Sadr being a counterweight to Iranian influence.

It is certainly true that Sadr enjoys a large patronage network, largely built off of his father's network. It is also true that he has been working hard to build up his religious credentials. However, it is also true that the Badr Organization, for instance, with Iranian money could outspend and outmaneuver Sadr on the ground and it would take Sadr years to reach a significant level of religious authority. Which is why it is odd for Alaaldin to write, "Al-Sadr has long aimed to compete with Sistani for power and influence, in the way his father did in the 1990s. During this period, the senior al-Sadr attacked Sistani and the power and privilege of what he called the 'elitist' religious establishment (or *marja'iyya*), a disconnect that also shaped the Sadrist movement's relations with the exiled Shiite opposition that now dominates the Iraqi government" (Alaaldin 2017, 4). This would require an undoing of centuries of religious practice. We have seen how influential Sistani is and how important the clergy is to the Shi'a religion, and it is hard to imagine that being undone any time soon.

It is no secret that Iran has been trying to bring Sadr under its sphere of influence since he gained international attention in 2003. Sadr is both cooperating with Iran yet working against their interests. One possible explanation for this is that "With intra-Shi'a conflict and violent JAM splinter groups, al-Sadr grew dependent on Tehran's financial and military support, further undermining his ability to emerge as an independent Shi'a leader in the postwar period. Accordingly, al-Sadr's decision in late 2007 to move to Iran provided Iranian hardliners a major advantage to monitor the young cleric, while encouraging him to undergo religious training through Iranian seminary circles" (Rahimi 2010, 2). Yet it has to be remembered that Kazali and Muhandis were recruited by then Quds Force Commander Soleimani. Did they splinter them off of Sadr's forces to weaken Sadr so that he had to turn to them for support? That seems likely.

There is no doubt that Sadr is attempting to deploy the Hizb'allah model in his areas of operation. His strong reliance on his father's network of charities, his anti-Americanism, his use of force, all point to the Hizb'allah model. He cooperates but is not a part of the PMF, the PMF is made up of the Badr Organization, AAH, and KH all bitter rivals of Sadr. Sadr appears, still, to be in the process of finding his true voice and vocation. He may yet emerge the most powerful militia leader, with a strong political, religious, and ideological army supporting him, and as such be a stalwart against Iranian influence. His bloc won the plurality of votes in 2018 and he has functioned as a sort of kingmaker or gatekeeper since.

## SUMMARY

From the point of view of Iran, strategic patience is the way of influence. They appear to support any number of groups sometimes at cross purposes to keep a hand in every militia. The number and size of these militias that pledge loyalty to the *velayat-e faqih* system and Khamenei, himself is a testament to the payoff of their strategy. The establishment of the PMF institutionalizes Iranian influence and gives them a strong voice shaping policy. Yet even when the PMF is excluded from major battles, such as the taking of Mosul, their ability to make and perpetuate myths of the sacred defense, keeps them indispensable to the future of Iraqi security.

The fact that the PMF is not a monolithic actor presents opportunities for the Iraqi nationalist movement and its allies like the United States. As Monsour puts it, "Understanding subgroups is pivotal. The PMF is not a monolithic Shi'a militia. Policy recommendations must separately address Iranian proxy; rightwing, pro-Khamenei Iraqi; pro-Sistani; and pro-Sadr subgroups" (Mansour 2017, 1). While it is not clear to me why the term "rightwing" is at play here, nevertheless the call for deeper understanding of the groups Iran is supporting and those who may be able to resist Iranian influence is key. However, the call for integrating the PMF into the Iraqi security forces, though logical, is fraught with dangers. So long as these groups are in line with Iran, giving them legitimacy and formal recognition is a dangerous gamble.

Enforcing the prohibition against political parties having armed wings would be a great boon for Iraqi sovereignty and nationalism. However, this seems unlikely at this time as the militias enjoy widespread support among the people and their leaders are galvanizing that support into political action. If the question is who can mobilize the Iraqi people best, the answer seems to be in matters of faith it remains Grand Marja Ali al-Sistani, but in matters of politics it is Supreme Leader Ali Khamenei. Should Sistani pass and no single Marja with the ability to resist Iranian influence emerge, Iran's influence will continue to grow. That situation would be much worse if an Iranian ally or proponent of the *Velayat* system like Grand Ayatallah Hakim should emerge as the *a'lam*. The forces of culture, economics, military, political will, and geography favor Iran and the ability to withstand those forces alone falls outside of the capability of the Iraqi government. Whether there is the will and ability to resist Iranian influence by powers sympathetic to Iraqi nationalism is an open question. The origin myths of the IRGC and Hizb'allah, born of revolution and civil war, respectively, as triumphant embodiments of resistance resonate with the Iraqi masses. The symbolism of the clenched fist clutching a Kalashnikov rifle captures this well and is adopted by the major militias in Iraq. Yet, it is more than martial vigor, it is also religious authority, economic infrastructure, and the importance of history, culture, and the stubbornness of geography that make Iran so influential in Iraq. Curtailing that influence requires a carefully elaborated influence strategy that, like Iran's, is long term, holistic, and adaptive. I address this at length in the conclusion of this book.

*Chapter 9*

# Syria

What do a secular military dictatorship and an Islamic Republic have in common? At first, it was a relationship primarily built on having common enemies. For example, Syria supported Iran in its nearly ten-year war against Saddam Hussein. Both countries have a hostile posture toward Israel, although Syria has engaged in direct negotiations with Israel. And both countries, together with Lebanese Hizb'allah form the Arc of Resistance, a coalition that opposes Western, primarily American and Israeli, influence and power in the region. More recently however Iran has been Syrian president Bashar al-Assad's primary ally in his fight to retain control of Syria. This support from Iran, of course, plays directly into Iran's regional strategy of hegemony through influence. Since the inception of the Syrian Civil War, Iran has been arming, training, and funding militias in Syria, ostensibly to fight Daesh, but clearly, they are fighting to keep Assad in power as well. They have done this by mobilizing Shi'a faithful throughout the region using familiar themes of religious duty and sacrifice—namely, Islamic Resistance. And this mobilization of religious identity, as we have seen in Iran and Iraq, is likely to have long-term effects on the political make-up of Syria and the relationship between Iran, Iraq, and Syria.

As of this writing the civil war in Syria appears to be drawing to an end, Assad's position seems secure, and Syria and Turkey are trading blows in Idlib province; Assad remains dependent on Russia and Iran and its militias, leaving a network of Iranian proxy cells throughout Syria. One of the questions this chapter seeks to examine is how the Syria-Iran relationship will survive recent regional events such as the defeat of Daesh and the increased hostility between the United States and Iran? Another question this chapter addresses is how firmly Iran has established its influence network in Syria. To begin addressing these questions, I examine the background of Iranian-Syrian strategic relations, describe the beginning and unfolding of the civil war, and offer a brief profile on some of the groups operating in Syria. I conclude by discussing potential future states for Syria and, of course, how these possible states play into Iran's strategic goals and how their influence strategies are faring.

## IRAN AND SYRIA, BACKGROUND

At first blush, it may appear that mapping Middle Eastern strategic relationships requires a scorecard written in pencil. Certainly, the tacit cooperation between Saudi Arabia and Israel is exemplary of a strong type of relationship—the enemy of my enemy is my friend. But there is another strong type of relationship that permeates this space—like knows like, homophily. The Iran-Syria connection is an odd mixture of both types. Thus, Byman points that "the Middle East is home to many unusual alliances, but one of the oddest is the enduring partnership between Syria and Iran" (2006). Yet, observers concede that it is indeed enduring and difficult to disrupt relationship (Byman 2006; Polk 2013; Fulton 2013; Barabandi, 2014).

The enemy of my enemy is my friend as a foundation for cooperation is significant. "Syria was the first Arab state to recognize the post-Shah government in Iran and backed it in conflicts throughout the 1980s, particularly that against Saddam Hussein in Iraq" (Barabandi 2014). Soon after Iran's Islamic Revolution in 1979, it found itself at war with Iraq. Saddam Hussein, like Hafez Assad of Syria, was a Ba'athist military dictator. However, the two men saw each other as rivals, if not enemies. Therefore, Assad was one of the very few supporters of Iran during that war. "Israel, too, provided a common foe. Iran's revolutionary ideology saw Israel as anathema; Syria also opposed the Jewish state, especially after its humiliating defeat in the 1967 war, since when it has strived to regain the Golan Heights" (Byman 2006). Both countries see Israel as a Western imperial transplant and cooperation against Israel imperative to their strategic ambitions. Syria has permitted Iran passage through its territory to support Lebanese Hizb'allah, Hamas, and Palestinian Islamic Jihad, groups whose missions include the destruction of the state of Israel (Fulton 2013).

Further, both states have a common adversary in the United States. "In 1982, a new relationship was formed between Syria under Hafez al-Assad and Ayatallah Khomeini in Iran; Syria was the only Arab country which supported Iran in the Iran-Iraq war. The aim of such an alliance was eventually to defeat American hegemony in the Middle East" (Rostami-Povey 2010, 114). This relationship would only strengthen over time, partly in reaction to U.S. actions. "In 2002 when the concept of the 'axis of evil' was adopted by George W. Bush and the USA continued its hostility towards Syria and Iran, Tehran and Damascus cemented their economic, political and cultural relations. Iran built petroleum and gas refineries in Syria. They established a joint car industry (80 per cent Iranian and 20 per cent Syrian), and began to cooperate with each other on Lebanon" (Rostami-Povey 2010, 115).

While both benefited from the ouster of Saddam Hussein, the presence of U.S. military assets in Iraq and Syria pose a threat to both regimes. Yet neither state wants to take on the U.S. military directly. This is why Iran's use of proxies is central to its strategy. They toe the line without prompting massive U.S. retaliation. Likewise, in Syria, fights against Daesh and the rebels are orchestrated not to get the United States to turn directly against the Assad regime. Nevertheless, U.S. policy is as hostile to the Arc of Resistance as the Arc is to the United States. In addition to these motivations to cooperate against the United States and Israel, there is the chaos that swept the region since the 2003 invasion of Iraq, including the rise of Daesh in 2014 (Byman 2006).

However, I believe the relationship between Syria and Iran is deeper than just a strategic partnership based on having common adversaries. There is a common historical narrative and emergent imperative that enables them to recognize each other, cooperate, and even to some degree trust each other. *Resistance* is that historic and strategic imperative for both states; it is the basis of homophily. Further, I contend that Syria's secular military dictatorship is difficult to maintain in the contemporary Middle East, particularly in what is known as the Levant. This will be made clear in the next section *A Brief History of Contemporary Syria*. If the relationship between Iran and Syria is, in fact, deeper than just a strategic cooperation born from shared enemies, then the following puzzle must be addressed.

How can Iran and Syria be allies given these conditions: Syria portrays itself as a champion of secular Arab nationalism, although in practice it is a minority-dominated military dictatorship. Iran, in contrast, rides under the banner of revolutionary Islam, although as a Persian country, it is often at odds with the Arab world, particularly since the vast majority of Iranians are Shiites, while most Arabs are Sunnis. Syrian president Bashar Assad's father and predecessor, Hafez Assad, gunned down thousands of revolutionary Islamists in the 1970s and early 1980s to prevent an Islamic revolution in Syria. Iran's religious elite often criticizes Arab leaders as despots who have turned away from true Islam—a description that could easily apply to Assad's Syria (Byman 2006).

Ultimately, the solution to this puzzle, explored in the chapter summary, comes down to answering these questions. Is *resistance* a sufficient cause to create homophily and is homophily sufficient to maintain an alliance? If a military dictatorship and an Islamic revolutionary republic *identify* with *resistance*, is that enough to draw them together, to guarantee cooperation, to build trust. It appears that this is so, but is it sustainable? The difficulty as we will see is that Iran is now deeply embedded in Syria through its network of proxies. This represents both an opportunity and challenge for Assad. It is an opportunity because the Shi'a militias that Iran has sponsored give Assad's security forces a much-needed augmentation and provides for the safety and even loyalty of many communities throughout Syria. It is also a challenge because it gives Iran a lot of reach and power within Syria, a potential challenge to Assad's sovereignty. Nevertheless, if the common identity, motivation, and cultural frames associated with *resistance* are sufficient causes for homophily, then they will likely work through these challenges.

Barabandi, a former Syrian diplomat tells a story about a dinner he attended with Iranian ambassador Ahmad al-Mousawi. "He told me, 'Iranians are all blooming flowers planted by Mohamad Nassif.' Nassif was a close advisor to Hafez al-Assad, and until recently the deputy vice president for security. Ambassador Mousawi's statement hints at the complexities of Iran and Syria's relationship over the last forty-five years" (2014). Indeed, in the Muslim Middle East, a secular dictatorship whose only religious affiliation was to an Alawite sect considered non-Muslim by both Sunni and Shi'a scholars lacked legitimacy and was open to domestic and foreign intervention. In fact, as we will see in the next section, the Muslim Brotherhood used this line of attack to mobilize the masses against Assad. As a concession to them, Hafez al-Assad, an Alawite, sought out religious legitimacy. He did so by supporting Musa al-Sadr an influential Shi'a scholar in Lebanon of Iranian nationality. "Assad supported Sadr's rise, and in return, Sadr declared that all Alawites were brothers in the Shi'a Muslim faith. Sadr later suggested that Assad meet an influential Iranian Shi'a named Khomeini, then exiled in Iraq. Assad saw strategic benefit in supporting a future ally in the region, and supported Khomeini with intelligence, money, and assistance" (Barabandi 2014). Thus, was born the odd alliance that is reshaping Middle East strategic policies today.

The legitimacy of the Syrian regime is contingent on a certification of Islamic credentials bestowed by an Iranian Shi'a scholar.[1] These Shi'a credentials become even more important during the current civil war for drawing in fighters from the region to defend Shi'a shrines leads to recruiting fighters for Assad. Yet, over time these postures for strategic advantage produce effects. Whether Bashar Assad remains in power, or for how long he remains in power, is still a relatively open question at the time of this writing. However, that Iran has fought to keep Syria in its regional alliance is clear.

In March 2011, just a few days after the uprisings began in Syria, the secretary of Iran's Supreme National Security Council, Saeed Jalili, made an unannounced visit to Damascus. He came with a clear message: Do not give in to the Arab Spring in Syria. Jalili met with President Bashar al-Assad and his top advisors to propose what he called a new "Iron Curtain" with Iran and Russia against a Western conspiracy in the region. Assad took the offer despite his father's efforts to keep his dubious Iranian ally at arm's length. Now the world watches as Iran increases its influence in both Syria and Lebanon, building toward an improved bargaining position with the West. By design, this process will soon render Bashar dispensable to all sides (Barabandi 2014).

Assad may end up dispensable to all sides and a Russian-Iranian-Turkish arrangement could emerge that keeps Assad in power for a time while a new government is formed. It may also come to pass that Assad stays in power by appeasing Turkish concerns about Kurdish independence, continuing and/or increasing support to Iranian proxies in exchange for continued to support for his regime, and promises to extend Russia's basing rights. While these two possibilities do not exhaust the possible futures, they are two distinct directions in which these events could lead. This is precisely where Iran's tenets of Strategic Influence, adaptive resistance and designed redundancy, come into play. In other words, "Iran's strategy in Syria aims to keep President Bashar al-Assad in power as long as possible while setting conditions to ensure Tehran's ability to use Syrian territory and assets to pursue its regional interests should Assad fall. Iran has conducted an extensive, expensive, and integrated effort to achieve these objectives" (Fulton 2013).

The defeat of Daesh, as a territory-holding, quasi-state was completed with the capture of Raqqa. The anti-Assad rebels, too, seem to have been pushed back. For the moment, it appears that Assad is secure. His fate, however, is dependent; it seems to this observer, on the regional and global powers and their agreement on the future. Both Russia and Iran have invested heavily in keeping Assad in power and they seem to have achieved their objectives. Russia has supplied air support and intelligence. Iran has supplied a comprehensive Foreign Internal Defense mission run by the IRGC's Quds Force. This has included intelligence, advice and assistance missions, and the standing up of proxies. It is unlikely that whey would welcome Assad's fall from power.

However, should Assad fall from power, Iran's proxies in Syria could still serve as the basis for Iran's influence in Syria and the region. "This aspect of Iran's approach is congruent with Tehran's long-standing efforts in Lebanon and Iraq, where it also built Shi'a militias to ensure that its interests were protected even in the absence of effective or pliable host states" (Fulton 2013). Thus, Iran's adaptive resistance and designed redundancy models are clearly at work in Syria as they are in Iraq. They will work to keep Assad in power, sacrifice him for a more suitable long-term Alawite replacement, or maintain a presence through their proxies. Before moving to an examination of these proxies and potential future states, the next two sections serve as brief backgrounds to Syria's contemporary history and the civil war.

## A BRIEF HISTORY OF CONTEMPORARY SYRIA

The battle in the collective imagination of the people of Syria, like that of Iran, is a battle for meaning and belonging, between history and modernity, between modern secularism and Islamism, with competing spectral narratives deployed to mobilize the imaginary into a unity that never really quite was nor could ever really truly be. This is the legacy of a land of empires dealing with modernity. Syria, like Iran, was a land conquered, divided, and dominated by others. "Since before history was written, Syria has been fought over by foreign empires—Egyptians, Hittites, Assyrians, Persians, Macedonian Greeks, Romans, Mongols, Turks, British, and French. Only during the Umayyad Caliphate in the 7th and 8th centuries A.D. was it the center of an empire" (Polk 2013). Unlike Iran, however, there was no core Syrian nation, identity, and essence that endured or absorbed the conquerors.

It was a land of many peoples, religions, and languages, vestiges of conquerors past. In its modern history Syria as a political entity included various ethnicities and religions, with the Ottoman Empire functioning as the unifying principle. "During most of the last five centuries . . . Syria was part of the Ottoman Empire, groups of Orthodox, Catholic, and other Christians; Alawis, Ismailis, and other sorts of Shi'a Muslims; and Yazidis, Kurds, Jews, and Druze lived in enclaves and in neighborhoods in the various cities and towns alongside Sunni Muslim Arabs" (Polk 2013). Each enclave enjoyed a certain degree of autonomy in terms of their internal governance, marriage and inheritance laws, and so on. But there was no national Syrian identity. Of course, "the concept of a state, much less a nation-state, did not enter into political thought until the end of the 19th century" (Polk 2013). Most people identified with local communities, towns and villages, or provinces (Reedy 2010; Polk 2013).

This state of affairs would dramatically change with the fall of the Ottoman Empire. The Ottomans, allied with the Germans, were defeated at the end of the First World War by the allied powers of the United States, Great Britain, and France. The United States mostly withdrew from the Middle East while Great Britain and France secretly devised a plan to govern the newly conquered lands of the Middle East. "At this point in time, the political powerhouses of the world—namely, France and the United Kingdom—moved into the Middle East and (so Syrians said) carved it up in a random fashion without any consideration for the people who lived there" (Reedy 2010, 94). The pact to divide the Middle East between the French and the British, known as the Sykes-Picot Agreement, gave Britain dominion over the Gulf and Iraq; Syria and Lebanon would go to the French. The political elite of Syria, not surprisingly, had their own ideas.

During the latter part of the war, the leaders of the Arab revolt against the Ottoman Empire established a kingdom at Damascus and at the Paris Peace Conference sought recognition of their independence. France was determined, however, to effect its deal with Britain, so in 1920 it invaded and "regime-changed" the Damascus government, making Syria a de facto colony of France but legally, under the League of Nations, a "mandate." The terms of the League mandate required France to prepare it for independence, but the French showed little intention to do that. They spent the next three years actually conquering the country and reformulating the territory. Over the next several decades the French attempted to force the population into submitting to their rule. "The French bombarded Damascus, which they had regime-changed in 1920, in 1925, 1926, and 1945, and they pacified the city with martial law during most of the 'peaceful' intervals. Constitutions were proclaimed periodically, only to be revoked, and independence was promised time after time until it was finally gained—not by the Syrians nor given by the French but bestowed on Syria by the British army" (Polk 2013). Nevertheless, the French did not leave until April 17, 1946, Syria's national day.

At this point, there were, generally speaking, three forces at work. Part of the elite wanted Syria to be a Western-oriented modern nation-state. Others wanted national unity and independence, but were suspicious of the West, both because of recent memory of the French and British roles in dominating the Middle East, but also because of the way the French used Christianity to dominate Lebanon and Syria. Then there was the population that largely continued to live as they did during the Ottoman Empire, in semi-autarkic enclaves.

Nationalists took this diversity as a primary cause of weakness and adopted as their primary task integrating the population into a single political and social structure. But the nationalists were deeply split. The major Islamic movement, the Muslim Brotherhood, argued and fought for the idea that the nation must be Arab Sunni (or "Orthodox") Muslim. Minorities had no place except in the traditional and Ottoman sense of "protected minorities." The more conservative, affluent, and Westernized nationalists believed that nationhood had to be built not on a religious but on a territorial base. It was in this competitive space for the definition of a new Syria that the Muslim Brotherhood and Hafez Assad emerged as competing elites. The Muslim Brotherhood represented a version of "orthodox" Islam that was quite different from the practices of most Syrians. The Assads hailed from a sect considered heretical by most Sunni and Shi'a scholars. Naturally, Assad favored a secular regime, but since the Umayyad Dynasty Syria was heavily Sunni Muslim. Although the Syrian constitution stipulates that the president must be a Muslim, it does not specify Sunni, presumably because that would have seemed obvious at the time.

Despite this the Secular Hafez Assad became president in 1973. To do so, he made two major concessions to the Muslim identity of the Syrian people. First, he got the definition of "Muslim" in the constitution redefined as an "Islam of sorts. 'Islam,' the new language stressed, 'is a religion of love, progress and social justice, of equality for all'" (Polk 2013). Then, he got the blessing of an Iranian Shi'a scholar in Lebanon to recognize the Alawis as Muslim. In a majority Sunni country, the Alawite President asked a Shi'a scholar to recognize Alawis as Shi'a Muslims and defined Muslim in a new way. The reaction from the Muslim Brotherhood was predictable. Throughout Syria riots broke out as the Muslim Brotherhood (MB) mobilized their masses casting the Assad moves as affronts, if not direct attacks, on orthodox Islam. The MB took to the streets recalling stories about the transgressions of the Alawis and their heresies. Syria was a Sunni Muslim state and the Alawis were interlopers unfit to govern. The epicenter of this storm of unrest was Hama. Hama lingers in the imagination of contemporary Syrians as the Massacre of Hama or as the Great Revolt. It no doubt was heavily on the mind of Hafez' son Bashar al-Assad when the 2011 uprisings began. The battle for Hama, or the Massacre of Hama, as it is often referred to, was a turning point in the history of contemporary Syria. Certainly, the effects of the Muslim Brotherhood attack enabled Hafez Assad to crush the rebellion, break the will of the Muslim Brotherhood, and secure his government's control of the country.

Yet, the underlying issues were not only left unresolved, but they also became undercurrents of political discontent expressed through narratives, frames, and myths that recalled a time before Assad and the European Imperial Project, when there was harmony among the peoples of the land called Syria. In other words, symbolic myths kept alive through story telling stoked the symbolic predispositions of the population under the surface of Assad's governance. "[These stories] came up in a number of contexts . . . I came to realize that they tended to be similar in form and content. I also noticed that these narrated histories were not merely re-presentations of the past, but were intentionally made relevant to the present" (Reedy 2010). For Reedy, these stories, like the mobilization literature discussed above, rely on the notion of speech acts. "Theories of language use provide an insight into how this process might be effected. Austin's (1962) work on speech acts opens up the idea that speech can also be performative and thus can constitute action" (Reedy 2010, 93). Through these speech acts storytellers re-create a Syria of tolerance and freedom, juxtaposed to both Great Britain's and France's interventions and the governance of Hafez Assad.

To do so effectively, story tellers, those deploying myths, begin their stories prior to both the Assad and European Imperialists. "Despite the long history of the Syrian land, many of the stories I was told began with the Ottoman Empire. My informants described it as a time when Bilad al-Sham (the region of Greater Syria, covering much of what is now Syria, Lebanon, Palestine, Jordan, and parts of Iraq) existed as a unified place under a single rule" (Reedy 2010). These stories re-presented an idealized version of Syria under Ottoman rule. There was freedom of movement, tolerance for ethnic and religious differences, with no official divisions between the peoples. "The idea of a division-free world is used not necessarily (or only) as an analysis of Ottoman times, but more as a dramatic point of unspoken comparison to what came afterward" (Reedy 2010). The other maneuver needed for these stories to work is the creation of the "other." That is, it is not enough to build myths from certain starting points, although this is necessary. To create the narrative of a newly imagined Syria, to discursively maneuver myths and predispositions, there must be an "other."

This peaceful co-existence was then juxtaposed against what came afterward with the British and French occupiers, who were depicted—and thus momentarily and discursively created in speech acts—as foreigners. These unwelcome "outsiders" may have had the ability, but certainly lacked the authority to dismember the unity of the "insider" population. Thus, we see that through these stories, Syrian speakers are creating a set of social identities that are relevant today: the people of historical (and, by association, modern) Britain and France are (re)affirmed as being external to and different from those living within the Bilad al-Sham. At the same time, these narratives grant to everyone who is native to the area, regardless of ethnicity or religion, a modern groupness that parallels their historical unity. The Ottomans, as such, are not featured as an active group in the stories but appear more as background figures. As a population that no longer exists, they have become socially irrelevant to Syrian speakers today (Reedy 2010, 95). The frame of the idealized past, one in which a Muslim Empire was dominant, as tolerant, is juxtaposed to the European Empires that were divisive and brutal. The Europeans are "others" and the true Syrian experience is destroyed through the meddling of "outsiders." For those advocating for a new Syria based on "orthodox" Islam, like the Muslim Brotherhood, this is a sine qua non of mobilization.

However, the creation of the outsider does not stop with the Europeans. "These global figures placed a series of cowardly puppets at the head of Syria, enabling them virtually to control Syria while making these leaders militarily and financially so powerful that they cannot be challenged locally. As a result, the non-Alawi population of Syria must put up with a corrupt leadership that hoards resources and money without sharing it with its people" (Reedy 2010). Here, Reedy, tells us that the Ottomans and the Europeans fade into the background and the real villains in the story are the Assads and the Alawi minority from which they hail. "The narratives reveal that the Asads are tied to the foreign powers, which, as we saw last time, are constructed as outsiders. The speakers, then, are engaging in a process of differentiation whereby they set the Alawis as being different from and external to 'ordinary' Syrians in a sort of guilt-by association move . . . these narratives are actually critiquing and challenging the legitimacy of the Syrian leadership" (Reedy 2010, 98). Of course, the Alawis have been in Syria for centuries and were part of the idealized past these stories re-create. These speech acts, these myth-making maneuvers, must recognize this truth as well. Therefore, "The Alawis come to occupy an almost liminal state, in which they are not foreigners but are not exactly like other Syrians either" (Reedy 2010). Alawis, and by extension, Hafez Assad and his regime, are not true insiders or true outsiders. They cannot then be legitimate rulers of a Sunni Arab orthodox population. Thus, Polk's and Reedy's stories meet at Hama.

But theirs are not the only stories explaining the events at Hama. In fact, the current Assad regime has their version as do the current rebels. Histories are weaponized; they are deployed with targets in mind to support a greater strategic goal. But certain events are so laden with meaning and emotion that their nature becomes obscured from so many explanations, narratives, and frames. Conduit, using spectacle theory, explains how the Muslim Brotherhood became conflated with Hama and how that episode became obscured by myths. "Using Guy Debord's concept of the spectacle, this article demonstrates that Hama has become surrounded by a mythology that has made it difficult to separate fact from fiction, and makes it almost impossible to conceptualize the Brotherhood outside the lens of 1982" (Conduit 2016, 212). In this case, the confusion regarding the actual events was sown through various narratives borne from various perspectives. It is, of course, the case that this type of retelling of history from various perspectives is a maneuver meant to sow confusion and deflate the ideological will to fight. That is, creating a spectacle, to confuse, can be an important maneuver in strategic influence.

According to Conduit's telling, "The Hama massacre was the final chapter in a period of escalating violence in Syria that spanned more than half a decade" (Conduit 2016, 213). It is interesting that a scholar writing about how myths occlude events posits the Hama massacre as a final chapter of violence. This observer is more inclined to think that the events of 1982 and the events beginning in 2011 are, in fact, deeply related, interdependent even.

"The Hama uprising was the militants' last major stand against the Ba'th regime. Although details remain vague on how it started, the episode began on February 2, 1982, after a Syrian Army patrol stumbled upon an opposition hideout in the city of Hama. It is thought that a number of cells in Hama, in which Brotherhood members were dominant, were planning an uprising in the city for later that year" (Conduit 2016, 213). The government learned of the plot forcing the plotters either to abandon the plot and flee or to take action. The rebels rose up and seized government buildings and declared independence. The government reaction was rapid and fierce. Government military units besieged the city for weeks until they broke the resistance. The brutality has become the stuff of myths and legends but no official report was ever released and the data on the number of casualty, displaced persons, or property damage is not known.

Conduit uses Debord's definition of a *spectacle* to capture the importance of Hama. A "spectacle is a shocking narrative that emerges to convey the story and imagery of an event. It is constructed via the snippets of information that become available as an event unfolds and it is elevated by memory, rumor, and emotion . . . as a process of 'paralyzing history and memory'" (Conduit 2016, 214). Further, "Douglas Kellner added that major events are particularly vulnerable to becoming spectacles, helping to 'shape social memory, constructing individual's views of history and contemporary reality. Resonant images help construct how people see and interpret the world.' This means that spectacles, due to imperfect memory combined with personal prejudice, can become divorced from fact and reality" (Conduit 2016, 214).

The narratives of Hama, converging into spectacle, not only told a story about an event that occurred but also continues to tell that event as a thing that shapes contemporary events. Would Hama not have happened, would Bashir al-Assad have taken the steps he took in response to events in 2011? To be clear, I am not positing here that narrative is everything. Real-world events, revolts, natural disasters, and so on, all have effects, but it is often how these events are framed, as we saw in the discussion in chapter 4 Strategic Influence, that shape reactions and produce new narratives and effects. In the next section, we will see how Hama hovered over the 2011 uprisings as a specter and shaped reactions to events.

## A BRIEF HISTORY OF THE SYRIAN CIVIL WAR

Syria's current President Bashar al-Assad assumed power when his father Hafez al-Assad died in 2000. Bashar was not groomed for power but came in line for succession when his older brother was killed in a car accident in 1994. In fact, Bashar's training was in medicine, having earned a medical degree from Damascus University. His postdoctoral studies in London were interrupted by his brother's death, as Bashar was recalled to Syria to begin his role as heir apparent. It is fair to point out, therefore, that Bashar did not have the background and training that is typical of an heir. It is therefore understandable that he would use his father's legacy as a guide in times of crisis. "Like his father had done after the Battle of Hama, Bashar initially made conciliatory moves to his opponents, including allowing the Muslim Brotherhood to resume political activities and withdrawing most of the Syrian troops that had occupied strife-torn Lebanon" (Polk 2013).

But circumstances in Syria were not favorable for reconciliation. The country was suffering from the effects of a four-year drought that drove hundreds of thousands of farmers into the major cities looking for work. These cities were already overcrowded from Palestinian and Iraq War refugees. The cities were, in Polk's terms, tinder boxes, ready to explode. "Hundreds of thousands of Syria's farmers gave up, abandoned their farms, and fled to the cities and towns in search of almost non-existent jobs and severely short food supplies. Outside observers including UN experts estimated that between 2 and 3 million of Syria's 10 million rural inhabitants were reduced to 'extreme poverty'" (Polk 2013).

But the economic conditions in the cities were not welcoming to these internally displaced "economic" and/or "climate" refugees who immediately found that they had to compete not only with one another for scarce food, water, and jobs, but also with the existing foreign refugee population from Palestine and Iraq. These were the conditions that precipitated the protests in Daraa on March 15, 2011. The protesters were angry with the government for failing to help them cope with the overcrowding, the strain on resources, and the fear of worsening conditions. The Assad regime did not meet with the protestors, treating them instead like subversives. Thus, the spectacle of Hama appeared as a focal point. Bashar did as his father had done and ordered a crackdown and the army responded. But instead of calming the rebellion, it fueled it. The rebellion spread and the military response used to crush the rebellion only exacerbated them. "So, during the next two years, what had begun as a food and water issue gradually turned into a political and religious cause" (Polk 2013).

The spectacle of Hama cut both ways. The Assad regime responded with force and the local population saw an outsider attempting to destroy them. Given the context of the Arab Upheavals that began in Tunisia, this could not be seen strictly as a local event by regional and international actors. Violent Extremist organizations such as al-Qaeda saw an opportunity; Saudi Arabia and Qatar, often lumped together as Gulf States, pursued different influence campaigns in Syria backing different tribal leaders. Local grievances were consumed into larger regional and global narratives, but local voices continued speaking about an imagined Syria, a new Syria, a reconstructed Syria. Like Reedy, Polk reminds us about the making of an outsider within Syria.

"The Syrians focus on Syria and seek the overthrow of the Assad regime much as their fathers and grandfathers focused on the task of getting the French out of their country—their watan . . . The foreign jihadists . . . seek a restored Islamic world, a Dar ul-Islam, or a new caliphate" (Polk 2013).

But for Iran the events of 2011 were a boon to their strategic influence goals. "The March 2011 uprising presented an irresistible opportunity for Iran to assert permanent dominance throughout greater Syria" (Barabandi 2014). According to Barabandi, Iran sent the secretary of their Supreme National Security Council (see discussion above) to coordinate with the Assad government. Coordination would entail suppressing the uprising but also curtailing the influence of the United States, Israel, and others against whom the resistance had been organized. In other words, the demonstrations throughout Syria presented an opportunity for Iran to deepen their relationship with Syria's Assad through the Islamic Resistance frame.

Jalili pitched the Iron Curtain plan to Bashar's inner circle, assuring them that he knew the formula to neutralize protesters effectively. Iranian officials encouraged Assad to avoid concessions that could limit their influence over Assad's inner circle. As the tensions evolved into armed conflict, Iran immediately sent advisors, snipers, and special forces to support Bashar. To compensate for defections from his officers, Bashar padded his loyalist camp with fighters and strategic planners from Iran and Hezbollah. Hafez spent decades protecting himself from such an incursion, but by late 2011, his son was desperate for a friend (Barabandi 2014).

Barabandi was himself part of the Assad government, a diplomat. His retelling, therefore, must be understood in the context of a deep suspicion of Iran, a suspicion that may be wholly justified, but which nevertheless colors the commentary.

> In 2011, we received separate reform proposals from Qatar and the UAE. Assad refused both. As the death toll escalated, Turkey seemed to dent the Iron Curtain with its proposal on January 27, 2012 to downgrade Assad to prime minister, but allow him to preserve his control over the military and air force intelligence. The plan proposed that Vice President Farouk al-Shara, a Sunni who had previously called for reconciliation, assume the presidency and place Assad's brother-in-law, Assif Shwakat, as defense minister. The Iranians balked at the plan—they could not trust a reformer in the top position or Shwakat. Assad himself did not trust the Turks, but was willing to consider options as the conflict escalated out of control under the Iron Curtain. By February, Bashar engaged with the Turks on their plan in an effort to ease Western pressure. In March 2012, Vice

President Shara hosted reconciliation meetings with the opposition. Iran was furious and used its influence to stop any further meetings. Reconciliation posed a direct threat to Iran's Iron Curtain strategy, threatening to reunify the country outside of the Iranian umbrella. On July 18, a bomb in Damascus killed Assif Shwakat and several other key members of the security apparatus. Iranian officials used the bombing to convince Assad that reconciliation would only bring more attacks on his inner circle. In response, Bashar became more intransigent, and avoided any restructuring that would reduce his power. (Barabandi 2014)

The political and diplomatic moves that Iran made to gain more influence on Assad were coupled with moves on the ground to beat back the opposition. One prominent example is the Battle of Qusayr in 2013. Qusayr is a predominantly Sunni city—surrounded by Alawi areas. Syrian armed forces had attempted to retake control of the city on three separate occasions and failed. Then came Hizb'allah that overtook the rebels and took control of the region. They also used Strategic Influence to relay to the people that it was not Assad, but Iran and Hizb'allah who came to their aid. "Iran capitalized on this gain by establishing Syrian Hezbollah, investing heavily in the pro-government militias known as the National Defense Forces" (Barabandi 2014).

Please note the names Syrian Hizb'allah and National Defense Forces. This is meant to emphasize that these are local forces not Iranian proxies, despite Iran's ideological, religious, and material support. That is, Iran and Lebanese Hizb'allah would help the local forces, but the local forces owned the fight, they had to fight for their homeland, they had to retake, reclaim, remake Syria—thus, the *triumph* would belong to the Syrian people. These two narratives serve two goals. First, they further the immediate purpose of gaining the trust and support of the local population. Second, they also serve the purpose of making Assad more dependent on them. Not only were they beating back the enemy, but they were also now positioned to directly mobilize the population. Hafez Assad made the Alawi Shi'a, Bashar Assad may have made them Iranian Shi'a.

Through Hizb'allah and the National Defense Force, Iran placed militias indebted to them throughout the Alawi regions of Syria, creating a network of influence and force projection throughout Syria. As we saw, this is the same approach that Iran used in Iraq. By building up a strong militia presence, Iran had various leverage points it could use against the government. First, Iran used its militia forces to build a relationship with the local population. They deliberately tell the Alawi community that it is Iran and Hizb'allah that is saving them, protecting them, and in the name of Shi'a, Islamic Resistance. Iran then uses this good will that it builds with the population to form a political base for the militias, making them a permanent part of the landscape. Yet, the militias do not disarm, enabling a direct physical threat to the government and other adversaries, should they arise. It is to these militias that we now turn.

## THE HIZB'ALLAH MODEL IN SYRIA

If Iran is seeking Middle East hegemony it is hampered by its Persian and Shi'a identities. In the majority Sunni and Arab Middle East being both Persian and Shi'a cast Iran as perpetual outsiders, the "others." In Hizb'allah, Iran has an Arab ally with a proven track record of resistance and loyalty. "Hezbollah fighters are well situated to provide advice and training to Syrian armed forces, pro-regime paramilitaries, and Shi'a proxy groups because of their native Arabic language and experience with light infantry combat operations.... Hezbollah's Lebanese Arabs are better suited to work closely with Syrian counterparts than Iranian Revolutionary Guards" (Fulton 2013, 22).

The use of Hizb'allah as an expeditionary force is also not new. Iran used IRGC troops to arm, train, and finance Asaib Ahl Aal-Haq and Kata'ib Hizb'allah. Lebanese Hizb'allah was critical in setting up those groups. Iran relied on their Arab ally there and they are replicating that pattern in Syria. Further, those very groups are now battle-hardened and can bring that combat experience to bear in Syria as well, thereby amplifying Iran's options. This complex web of militias is in keeping with Iran's designed redundancy strategy. As Levitt puts it, "For Western and regional policymakers, the large number of groups, connections, and overlapping areas of influence creates further confusion, giving Iran and its proxies further room for plausible deniability if the need arises" (2015).

According to Fulton the use of militias dates back to Hafez al-Assad and the Muslim Brotherhood uprising. The reliance on external militias then is not surprising given that the Muslim Brotherhood had a very large, nationwide following. Being able to both defend ethnic and religious minority enclaves while going on the offensive against Muslim Brotherhood positions put an inordinate strain on the Syrian forces. This is the exact same dilemma faced by Bashar al-Assad in contemporary Syria. However, the use of popular, local militias defending these enclaves takes pressure off of Assad's forces but also gives Iran and Hizb'allah an opportunity to increase their influence. Perhaps it was in response to this reality on the ground that President Assad formalized the Popular Committees in the beginning of 2013. Whether this was done to recognize service, more easily control the militias, or curtail Iranian influence, the effect has been to formalize the structure of resistance and to give credibility to the militias Iran has recruited, armed, funded, and trained. This is, of course, the exact same pattern we saw in Iraq, and even to some degree in Lebanon. It is difficult to imagine this not being a long-term boon to Iranian influence inside Syria regardless of what happens to Assad.

It would be a mistake, of course, to think that Iranian participation in the Syrian conflict was limited to the defense of religious and ethnic minority enclaves. Syria has given Iran its first taste of successful expeditionary fighting ever. "Iranian forces successfully exercised the ability to design operational plans, fight a determined enemy alongside local and foreign partners, take casualties, and return to the battlefield. The Aleppo campaign also exposed a large portion of Iran's operational units and junior officers to participating in a sustained operation abroad, better positioning these forces to wage similar campaigns in the future" (Bucala 2017).

Iran's participation in Syria, then, involved setting up militias to defend minority communities, mostly Shi'a and Alawi groups, but also Christian and others, against Daesh and other regime enemies. It also involves actual combat operations such as the taking of Aleppo. In terms of training for IRGC officers this is invaluable. What appears certain, however, is that standing up militias in Syria, just as in Iraq, gives Iran a long reach, many tools to use to achieve its policy goals, and powerful influence in neighboring regimes. There is not a great deal known about all of the militias operating in Syria. In what follows I give an overview of some of the more well-known groups.

### Harakat Hezbollah al Nujaba

Nujaba is an Iraqi group of roughly 10,000 fighters, whose name means "the Virtuous." They are loyal to Iran and believers in the *velayat-e faqih* system, "according to the Iranian Tasnim news agency" (Dehghanpisheh 2017; Majidyar 2017). Heeding Khamenei's call for fighters to defend the Holy Shi'a Sites of Syria, Nujaba was deployed to Syria to defend "Sayeda Zeinab, a shrine south of Damascus that is revered by Shi'ites" (Dehghanpisheh 2017). But their presence in Syria created three strategic windows of opportunity for their Iranian sponsors. First, they have fought against the Islamic State and in support of President Assad more generally, gaining more battle experience. Second, they are opening a road from Iraq to Syria to Lebanon, the supply line that Iran seeks. And third, they are forming a separate militia to focus on challenging Israel in the Golan Heights, extending Iran's strategic reach and threat to Israel.

For groups like Nujaba the rise of Daesh presented an opportunity. They were able to organize, gain fighting experience, marshal troops, attract resources, and gain notoriety or fame based on their victories. "'Daesh became an opportunity for many of these people. When Daesh came, they became needed,' said an Iraqi former senior government official. 'They flourished and expanded the group: more arms, more money, more people. The money was coming from Iran'" (Dehghanpisheh 2017). However, "Hashim al-Moussawi, spokesman for Nujaba, said: 'We couldn't find any support for Iraq from America or Arab or Islamic countries, except Iran. Iran supported Iraq with arms and advisers'" (Dehghanpisheh 2017). This raises some interesting questions such as would these militias be so-pro Iranian if the United States or some other party had stepped in early to coopt them? What would a U.S. Strategic Influence campaign have looked like? What would success have been defined as? What effect would that have had? While it is too late to know, it is not too late to pivot to such a strategy, something I discuss in the conclusion of this book. This is worth considering in the light of understanding what motivates these fighters, it is true that many are motivated by a religious fervor, but many are motivated by financial and other material incentives.

Nevertheless, Iran saw a window of opportunity and seized it. They fund, train, and arm these Nujaba fighters and win their loyalty. Nujaba fighters are sent to Damascus from Baghdad or Najaf directly, while others are sent to Southern Iraq for training "on the use of heavy machine guns, rocket-propelled grenades and sniper rifles. Some train with Hezbollah in Lebanon and then cross by land into Syria, according to the security adviser; in Iran there is specialised training in de-mining, communication and operating drones. Kaabi has said that the group has Yasir drones, an Iranian copy of the Boeing ScanEagle, used for reconnaissance" (Dehghanpisheh 2017). Nujaba victories and defeats become the stuff of more *resistance* myth-making. Their *triumphs* and martyrs are celebrated publicly to burnish their credentials and help recruit new fighters. "Videos posted online in 2016 show Nujaba military parades around Aleppo, featuring armoured personnel carriers, anti-tank rockets and pickup trucks mounted with heavy machine guns. Other clips show Nujaba members engaged in street fighting in southern Aleppo" (Dehghanpisheh 2017). And also, "The Nujaba spokesman said around 500 Nujaba fighters have been killed in combat between Syria and Iraq. The war dead are memorialised in online postings, and last April the militia group posted a large billboard praising its martyrs near the gate of Baghdad University" (Dehghanpisheh 2017). These efforts to fight Daesh, then, morph easily into building up a fighting force that supports Assad and protects the Shi'as of Syria. However, they also serve the strategic interests of Iran. Martyrs, after all, reinforce the sacred defense—*resistance*—narrative and victory in this sacred defense reinforces the *triumph* narrative.

The second strategic window of opportunity that Iran is seizing/creating is building a road that ultimately connects Tehran to the Israeli border. This window of opportunity supports Iran's strategic objective of uniting the Shi'a Arc of Resistance. It means being able to supply arms, funds, training, and other logistic support from Iran and Iraq through Syria to Lebanon, which means from Iran to the Syria-Israeli and Lebanese-Israeli borders. "According to Iraqi lawmaker Shakhwan Abdullah, retired Lebanese general Elias Farhat, and other current and former officials in Iraq. The route will run through a string of small cities including Qayrawan. To open it up, Iranian-backed militias are pushing into southeast Syria near the border with Iraq, where U.S. forces are based" (Dehghanpisheh 2017).

The third window of opportunity appears because of the second. Iran is now in a position to open a second front in its battle with Israel. Beyond supporting Assad, then, this group embodies the Iranian strategic objective to materially linking, at low cost and high security, the Arc of Resistance from Tehran to the Israeli borders with Syria and Lebanon. They are doing so through expanding Nujaba, which created the Golan Liberation Brigade, "This is a trained army with specific plans. If the government of Syria requests, we and our allies are ready to take action to liberate Golan" (Majidyar 2017). While it is unclear how many of Nujaba's 10,000 fighters, with as many as 3,500 in Syria, are committed to the liberation of the Golan Heights, the mission is clearly a top priority for the group. "In a similar remark last month, Nujaba's leader Akram al-Kaabi emphasized that his forces were prepared to cooperate with the Bashar al-Assad regime to 'liberate' the Golan region from Israeli forces" (Majidyar 2017).

Along with Lebanese Hizb'allah this would give Iran a potential two-front war against Israel. In this instance, Iran's strategy is clear. It supports groups in Iraq, provides arms, training, and funds and then calls them into service in Syria. Part of that service is to support Assad, but it is also partly about working to achieve Iran's strategic interests both in terms of establishing logistical support to key resistance groups and in terms of giving Iran reach to the Israeli border. The last conflict between Israel and Hizb'allah resulted in a stalemate. Hizb'allah has since re-armed. The presence of another armed militia on Israel's border complicates Israel's and by extension America's security posture in the Middle East. Nevertheless, armed resistance is only one facet of this threat. The other, establishing political wings with popular support, I will discuss in the chapter summary.

### Abu al-Fadhil al-Abbas Brigade

Much like Nujaba and other Iranian-backed militias in Syria, the Abu al-Fadhil al-Abbas Brigade (AFAB) is a unit of a larger Iraqi Brigade. This is very important because these groups share both the Shi'a religion and an Arab identity with their target populations in Syria. Thus, many in AFAB went to Syria to protect Shi'a shrines and religious leaders. "The brigade is named after Abu al-Fadhl al-Abbas, a brother of Imam Hussain Bin Ali, a grandson of the Prophet Mohammed. Al-Abbas was killed with his brother more than

1,300 years ago, and since then has become a symbol of sacrifice for Shi'ite Islam" (al-Salhy 2012). And to reinforce the idea of relationships based on identity Fulton offers this. "A public statement released by AFAB confirmed that leadership and general membership of the militia is split between Syrian and Iraqi Shi'a 'mujahidin'" (2013).

As noted above if Iran is seeking regional hegemony it suffers from two handicaps—their Shi'a and Persian identities. However, Iraq is majority Shi'a, Lebanon has a Shi'a plurality, and Syria has a significant Shi'a minority, Iran's Shi'a identity is a plus. However, Iranians are Persian not Arab and as such they are foreigners—others. Using Hizb'allah, for example, helps in this regard. Nasrallah, Hizb'allah's Secretary General, is a formidable and charismatic figure, he is most certainly Shi'a, but he is also Arab. As such, he is a logical figure to project throughout the Arab Shi'a population as the face of resistance. However, other groups with ties to Hizb'allah are also active in Syria. "In April 2013, both KH and AAH confirmed their involvement in the Syrian conflict. The two groups published videos and photographs on the internet acknowledging that four of their fighters had been killed while 'defending Shi'ite shrines in the Damascus suburb of Sayyeda Zeinab'" (Fulton and Wyer 2013, 24). This strengthens the idea that the Hizb'allah model, very successful in both Lebanon and Iraq is now being deployed in Syria as well.

AFAB is related to KH and AAH in that they were once part of the Mahdi Army. As noted previously, the Mahdi Army was Sadr's Iraqi militia that disbanded upon being defeated in 2007–2008 by the Iraqi Army with U.S. support. Some AFAB members have been in Syria since 2007 and others, loyal to Khamenei, have arrived more recently (al-Salhy 2012). They cite the same justification, "'We formed the Abu al-Fadhal al-Abbas brigade which includes 500 Iraqi, Syrian and some other nationalities,' an Iraqi defector from the Mehdi Army who goes by the name of Abu Hajar told Reuters by satellite telephone from Syria" (al-Salhy 2012).

And much like the other militias, the religious mission of protecting the shrines and religious leaders requires working with and through the Syrian Army by fighting Syrian rebels.

"Another Mehdi Army defector, Abu Mujahid, who recently returned from Syria to visit his family in the Iraqi city of Najaf said his group's mission in Syria was restricted to securing the famed Sayyida Zeinab Shi'ite shrine and its nearby Shi'ite neighborhoods. But sometimes, he said, they carry out preemptive raids on Free Syrian Army rebel fighters, whenever they get information rebels will attack the shrine, offices of Shi'ite religious leaders, known as Marjaiya, and Shi'ite neighborhoods" (al-Salhy 2012). These defectors provide valuable insights into the motivations and day-to-day experiences of foreign fighters in Syria. One such story, captured in detail, is of Baghdad student Ammar Sadiq. He was in Baghdad when he heard about Syrian rebels attacking a Shi'a shrine in Syria. He immediately took off to Syria to defend the holy sites. In Sadiq's own words, "It was like a thunderbolt hit me.... My friend was telling me that wahhabis from Saudi and Afghanis were trying to destroy the [Shi'a] shrine of Sayyida Zeinab. I did not wait even to tell my parents. All I was thinking of is to go to Syria and protect the shrine, though I have not used a weapon in my life" (Mahmoud 2013). It is because AFAB's reputation had spread throughout Syria and Baghdad that Sadiq had heard of them.

According to Mahmoud, "Many of its volunteers hail from Iraq's Shi'a heartland, where the group started some time last year with a fatwa delivered in Najaf by the renowned cleric Abu al-Qasim al Ta'ai, who gave religious authority to the Shi'a going to fight in Syria. The effect led to a surge of young Iraqis wanting to wage jihad and a groundswell of community support for a sectarian war in a neighbouring state, less than five years after similar bloodletting had ravaged Iraq" (2013). Presumably because of this, Mahmoud concludes that AFAB, "has emerged as one of the most powerful in Syria. Interviews with serving and former members of Abu Fadl al-Abbas suggest that upwards of 10,000 volunteers—all of them Shi'a Muslims, and many from outside Syria—have joined their ranks in the past year alone" (2013).

However, the link between religious duty and serving in the Syrian Army in support of Assad's regime was immediate. "'The moment you join the brigade, you have to join the Syrian government army,' he said. 'You have to fight with President Bashar al-Assad before you fight for [the brigade]. The Syrian army will tell you that you have to know that you are protecting Syria, not only the shrine'" (Mahmoud 2013). And the connections to Iraq and Iran were just as clear to him from the beginning. "The increased organisation of the group was evident in Baghdad, according to Sadiq. 'The first step is to register with one of the Shi'a Islamic resistance offices, like Righteous League [Asaib al-Haq], Mukhtar Army or Iraqi Hezbullah.' Then comes a trip to a boot camp in Iran. 'You have to enroll on a 45-day training course in Iran to be specialised in using a specific weapon like rocket launchers, Kalashnikov, sniper rifle or RPGs [rocket-propelled grenades]. After the course, you will be handed over to an Iranian middleman who will take you to Syria to join the brigade'" (Mahmoud 2013). Sadiq's journey from Baghdad to Damascus to Iran to Southern Iraq then back to Syria is a common journey for Shi'a faithful looking to protect holy shrines and religious leaders in Syria and those looking to defeat the enemies of the Assad regime.

In the next two brief sections I will introduce two other such militias and in the chapter summary I will discuss the work in construction and charity that could potentially make these militias more fully compliant with the Hizb'allah model. Here it is sufficient to understand that a militia of 10,000

Sadiqs is motivated by more than just money and cannot be so easily defeated when their faith, ideology, and identity are all activated by stories that recall oppression, stories that activate their desire for *resistance* and *triumph*. Iranian Strategic Influence activates their identity and mobilizes them based on myths that activate their predispositions. Sadiq was ready to be mobilized even though, in his own words, he had never held a gun before in his life. This is the power of Strategic Influence.

### Kataib al-Imam Ali

Kataib al-Imam Ali (KIA) appeared in June 2015. They were sponsored by Muhandis of Iraq and Soleimani of Iran. They are well armed, equipped, trained, and funded. In fact, Muhandis had been photographed wearing the KIA patch on his uniform. They have earned a reputation for ruthlessness. "In Salah al-Din province, fighters from the group posed in videos with the severed heads of their slain enemies. And in late December, the group even set about training Christians for a subgroup called Kataib Rouh Allah Issa lbn Miriam (The Brigade of the Spirit of God Jesus Son of Mary)" (Levitt 2015). KIA is led by Shebl al-Zaidi, just like AFAB, KH, and AAH Zaidi were once a part of Sadr's Mahdi Army. According to Levitt, Zaidi was "reportedly one of its more vicious sectarian leaders. He was jailed during the U.S. occupation of Iraq, only to be released by the Iraqi government in 2010" (2015). Like many militia leaders Zaidi has been photographed with Soleimani and Muhandis. But in what might be of greater concern to the United States and others is this. "The group also appears to have strong links with the Iraqi government; in August and September, it published pictures of Zaidi riding in an Iraqi army helicopter and one of the militia's field commanders, Abu Azrael, manning a different helicopter's machine gun" (Levitt 2015).

Levitt makes the following very important point regarding the proliferation of Iranian-sponsored militias in Iraq and Syria. "Yet new groups enable Tehran to diversify its political and military portfolio in Iraq. The wide range of these organizations also serves as a way to slowly impart and legitimize its ideology and power within Iraq. This phenomenon is slowly happening in Syria as well" (2015). This is, of course, the designed redundancy tenet of Strategic Influence that we have seen at play in Iraq but even during the creation of Hizb'allah. Hizb'allah was only one of many Lebanese groups Iran supported in the early 1980s. It was only after Hizb'allah emerged as the predominant militia that it got Iran's full and plentiful support. The same is happening in Iraq and Syria. Iran will support any group that meets basic criteria and let them produce, if any group emerges dominant Iran will move in and increase their support. So, increasing the number of groups is part and parcel of Iran's strategy.

## The Fatemiyoun Division

Among the many militias that Iran supports in Syria the Fatemiyoun Division is an oddity. First, it is made up of Afghan Shi'a, not Syrian, Lebanese, or Iraqi—that is, Arab—Shi'a. Second, their use is almost exclusively as shock wave frontline soldiers with little interaction or staying power with the local population. Third, because of the first and second points just mentioned, after their tour of duty, they are more likely to be re-transported to Afghanistan to give Iran some influence in that country, perhaps the beginning of an armed dimension to Iran's influence campaign to their east.

"The Fatemiyoun Division (formerly Brigade), a militia of Shiite Afghan refugees, was formed around early 2014 and trained by both the Revolutionary Guards and Hezbollah veterans. Its strength has been estimated at 8,000 to 14,000 men" (Latifi 2017). Most of these are Shi'a Hazara Afghans who fled after the Soviet invasion. These Shi'a Afghans, however, have a longer pedigree in Syria than Latifi notes. The Hazara fighters deployed to Syria by the IRGC were not the first wave of Hazaras to mark a presence near Syria's Shi'a holy sites. In the 1990s, a community of Hazara fled Afghanistan because of threats posed by violent Sunni extremists and moved to Syria to live near the Sayyeda Zeinab Shrine. Part of the IRGC's narrative is that the Fatemiyoun Division fighters voluntarily entered the militia group's ranks due to their commitment to protecting those Hazara near Shi'a holy sites in Syria such as the Sayyeda Zeinab Shrine near Damascus from the Islamic State and other extremist forces. To date, Iran's government has not recruited Hazara who were residents of Syria prior to 2011 to join the Shi'a militia (Cafiero and Behravesh 2020).

Iran has expanded recruitment to undocumented Afghans, "recently arrived from Afghanistan in search of economic opportunity" (Latifi 2017). The wages associated with being a foreign fighter are significant for those coming from places such as war-torn Afghanistan and Iraq. This is, of course, another unintended consequence of the U.S. wars in those states.

Because these fighters are not Arabic or Iranian, because they will not be able to stay in Syria and become part of Iran's long-term influence strategy, "Iranians and Mr. Assad's forces used the Afghan recruits as the first-wave shock troops. 'We would be the first in any operation . . .' Several short memoirs by current and former Afghan fighters in Syria published on the Telegram app, which Mr. Shuja studied, recount the Afghans' being sent to fight the most difficult battles, and speak about heavy casualties among Afghan fighters and the eventual victory after multiple assaults" (Latifi 2017). With an eye toward the near future, this should be of particular concern. "Among those in the Fatemiyoun Division who have returned to Afghanistan, most have settled in Herat, located near the Afghan-Iranian border. Battle-hardened from the past seven years of war in Syria's most gruesome battles involving the Islamic State, these Afghan Shi'a fighters have the potential to heavily influence Afghanistan's future security environment" (Cafiero and Behravesh 2020). As the United States prepares to hand Afghanistan back to the Taliban, who view the Shi'a as heretics, this group's impact on Iranian-Afghani security relations will be very interesting to watch.

The U.S. Institute of Peace published a report on the Fatemiyoun and examined the question of their reintegration into Iranian and Afghanistan societies. "Clerics and politicians believe that the Fatemiyoun could become an armed force inside Afghanistan under two conditions. First, if the Afghan government continues its perceived prejudice against Hazaras, and continues to neglect development in Hazara areas, it could alienate the Hazara and Shi'a communities. Second, if the government fails to protect Hazara mosques and communities against IS- and Taliban-perpetrated violence, militia forces could form" (Jamal 2019). However, another possibility is that Iran continues to pay, train, and arm them as a buffer against the Taliban and to have more leverage in Western Afghanistan. While Afghanistan is outside the scope of this work, it is important to note the fluidity of the space created by the Shi'a Revival, the Arc of Resistance, and the windows of opportunity created by the U.S. invasions of Afghanistan and Iraq—all boons to Iran.

## SUMMARY

Iran's strategy in Syria seems clear enough. It is seeking to maintain a military presence and ties to local communities in order to guarantee a supply line from Iran to the Israeli border, to maintain the Arc of Resistance supplied, trained, and funded, and to protect its strategic investments in Iraq and Lebanon by adding the in-between link of Syria. It is also clear that Iran is playing a long game in these countries, building up militias, religious identities, economic incentives, and social services. In the sections above I did not delve deeply into the financial or social, but in addition to funding and training militias that helped keep Shi'a in Syria safe, Iran is already investing in Syrian reconstruction.

"One organization engaging in some reconstruction and development efforts is Mu'assasat Jihad al-Bina' (Jihad of Development Foundation), which has advertised some of its recent works in the Hajera area adjacent to Sayyida Zainab" (Al-Tamimi 2019). Al-Tamimi conducted an interview with the head of Jihad al-Bina. Here are some highlights from that interview:

*Q:* In which areas in Syria have you worked until now?
*A:* We have been honored to provide services to the people in Aleppo, Deir az-Zor, Homs, Damascus, and the Syrian coast. Of course we have had a big role

in caring for the people displaced from their towns and villages in these areas and others.

*Q:* In summary what are your main activities and main accomplishments?

*A:* A number of hospitals and clinics have been set up in Aleppo, Homs, Deir az-Zor. As for our foundational work, it has entailed caring for the families of the martyrs and tracking their affairs in addition to much material and moral aid that is for the purpose of supporting the steadfastness of the Syrian people. And let us not forget our current projects in Damascus that have begun in the town of Sayyida Zainab we have undertaken some works that are for the purpose of facilitating the return of the families and displaced people to their homes and livelihoods through cleaning and removing rubble and removing the remains of war from the development areas. This is in Damascus. As for in Homs, work is now being done to renovate the homes of the families of martyrs (naturally the families of martyrs have the priority) and raising the living standard for them. Of course there are many activities that we have been undertaking at the same time whether on receiving the displaced families or on liberating the towns from the terrorist gangs. (Al-Tamimi 2019)

On the face of it, this seems very normal, it appears to be the postwar reconstruction one would expect. But who owns and operates Jihad al-Bina? Jihad al-Bina is Lebanese Hizb'allah's construction arm and it is sanctioned by the U.S. Treasury.[2] What should be clear from this is that these efforts are not merely for profit construction or part of postwar donations to reconstruct war-torn Syria. Iran is funding reconstruction through Hizb'allah as part of its long-term influence campaign in Syria. These efforts are meant to convey to the Shi'a in Syria that their protection, wealth, and spiritual and material well-being is a primary concern of the *Rahbar* in Tehran, the Supreme Leader Grand Ayatllah Khamenei. It is part of their long-term influence campaign to activate and energize the key themes we saw above. Religious identity and *resistance* go hand in hand, *resistance* is a duty. So is caring for the less fortunate, if able-bodied Shi'a serve the Supreme Leader, he will care for them and their families. This *is* Strategic Influence at work. But, of course, winning the hearts and minds of the population is as much about letting Assad know that Iran has a cultural redoubt in Syria as it is about maintaining a presence to protect the Shi'a and project power to Israel. The Iranian presence in Syria serves multiple purposes ideological, religious, logistical, tactical, strategic, but above all it is tied to their influence, adaptive resistance, and designed redundancy strategies which I described above.

But this is also important in the light of the narratives we saw deployed by the Syrian people and Assad himself—the notion of the "other," the notion of what it means to be Syrian, and the narratives of division. Hafez Assad sought religious legitimacy to hold Syria together, much like the Qajars and Pahlavis in Iran. The Iranians used the Shi'a faith to recruit and deploy militias and to gain the support of the population. They deployed Arab Shi'a, in part, to overcome the "other" narrative. Thus, their influence strategy resonates with the Syrian cultural narratives, especially among the Alawites and Shi'a. This does raise questions, however: How deeply embedded are these militias and how successful will the reconstruction earn the loyalty of the population? Will Iran's influence strategy earn the loyalty of Syrians?

While this is a threat, to some degree to Assad, he also benefits from having these militias at his disposal and having Iranian support. But just as we saw with the Qajar and Pahlavi dynasties in Iran, when nationalist secular leaders activate religious identities to preserve their power, they could easily find themselves subservient to the religious authorities. As of yet, there is no sign that a Grand Marja is being installed in Syria. This is another thing to watch for. If one is installed and he is loyal to Khamenei, as opposed to a quietist who supports Sistani, this would increase Iran's influence considerably. Nevertheless, Iran, through its proxies can help stabilize Syria and cement Assad's hold on power. Another thing to watch for is whether an Iranian loyalist is placed high up in Assad's security apparatus after the civil war is finally over. At this point it is clear that this is a relationship of mutual interest and mutual suspicion.

Nevertheless, I must agree with Byman when he writes, "Driving Damascus and Tehran apart in a more fundamental way, however, will be extremely difficult. . . . Both have proved resilient against internal foes, and the United States is militarily and diplomatically stretched in Iraq and elsewhere. The friendship between Iran and Syria is not akin to the United States' relationship with close allies such as the United Kingdom, but their common interests are more than enough to keep these strange bedfellows close and cuddly" (Byman 2006). Further, Iran now realizes it has the ability to send and maintain an expeditionary force "hundreds of miles from its borders and sustain them in grueling high-intensity warfare—a capacity shared with only a handful of other states. This 'whole-of-military' approach expands Iran's ability to conduct long-term expeditionary operations and transforms the nature of the Iranian military threat in the region" (Bucala 2017). This not only expands the horizon of what is possible for Iran and its allies, of course it is also a change in the threat calculus of Israel and Saudi Arabia.

Israel in particular, with the creation of the Golan Heights Brigade as an overt expression of this threat, realizes that Iran is becoming, for them, a much greater and formidable enemy. Israel has responded in declaration and in action that they will not let Iran set up permanent bases in Syria. And yet this observer has to wonder how much Israel will be able to do when the militias become regularized by the Syrian Defense Forces and their missile and drone capability increases. Can Israel continue to bomb Syria indefinitely?

Even after the war there is over? At what point will the international community, or more importantly Russia, permit that.

There is the view that the United States will not intervene and Russia will only act to preserve its own interests. "The Trump administration has so far seemed willing to cede Syria to Russia, save for the defeat of the Islamic State. Moscow wants little more than to maintain its military bases in Syria. It will not actually provide a counterweight to Iran once the war is over" (Lesch 2017). However, Lesch warns, "But Washington should understand what this really means: ceding it to Iran" (2017). He further explains, "For decades, Syria has seen the United States as leverage in terms of pressuring Israel on the Golan, keeping Israel off its back in return for the prospect of a comprehensive Arab-Israeli peace, and in clearing the way for foreign investment in the country. But if the United States isn't interested in Syria anymore, and if Russia continues to focus solely on security issues while ignoring politics, Iran will be dominant in Damascus" (Lesch 2017).

This view has merit, but it is not clear that Russia will play such a hands-off role. As of this writing Syria and Turkey are trading blows over Idlib province, the last rebel hold-out. Russia has given up the role of arbiter and is firmly supporting Assad. It is not doing so in the north of Syria to keep its bases secure. It appears that in Putin's calculus Assad's control of Syria is in Russia's interest. This is potentially Iran's greater challenge to influence in Syria. Iran may not be able to compete with Russia for influence with Assad. However, Iran is better positioned on the ground than Russia, through the networks established by their militias. Given that the United States has strong ties to the national governments in Lebanon and Iraq with little effect on Iranian influence, why would this be different in Syria?

For Lesch, the outcome of this tension, whether Iran dominates in Syria, has important regional implications. "In a vacuum this wouldn't matter. But the Middle East today is not a vacuum. Israel will not tolerate Iranian control over Syria—and if his recent speech is any indication, nor will Mr. Assad be able to prevent it. The result will inevitably be a Syria-Israel war, which would really mean an Iran-Israel war, one that would not be limited to Syria" (Lesch 2017). But this depends on whether Iran is patient and builds its influence slowly from the ground up, more consistently with its operations in Iraq and Lebanon. In the next section, I take a renewed look at Iran's regional strategy, sum up some key findings, and prime the discussion for policy recommendations for Washington. For now, it is sufficient to say that if Iran follows its own playbook of strategic influence it can play a very long game, one that its rivals will be hard to match.

*Chapter 10*

# Conclusion

## IRANIAN OPPORTUNITIES AND CONSTRAINTS

We began this journey by examining Iran's history, ideology, and structure, their Strategic Culture, to better understand the *stuff* that infuses their policymaking and informs their Strategic Influence campaigns. We saw how the Parthians used the Zoroastrian religion to produce a unique Persian identity, despite Persia being a multiethnic and multireligious empire at the time. We also saw how the Safavids made Islam the religion of the state, favoring Shi'a over Sunni Islam to distinguish their empire from the Ottoman Sunni Empire to Iran's west and also because of the similarities between Zoroastrianism and Shiism, which presented an opportunity to foster national unity. We further saw how the Qajar and Pahlavi dynasties relied on religion to legitimize their rule even as they tried to take power from the *ulama* to modernize Iran. Because of this history, I concluded that what the Iranian Revolution of 1979 did most effectively was to unite these two strains—nationalism and religion—through the discourse and structure of the *velayat-e faqih*—the guardianship of the jurisprudent.

It is one of the great ironies of history that the Shahs empowered the clerics to unite Iran and that clerics would then use that as an opportunity to take power away from the Shahs. It is also one of the great tensions of modernity. A modern Iranian state could not leave marriage, divorce, and inheritance laws to the clerics, just as it could not leave education in their hands. To join the ranks of modern nations Iran would need a strong central government, clear borders, a well-equipped military, and so on. What we saw play out in Iran, then, was a larger historical tension, modernism versus conservativism. What the 1979 Islamic Revolution did was to resolve that tension by stipulating that only a state ruled by the *ulama* can have *just* marriage, divorce, inheritance, education, and governance in general, because any other form of government was inherently corrupt. And a state guided by the *ulama* could also have clearly defined borders, a well-equipped military, a strong central government, and so on. In other words, to its proponents the *velayat-e faqih* system resolved the tension between modernism and conservativism through the governance of the jurisprudent.

It is important to note the popular opinion that secular, socialist, military, and democratic leaders have failed the people of the Middle East repeatedly. Islamic governance has a long and respected history in the region and as we saw in the Syria chapter fondly remembered (imagined?) for order and tolerance. Further, the contemporary history of Iran and the greater Middle East was in large part about one-sided power relationships with the West. Imperialism and Colonialism left a mark on these relationships that persist until today. Once again, the *velayat-e faqih* system provided a definite alternative and a sense of *triumph* through *resistance*. The Iranian revolution not only united nationalism and religion, but it also deposed the Western-imposed dictator and threw off the Western imperialists. As a narrative, as a myth, this is as good as it gets. This is David and Goliath; this is Iran victorious over the United States and Great Britain, and this is a blow for freedom and self-determination in a space where colonialism was still (is still?) thriving. Whether one believes this narrative or not, it makes for a powerful myth for activating identities and mobilizing audiences.

Juxtaposing these opportunities Iran faces many constraints. If Iran seeks regional hegemony it faces two major challenges in being Shi'a and Persian. Iran's attempts to take on the mantle of the leader of a Pan-Islamic movement has not worked; and it is unlikely to ever work. Shi'a Islam is a minority in the Middle East. Of course, if you accept the basic premise of this work—that Iran is not seeking occupation, physical dominance, but influence, with a very specific logistical focus—then these constraints may not be debilitating.

But there are other constraints in Iran's gaining influence. For example, the rulers of Iran kept the Shah's secret prisons and the structure of his intelligence service. These symbols and infrastructure of domestic terror remain active and too often terribly busy with brutality. Iran cannot promote self-governance or democracy while arresting and torturing pro-democracy students. Further, to modernist Lebanon, Iraq, and Syria, it does not bode well for Iran that their clerics flog women for not wearing their chadors in public. While it is true that Iran's education system, economic structure, and even political processes have roles for women, more than other non-Islamic-government Middle East countries, the reality of clerical police patrolling Tehran in vans and beating women feeds the narrative that portrays them as hopelessly archaic and unable to modernize. The tension of a modern scientifically advanced yet socially conservativistic society was not resolved in the 1979 Revolution, or since.

For some, it does not matter that they may have been (may still be) working toward developing a nuclear weapon, while for others in the Middle East this is a non-starter. Iran says it does not want nuclear weapons. Perhaps that is true. Perhaps it is false. But the thought of a nuclear-armed Iran reshapes Middle East security strategy in such a profound way that every major player in the region, for example, Turkey, Saudi Arabia, Israel as well as international players such as Russia, China, the EU, and the United States have been working together to prevent Iran's weaponization of its nuclear program. What underlies this fear in the Middle East is a general sense of not wanting to be dominated by an "outside" power. Iran is Persian, not Arab. And the Arab Middle East will not sit idly by while Iran dominates them with a nuclear arsenal. On the other hand, Iran's work in nuclear technology, nanotechnology, and other scientific fields, reveals how strong their university system is and how modern they are when it comes to *certain things*.

None of these constraints may matter in their narrative building; to audiences receptive to their messaging, receptive due to sharing a history of oppression, these narratives will resonate no matter the truth of secret prisons or other brutalities. Or it may be that all these accusations will be proved true and undermine Iranian Strategic Influence. But the Israeli invasion and occupation of Lebanon, the U.S. invasion and occupation of Iraq, and the Saudi and Emirati, with U.S. backing, attempts to depose Assad through force, all provide rich fodder for Iranian influence. *Resistance* in Lebanon led to *triumph*: Israel withdrew; the Americans withdrew, too. Iran backed the Popular Mobilization Forces (PMF) in Iraq and they *triumphed* over Daesh. And as of this writing it appears Assad is safe in Damascus and the *Resistance* has scored yet another *triumph*. To Iran's elite and to their receptive audiences in the Middle East—those predisposed to believe Iranian narratives—*triumphalism* resonates. As we have seen the Shi'a have long been subjugated, it is only with the 1979 Islamic Revolution in Iran that Shi'a have begun to rise in power and prominence. To those predisposed against Iran's narratives, *resistance* and *triumphalism* are masks for terror and imperialism, and to others it is a long-awaited return to glory.

To debate which of these narratives is true or false is not really the point of this work. The point is that Iran's narrative has been effective. Here, again, is the working definition of Strategic Influence I introduced above. Strategic Influence is the use of the elements of national power—diplomatic, military, economic, *with and through information* to erode the will of the enemy by shaping the information and operations environment to generate desired strategic effects. To which I added, these effects likely include galvanizing domestic audience support for operations, eroding confidence in foreign governments' domestic audiences, mobilizing proxies to act and speak in ways to commensurate with one's strategic goals, sowing confusion among the enemy—all of these, of course, as noted, is about eroding the adversary's will to fight. Whether Iran is confronting an otherwise occupied Bush administration, an engaging Obama administration, or the Trump administration's "Maximum Pressure" efforts, Iran remained steadfast in its Strategic Influence campaigns and enjoyed some success in confusing its enemies, mobilizing allies, and gaining support among large segments of their target audience. Success or failure of any strategy, however, can only be measured against goals.

## Of Goals and Strategies

What does Iran want? What are its strategic goals? Why is it expending so much treasure when it is facing such stark economic conditions at home? While these simple questions belie a deep web of interconnecting goals and ambitions for different actors within Iran's political elite, there are two clear, high-level, and generally accepted goals for Iran in their near abroad. They want to be able to build and sustain a logistics chain from Tehran to Israel's borders; and, they want to be able to open a two-front war against Israel. One front is already firmly established in Lebanon. They want to establish a second front in Syria. On this point we can believe Iran's strategic leadership to be sincere, defeating the state of Israel is a vital strategic goal. The other goal is far more abstract. They want to have economic, political, religious, and cultural influence to buffer against U.S. pressure but also to re-establish themselves as the regional power their population, history, culture, science, and military prowess merit. In other words, Iran wants a Strategic Influence form of regional hegemony and the ability to deploy resources and expeditionary forces to Israel's border.

Does Strategic Influence really offer insight, potential answers to these questions? Strategic Influence campaigns enable some deniability, build off of common themes of *oppression*, *resistance*, and *triumph*, and are far cheaper than building and maintaining a large conventional force that would be at the mercy of U.S. and Israeli air power anyway; it is designed to be adaptive and redundant, just like Iran's strategy in general, and it is designed as a long-term strategy. These characteristics are important to understand, not unique to Iran (although Iran is adept at their use), but useful if one seeks to understand and defeat Strategic Influence campaigns anywhere.

One of the motivations for this work is to help readers get to a more profound understanding of what is referred to as the new way of warfare. In general, Strategic Influence includes building narratives, disorienting targets, activating identities, and mobilizing proxies. These are also congruent with what some think of as Gray Zone warfare or Hybrid Warfare. Narratives are built to extend the range of influence communities—that is, communities real and virtual who are predisposed to believing and repeating tropes delivered by the influencer. It is also often the case that even if people are arguing against your narrative, you are still dominating the conversation. These narratives are meant to disorient the adversary. The term *disorientation* bears consideration. At its root, the term means that one is not facing the right direction; therefore, not fighting the right fight. Concentrating on amassing troop strength and kinetic lethality when the battle is about influence, for example, is evidence of disorientation. Concentrating on amassing troop strength and lethality as part of Strategic Influence, however, is indicative of understanding the current fight against opponents such as Russia and Iran. The idea of activating identities and mobilizing proxies are intertwined. Proxies are often mobilized because their identities have been activated and the mobilization of proxies often activates identities. Nevertheless, they can be and often are distinguished in analysis and practice. Russian incursions into Crimea showed both these elements. It was to Russian-speaking Crimeans that narratives were directed to activate their Russian identity and get them to act against the Crimean government. Their activation was soon followed by the mobilization of proxies, militias. The goals of Strategic Influence, however, can be summed up in one word—mobilization. Iran uses kinetic action to further its influence goals. This critical point needs to be understood by U.S. policymakers.

Distinctions between soft power, hard power, and smart power rely on a separation between act and information that is unwarranted. Every action, every troop deployment, every shot fired, each action contains and communicates information. Further, it is important to keep in mind that any individual piece of information can be connected with preexisting assembled pieces of information. These preexisting assembled pieces of information are what I refer to as myths, discourses, frames, beliefs, and so on. The act of connecting any individual piece of information with preexisting assembled pieces of information is what I mean by framing. Further, the reader should also keep in mind that the tendency to isolate bits of information in order to understand does not just happen in academic analysis of things like soft, hard, and smart power, but it also happens in how strategists and practitioners analyze Iranian Strategic Influence.

In other words, each action contains information. Each bit of information can be tied to assemblages of information—tropes, narratives, and so on. So, when Iran takes action the United States deploys tropes to shape the information into a narrative of Iran being the world's leading state sponsor of terrorism. Iran packs that information into the *resistance* narrative. The same act, then, framed differently, directed at audiences (sometimes different audiences, sometimes not), produces Strategic Influence effects as described above. Iran enjoys a certain advantage, opportunity, in the sense that they have a long-term strategy that is not interrupted by democratic processes—changes of administrations and priorities—as national security is the purview of the Supreme Leader, who is the commander-in-chief and as such commands the IRGC and Quds Force, and not in the hands of elected officials. This gives them a unity of purpose, a unity of message, a unity of effort, and a durability to their strategic efforts that the United States lacks.

The ability to craft a consistent narrative over time and drive that narrative through multiple channels to multiple audiences is a great advantage in Strategic Influence. Iran presses this advantage in Lebanon, Iraq, and Syria and while it generates great opposition, and therefore constraints, against its praxis, it also generates great enthusiasm and mobilization among many of the denizens of these countries. If the goal is to activate their identities and mobilize them in Iran's favor, can kinetic action win this war? Simply put, Iran seeks to Lebonize Iraq and Syria. That is, they are seeking to replicate their successful Lebanese Hizb'allah model. We see this already in Iraq with the creation of the PMF and we see similar activity in Syria. But it is worth recalling what the Hizb'allah model is. In Lebanon Hizb'allah is a political actor, a social service provider, a militia, a media conglomerate, and other things. It does not control Lebanon, but it can and has shut down the government, vetoed key initiatives, used force to defy the government, and continues providing support to the Shi'a plurality. It is true that since the Iraqi and Syrian wars, from which the world is still emerging, Hizb'allah has lost popularity for their "foreign adventurism." Yet, until the government, or some other party, is seen by the Shi'a plurality as a viable alternative to Hizb'allah in terms of providing social services, representation, and grievance resolution, Hizb'allah will remain powerful.

We see Iran busily supporting the PMF in Iraq, with, it is fair to say, the same goal in mind. When Maliki made the PMF an official part of Iraq's security infrastructure, he knew he was giving Iran a large field of play. But even Abadi had to recognize the role of the PMF in the defeat of Daesh and reward them with recognition and official status. While it is illegal in Iraq for a political party to have an armed wing, virtually every political party does so anyway. It is also the case that the larger of these groups maintain education, social and medical service, media, and other essential Strategic Influence infrastructure. In Iraq, where the majority of the population is Shi'a, the story of *oppression, resistance*, and *triumph* not only resonate, but they also inspire, as we have seen. Like Hizb'allah in Lebanon, the PMF in Iraq represent, defend, and provide for the Shi'as who have a long history of being oppressed. And just like in Lebanon that oppression has given way to political power and victory over foreign forces and the United States in particular. Iran's material and religious support comes with clear messaging that the *velayat-e faqih* has brought success in both countries and that *resistance* brings *triumph* to those willing to fight, to those who believe.

In Syria, the Shi'a population is smaller. Alawites, as we saw, were only fairly recently considered Shi'a. Yet, Iran, through its Iraqi and Lebanese proxies are deploying the Hizb'allah model. They are deploying troops to protect the religious shrines, the holy sites of Shi'a Islam in Syria. They are organizing militias, training and arming them, and are providing services and letting every citizen they help know that it is Iran that is supporting them. It is the *Rahbar*, the Supreme Leader, the spiritual and temporal leader of Shi'as everywhere who is supporting them, goes the narrative. However, there are real constraints in this theater. Israel has consistently said and acted on the principle that it will not allow Iran to establish a permanent foothold in Syria. Israel says it will deny Iran's strategic goal of being able to open a two-front war against Israel. How long Israel can continue bombing a neighboring country with impunity, however, is an open question. But the other constraint against Iranian ambitions in Syria could be Assad himself who once more firmly in power may resent and work to diminish Iranian influence among his people.

If there is a peace process in Syria and all the regional and international actors sign off on it, Israel's ability to use force in Syria will diminish. At that point, it will be seen as aggression. In addition, it will take years for Assad to rebuild his power throughout the country even if such a peace were attainable. He will need Iran for far longer than he might want. As we saw at the beginning of chapter 9 "Syria", this was precisely the fear of Bashar Assad's father, Hafez. Yet, it was Hafez Assad's strategic decision to have Alawis recognized as Shi'a that has given Iran this opportunity (another iteration of the great irony.) From the Iranian perspective, they see events in Lebanon, Iraq, and Syria as favoring their long-term strategy. This element is critically important. Iran believes it can wait out the Trump administration's "Maximum Pressure" campaign, as it did Bush's wars in Iraq and Afghanistan, and Obama's and Trump's wars in Syria. Iran believes that history and God's will are on its side. But in the meantime, they deploy the two strains of their Strategic Influence policies—Designed Redundancy and Adaptive Resistance—with strategic patience.

The concept of strategic patience deserves to be considered separately as it is a subject unto itself. It is here, perhaps more than anywhere else, that we see the history, ideology, and structure of the IRI playing the strongest role in informing strategy. Iran keeps alive, recalls, and projects its long history. And from that long history there is a sense of *triumphalism*. They have not only survived but thrived despite the many invasions, foreign interventions, and sanctions. Keep in mind that as soon as the 1979 Revolution happened there was international condemnation, followed by sanctions, followed by a nearly existential war with Iraq, followed by decades of escalating regional and international sanctions and pressures, yet they have, indeed, endured and their position is stronger today than ever, despite the "Maximum Pressure" campaign and the ravages of natural disasters and pandemics. They have learned that patience, preparedness, and time will produce opportunities. Coupled with an ideology of *resistance*, this strategic patience plays a long game of attrition that may not be discernible given the high turnover of strategists, planners, and practitioners among their adversaries. Further, the structure of the IRI is built from that history and ideology. A history that is replete with overcoming adversity, an ideology of adaptive resistance, and a decisionmaking structure that is designed to prevent interference and maintain balance is designed to favor a prudent, influence-based, strategic policy approach. Thus, information, from the Iranian point of view, is the most important element of national power.

## Opportunities and Constraints in Iran's Near Abroad

An holistic view of Iran's Strategic Influence would have to include work they are doing in Latin America, Africa, Central Asia, and potentially elsewhere. Such a scope is beyond the capability of a single book. But Iran's near abroad could be defined to include their activities in Bahrain and Yemen. In the early 1980s Iran's IRGC attempted to establish a *resistance* movement in Bahrain but failed. They achieved success in Lebanon, in part, because of the opportunity structure that emerged from the Lebanese Civil War and Israel's invasion of Southern Lebanon. This is partly because one of the key facets of an opportunity structure was missing in Bahrain, a divided leadership unable to suppress opposition. The Bahraini monarchy, supported by the Saudis were a unified, effective force against Iran's efforts to mobilize the Shi'a. That being said, Iran remains active there.

Nevertheless, I have deliberately excluded Bahrain and Yemen for two reasons. First, they are peripheral interests for Iran. Iran is eager to be a thorn in Saudi Arabia's side, support *resistance* movements everywhere they can, but focus resources where the largest payoff is likely to occur—*resistance*, yes, but adaptive resistance—that remains Lebanon, Iraq, and Syria. This is largely due to the second reason, while Yemen and Bahrain activities threaten Saudi Arabia, the Shi'a Arc of Resistance is seeking the destruction of the state of Israel and a direct supply route to Israel's border will facilitate this vital Iranian strategic interest.

## Lebanon

One of the opportunity structures that enabled the creation of Hizb'allah was the Lebanese Civil War. Hizb'allah did not participate in the civil war. In fact, it declared itself a non-aggressor, and as soon as it was able joined the political process representing the Shi'a in Beirut and the south of Lebanon. This is because for both the Iranians and Hizb'allah, democracy is seen as an opportunity. Because successful Strategic Influence mobilizes audiences, this has led to power in nascent democracies such as Lebanon in the early 1980 and Iraq today. Thus, "democracy" is seen as an opportunity, not an obstacle to Strategic Influence. Coupled with strategic patience, Iran believes that it can gain greater influence through civil society and the normal political process than it can through violence, although the selective use of violence is always an option to Quds and proxy operatives.

But this should not be read as stating that the path to power in Lebanon is direct or easy. On the contrary, many factions in Lebanon, especially those loyal to Saudi Arabia (Sunnis) are deeply suspicious if not overtly antagonistic to Hizb'allah. There is, too, an odd mix of fear and disdain for Hizb'allah's Iranian sponsors. Further, Hizb'allah has even lost support among its own constituency, although this may be temporary, because of its war efforts in Iraq and especially Syria. This is a fairly well-understood phenomenon: Why should our sons die to fight someone else's war? Does that mean that the Shi'a Revival does not resonate with the average person? Or does it mean that there is no solidarity with Shi'as outside national boundaries, if so, what does that say about the position that the *umma* is not bound by national borders, which are impositions by imperialists? Perhaps, nationalism is a stronger force than Shi'a internationalism.

In short, Lebanon remains a complex state with many competing factions, a failed economy, and many external actors meddling in its affairs. That this presents both opportunities to and constraints on Iran and Hizb'allah is to be expected. However, Hizb'allah remains in a strong position and its position will strengthen over time. It remains the only voice and representation for the Shi'a in Lebanon. Further, Hizb'allah's position will only strengthen as Assad stabilizes Syria, which will mean greater legitimacy for Hizb'allah's operations there. The *resistance* will have gained more battle-hardened soldiers, meaning a more formidable force to dominate Lebanon and threaten Israel, and perhaps even material support from Assad himself as his position solidifies. In any event, Hizb'allah has not been, to this point, mortally wounded and looks very well positioned into the foreseeable future.

For some time now Saudi Arabia has been trying to weaken Hizb'allah in Lebanon. They have done so through championing local alternative religious narratives and through arming other factions. However, their main strategy is to bolster the legitimacy of the Lebanese state. This effort, coordinated with the United States, is designed to mobilize the Lebanese people against Hizb'allah. This has proven an exceedingly difficult task. Despite the generous financial contributions and political support that Saudi Arabia has given the Lebanese government, Hizb'allah remains strong. In my estimation, until an alternative to Hizb'allah emerges as the voice and protector of the Shi'a it is unlikely that these efforts to delegitimize Hizb'allah will succeed.

## Iraq

Iraq presents a different set of opportunities and constraints for Iran. Iraq is a majority Shi'a country. Najaf, in Southern Iraq, is a vital center for theological studies. It is home to several Grand Marjas, the most important of whom is Grand Marja Ayatallah Ali al-Sistani. If one of the major themes of this work is the relationship between religion and nationalism, Sistani is, indeed, a pivotal figure. He is an Iranian by birth, but is a symbol of Iraqi nationalism, he is also the most respected and highly ranked Shi'a scholar in the world. But at age ninety-one, the efforts to succeed him are intensifying. In the Iraq chapter above, I discussed some of the contenders and some of the potential outcomes. For Supreme Leader Khamenei this is an enormous potential opportunity. If he can place a relatively "young" Grand Ayatallah in Sistani's seat, back him financially and in other ways, he will have given Iran an opportunity to influence Iraqi politics for decades to come.

But this comes with constraints as well. Any successor to Sistani cannot be *seen* to be pro-Iranian. If a Pakistani or Afghan Grand Ayatallah is selected that would be one thing, but anyone with overt ties to Iran would likely be rejected. Shi'a, it must be remembered, choose their own Marja, they cannot be forced to follow one. The Sistani network, inherited from Grand Ayatallah Khoi, is vast and a prize the Iranian leadership rightly covets. But, taking over that network will also be difficult because of the voluntary nature of contributions and allegiances. Since there is no formal method for selecting a successor, the process is open to external manipulation through threats, violence, bribes, and other inducements such as access to Iran's coffers, but it cannot be dictated. The Sistani succession does not get the attention it deserves from academic and policy circles; it can be decisive for Iran's influence in Iraq.

I spent some time in the Iraq chapter above discussing the difference between the Quietist and *Velayat* schools of Shi'a jurisprudence. At its core, Shi'a jurisprudence seems to be Quietist and considers the *Velayat* system an innovation. They do not believe that clerics should run the state, only advise and assist rulers. The *Velayat* system, on the other hand, calls for a far more direct role for clerics in supervising if not running the state. It is true that Khomeini insisted that technocratic leaders should run the functional aspects of government, but that they should do so under the direction and be subject to the authority of the clerics. However, realities on the ground blur these distinctions. The Quietist Sistani stopped the Bush administration from establishing a confessional system in Iraq, brought down the Maliki government, gave the order to mobilize Shi'a militias that led to the creation of the PMF, among other acts with major political impact. One can argue that Sistani has proved the point of the *Velayat* faction, that the senior cleric must guide, supervise, and even control the government. This internal religious debate and its implications for the succession question cannot be underestimated. Iran is working every angle to position its candidate(s) to succeed Sistani.

The other major opportunity for Iran is the PMF. The PMF as we saw is an official security organ of the Iraqi state. However, it comprises various Shi'a militia, some large and long-standing, some large and new, some small. Maintaining unity of purpose and command has not proven to be a great constraint on Iranian strategy thus far. The killing of Soleimani, the then head of Iran's special forces Quds Force, and the simultaneous killing of Muhandis, deputy chief of the PMF, could present a long-term organizational challenge to Iran, but there is little evidence that this is the case. One of the features of Adaptive Resistance and Designed Redundancy, the two pillars of Iran's strategic orientation, is not to become too dependent on any single individual or team. The reason Iran supports multiple militias in Iraq is precisely so that it continues its Strategic Influence campaigns should one or more of its key assets be neutralized.

But as we saw in Lebanon, the core strength of the PMF, like Hizb'allah, is not in their arms, their military prowess, but in their ability to represent and mobilize the masses. In Iraq, the PMF is referred to as the Sacred Defense. From the perspective of Strategic Influence this is an entirely different set of problems than the anti-terrorism tool kit that the United States deploys against them. The popularity of these groups is not ephemeral, it is deeply grounded in Shi'a Strategic Culture—identity, history, ideology, religion, and praxis and it speaks to the *resistance to oppression* that has led to *triumph*. This formula is deeply embedded, long-standing, and not easily dislodged.

The fact that the PMF is not a monolithic actor presents opportunities and constraints for Iran. The opportunity lies in the fact that as groups rise and fall in power, influence, and capability, Iran can balance against them to maintain its overall status—adaptive resistance and designed redundancy. The constraint lies in the fact that potential division, competition for resources, and electoral competition could weaken the groups that make up the PMF. However, the call for integrating the PMF into the Iraqi security forces, though logical, is fraught with dangers. So long as these groups are in line with Iran, giving them legitimacy and formal recognition is a dangerous gamble. But what does formal recognition matter if the PMF is more popular and has greater legitimacy than the government in Baghdad.

In Iraq, Iran has two main lines of effort that represent great problems for the United States. If they get their man to replace or gain greater influence over Sistani's successor and if the PMF continues to solidify its role as the "Hizb'allah" of Iraq, Iran will have more influence in Iraq than they do in Lebanon. The main constraint to Iran's Iraqi strategy is not the United States or Saudi Arabia, not at this time. Rather, it is Moqtada al-Sadr. Sadr says no to Iran and to the United States. He works with, but is not part of, the PMF. He comes from a long line of important Shi'a clerics. In other words, he has legitimacy and independence. He is a mid-level cleric and could not compete for Sistani's succession, but he could back a candidate and gain more prestige through that candidate's victory. He could also be preparing himself for the eventual taking over of that role. The Sadr's and the Khoi's history in Iraq is long and stellar. In the meantime, Sadr's relationship with Iran is complex. He has studied in Qom, has a public relationship with Khamenei, but is an avowed Iraqi nationalist. They can work together against U.S. interests and may eventually ally or turn against each other. Sadr may yet be brought under Iranian control. One other possibility that bears more scrutiny than I can give here is whether Sadr can step into the political-symbolic role that Soleimani and Muhandis left behind. To do so would dramatically increase his political power and prestige but would bring him squarely into Iran's Strategic Influence orbit. A potential challenge to Sadr is the rise of the Hakim faction. If Grand Marja Hakim succeeds Sistani as the *a'lam*, then the Hakim political movement and faction will likely dwarf Sadr.

Iran's path in Iraq is not obvious. Nor is it guaranteed success. However, it is very well positioned to achieve its two primary goals as described here. If it is successful, Iran and Iraq will be sister-states and creating a cleavage between them nearly impossible. There is an option of very low probability that merits consideration as a thought experiment. The Iranian constitution calls for the president of Iran to be an Iranian citizen, but not the Supreme Leader. Imagine, if you will, the impact across the Middle East, the Muslim world more broadly, but Iraq more specifically, if the next Supreme Leader of Iran were an Iraqi. While this is highly unlikely, imagine the impact of such a move. It should sharpen the mind around the cost of Iranian Strategic Influence in Iraq.

## Syria

Syria is an altogether different case. Syria is a majority Sunni state, with a large Kurdish minority, and a small Shi'a population. The advantage to Iran is that the president and ruling class are Shi'a, even if only nominally so. As we saw, recognizing that they lacked legitimacy in a Muslim state for being Alawi, Assad had Alawi formally recognized as a Shi'a sect. Syria's Shi'a population is not large, and they have no major clerics, no Grand Ayatallahs or Grand Marjas, no major centers of learning, although they do have a number of important shrines and a faithful religious Shi'a population. This appears to be an advantage for Assad; there is no single Syrian cleric, or even well-funded and organized clerical class to challenge him, at this point.

For Iran, however, this is both an opportunity and a constraint. Surely, training clerics in Qom, Iran, or Najaf, Iraq for service in Syria presents a long-term Iranian Strategic Influence opportunity. Not only could a stronger Iranian-friendly clerical presence, whether from Iraq or Lebanon (Arabic-speaking), potentially increase the number and fervor of Syria's Shi'a, they could prove a fertile ground for recruiting soldiers for the militia and prove a strong support for Assad. Religious fervor and a greater number of faithful *could* translate to more local recruits for the militias discussed above and give Assad more resources to fight against al-Qaeda and other Sunni insurrection groups, as his military works to fortify and rebuild key redoubts throughout the country. Further, one should have no doubt that Iran is advising Assad on how to set up an IRGC-type structure throughout Syria with local Basij-type paramilitary units as well. Religious fervor is a powerful tool for this type of mobilization, especially in a country where the Shi'as are a minority and threatened by powerful Sunni and non-Muslim neighbors. The more Assad relies on Iran in these ways, the greater their opportunity to mobilize the Shi'as and increase Iranian Strategic Influence in Syria.

Of course, the other major opportunity is in increasing and institutionalizing the Shi'a Resistance Militias. We saw that Assad institutionalized them under the title the National Defense Forces, or quwat al-difa'a al-watani (Fulton and Wyer 2013, 20). For Iran, this is a major win just as it was when Iraq did the same thing with the PMF. However, Iranian influence through the NDF is not a given. They must continue training, education, arming, and funding until these units are self-sufficient materially and only dependent ideologically. This is eventually what happened with Hizb'allah and what is currently happening in Iraq. This presents a great opportunity for Iran's strategic objective to be able to open a two-front war against Israel. And while Israel can currently destroy major military installations, it is quite another matter to take on militias scattered throughout the border region. Israel should be prudent if it plans to invade Syria, as we have seen (in Lebanon) how that could play out.

These opportunities are not without constraints, opportunities rarely are. In Syria, there are two main constraints—Assad's desire for independence and the outside influence of powerful regional and international actors on Assad. First, I should recall the questions I asked above: Is *resistance* a sufficient cause to create homophily? If a military dictatorship and an Islamic revolutionary republic *identify* with resistance, is that enough to draw them together, to guarantee cooperation, to build trust? It appears that this is so, but is it sustainable? Iran's religious and militia activities are an opportunity and a challenge to Assad simultaneously. It is unlikely that Assad does wants to depend on Iran for holding on to power, for obvious reasons. It is also unlikely that he wants a foreign actor holding that much power within his country, potentially challenging his authority. However, if the common identity, motivation, and cultural frames associated with *resistance* are sufficient causes for homophily, then they will likely work through these challenges. After all, their mutual animosity toward Israel and the United States have only increased and brought them closer together. And what is not knowable is the degree to which Assad and Iran are coordinating and genuinely sharing intelligence and strategy. Both parties have, in the short term, more to gain than lose by working together. But this relationship is not organic and is vulnerable to influence. Is Iran positioning itself for a post-Assad Syria? That question should trouble Assad.

The other pressures on Assad come from Russia, Turkey, and to a lesser degree the United States and Israel. The United States is working diligently to limit Iran's "malicious" activity in the region and that includes Syria. But with limited troops in Syria and with those troops having a limited scope, the United States is not directly challenging Iran's presence or putting pressure on Assad to dislodge Iran, assuming it could. Israel, as noted, is publicly stating and acting on the principle that they will not allow Iran to establish permanent bases in Syria. However, I do not believe that the position will be sustainable once Assad re-establishes sovereignty. At some point, Israel will be seen as an aggressor and not as protecting against a deadly enemy. In practical terms, this could translate into Russian S-300 or even S-400 anti-aircraft batteries denying Israel access. Further, both the United States and Israel have virtually no diplomatic or economic leverage on Assad.

Turkey and Assad have a difficult past. Those difficulties have only been exacerbated by current tensions. Turkey sees itself as defending Sunni nationals, which Assad sees as terrorists. Turkey sees itself as defending itself against Kurdish terrorists, which Assad sees as internal allies. Early in the Syrian Civil War, Assad granted the Kurds autonomy. At the time, I commented that this was a brilliant strategic move that would bog Turkey down for years. At the time, I was right. However, now Assad has to rethink this strategy. There is a possibility for a grand bargain involving both the Sunni insurgents laying down their arms and not defying Assad and the Kurds laying down their arms and not threatening Turkey. Iran's position to broker such a deal is strong. But for the moment, Turkey sees Iran's presence in Syria as a nuisance. Turkey has handed the Iranian-backed militias serious defeats in Northern Syria but not to where the two countries have engaged in direct hostilities either militarily (directly) or diplomatically. A grand peace is in everyone's interest and it would appear that Assad remaining in power is a recognized necessary evil. Turkey will tolerate Iranian influence and may even find ways to use that presence to their advantage, such as tampering Iranian support for Kurdish hostility toward Turkey.

Russia is more than tolerant of Iran's presence in Syria; it has encouraged it. From the Russian perspective, if Iran wants to deploy Afghani Shi'a shock troops to help keep Assad in power, so much the better. The Russian air power that has helped Iran's ground game in Syria spares Russian lives and spares Putin political trouble at home. However, Putin does receive significant pressure from Israel regarding Iran's presence in Syria. So far, that pressure has achieved only limited benefit. Putin has not stopped Israel's bombing campaigns in Syria, nor has it tried to curtail Iranian activity. However, that position is also untenable in the long term. Russia will have to support Assad's sovereignty or abandon him. They are unlikely to abandon him, therefore they will have to do something to either curtail Iran's military activity in Syria or prevent Israel's attacks or both. What makes this difficult is that the animosity between Israel and Iran is existential and Syria is currently, and for the foreseeable future, the primary battleground.

As I have stated multiple times, Iran wants to be able to threaten and/or attack Israel from at least two fronts. These two fronts are Israel's border with Lebanon and the Bekah Valley, where Iran has already established a small militia. While Israel is working to prevent supplying and therefore increasing that militia's capability, Iran is working to build them into a legitimate threat to Israel. These are deeply held strategic goals for these actors. Simply put, they are enemies. The advantage for Iran is that Assad also sees Israel as an enemy. The constraint is that Assad is not eager for a major war with Israel. However, Israel can escalate that tension only so far without risking Russian intervention. That is the balance that is currently at play. Iran, as usual, is happy to play the long game. Maintain a foothold, wait for small opportunities to increase their influence within Syria, continue fortifying their supply lines elsewhere, and wait for the right opportunity structure to emerge and then capitalize on that by establishing the presence with Syrian support along Israel's border.

While I do not intend to add a section on Iran's Strategic Influence in Gaza, it is important to note that they are very active there and potentially establishing a third front against Israel. In what should be a very familiar pattern by now, Iran supports charities and religious institutions and practices in Gaza through Iranian proxies. "During the first week of Ramadan, Harakat al Nujaba, an Iranian-backed Iraqi paramilitary group, distributed food baskets and other Ramadan gifts to the families of prisoners and those who have been killed fighting against Israel" (Truzman 2020). Another Shi'a organization targeting Palestinians in the Gaza Strip is the Palestinian-Iranian

Friendship Association (PIFA). This organization, according to Truzman, has ties to Hizb'allah. "Additionally, according to Hezbollah's media relations department, a delegation from PIFA met with senior Hezbollah official Ibrahim al Sayed on November 2019. 'We met the brothers in the leadership of Hezbollah to confirm our loyalty to the valiant Islamic resistance that carried the cause of Palestine and offered martyrs for it,' Abdul Karim al Sharqi, PIFA's Secretary-General stated" (Truzman 2020). Iran's attempt to encircle Israel with hostile militias is essential to its Strategic Influence campaign in these areas. Note how the charities do not hide, but rather advertise, their relationship with Iran, Hizb'allah, and other Iranian proxy groups. The key for Iran is to take credit, to be seen to be supporting these causes.

In Syria, Iran is playing the same long game it is playing in Lebanon and Iraq. It is setting up groups loyal to the *Rahbar*. It is funding religious and social service organization, it is providing security, it is supporting the regime that in turn acknowledges and supports the militias, the pattern is clear in Syria, as it is abundantly clear in Iraq and in the first place it was firmly established, Lebanon. Iran faces different constraints and opportunities in Syria than those they face in Iraq, but then those were different than the ones they faced in Lebanon. It is Iran's adaptive resistance ideology and designed redundancy structure that enables them to redesign their Strategic Influence campaigns to meet the opportunities and constraints that define the context. In the next section, I describe the opportunities and constraints that the United States faces in responding to Iran's Strategic Influence campaigns and how these can be more broadly applied to any Gray Zone warfare.

## U.S. OPPORTUNITIES AND CONSTRAINTS

The United States remains the world's greatest power and by far the greatest power in the Middle East. Since the 1979 revolution in Iran, the United States has been leveraging sanctions and attempting to isolate Iran, with varying degrees of intensity and success. Yet, relations between the two countries are best described as low-intensity military conflict with high-intensity economic, diplomatic, and informational conflict. So, why has the United States with all its power not brought this mid-level power to heel? Why has the United States not won? The answer to that question is exceedingly simple. The United States and Iran are fighting different wars. While Iran is fighting, with some important success and significant challenges, a Strategic Influence war, the United States is fighting, what appears to be, a modified anti-terrorism war. The U.S. policy is disoriented, facing the wrong direction; the United States is not defeating Iran because it is fighting the wrong war. Rather than a war that focuses on its strengths, military and economic power, the United States should be fighting a Strategic Influence war and developing better strategies, operations, and tactics in the process.

The importance of Strategic Influence cannot be understated in the contemporary international security environment. The ability to mobilize proxies, to activate and (potentially) radicalize identities, and the ability to sow confusion among rivals are just some of the maneuvers with which contemporary warfare must contend. This is not only true in the defensive sense, as in the United States must defend against Iran's Strategic Influence campaigns in Iran's near abroad, the United States must be engaging in offensive Strategic Influence campaigns of its own. This type of warfare is not just deployed by states like Iran, it is also used by near-peers Russia and China. Therefore, the United States must get better at identifying, mapping, countering, and ultimately engaging in and defeating Strategic Influence campaigns.

However, Strategic Influence is more than just winning hearts and minds, although that should not be underestimated either. This is about something much more central to conflict, which is a battle of wills not just a battle of arms. Again, "Commanders and their staffs should identify adversary support and bring every capability to bear in an effort to affect, undermine, and erode that support and the adversary's will. Note well, that eroding the will of the enemy often involves *mobilizing audiences*, by evoking memories and passions. The main effort for winning the battle of wills . . . will likely occur in and through the information environment" [Emphasis added] (JDN-2-13 2013, 1–8). Thus, the Joint Chiefs of Staff doctrine is in place and commensurate with the definition, theory, and empirical evidence presented in this book. The battle of wills against Iran is not a counterterror campaign, it is a Strategic Influence campaign.

If eroding Iran's will to fight is the ultimate goal, the United States must understand Iran's Strategic Culture, its motivation, and the force behind its will, thus the first three chapters of this book. But it must also understand how Iran uses the themes that emerge from its history and ideology and structure in practice. Thus, the three empirical chapters. We saw a familiar pattern of Iran deploying narratives of *oppression* coupled with financing, messaging, training militia, kinetic strikes, and developing long-term strategies in the service of *resistance*. That the resistance is asymmetric is not just a function of their believing that they have the moral high ground (which many among the Iranian political elite might) it is also a practical surrender to the overwhelming superiority of U.S. fire power. But it is more than that. It is also their understanding that the United States is casualty averse and lacks the political will to fight a guerilla war of attrition. They fight the way they fight, because it worked in Lebanon, it worked in Iraq, it is working in Syria, which leads to their narratives of *triumph*.

For the United States to defeat Iran it must embark on a long-term Strategic Influence campaign that is geared to break the will of Iran's political leadership. It must rethink the way it uses kinetic action, messaging, economic power, and so on. One great constraint in U.S. influence projection in the Middle East is the perception, some have, and Iran perpetuates, of the United States as a colonialist power trying to dominate the region through its proxy states—Israel and Saudi Arabia. If Iran is unpopular in the greater Middle East, Israel and Saudi Arabia are not far behind. Another great constraint is America's deep emotional resentment against Iran. When you hate your enemy, your enemy has already won the first battle. Since the 1979 Revolution Iran and the United States have been locked in an emotional dance of hatred, resentment, and suspicion. It has all the earmarks of a bitter divorce. This observer gets the impression that both sides would rather burn down the house than share it or let the other have it. While marriage counseling is not an option, more detached, logical, strategic thinking is and should be the only option here. The United States must separate its animosity toward Iran from its Strategic Influence approach to Iran.

But there are opportunities here as well. Some are of Iran's making and nature. Again, Iran is Persian where most of the Middle East is Arab. Iran is Shi'a where most of the Middle East is Sunni. Iran's *velayat-e faqih* is not popular among most Shi'a. Iran's internal struggle between modernity and conservativism, between autocratic rule and democracy is exploitable and exists throughout the region in different forms. From Egypt, through Palestine, through the Levant, to the greater Middle East the peoples of this area, generally speaking, do not want to be ruled by a system that is retrograde in respect to human rights, now very widely defined in common, they want to be modern, have access to modern technology, enjoy economic prosperity, and live a life of faith in peace. They want rule of law, equal protection under the law, education, the dignity of work, and so on. In other words, they want what most people everywhere want, dignity, peace, and the ability to pursue happiness as they define it. This entails an implicit and, in most cases, an explicit rejection of both the *velayat-e faqih* system of Iran *and* the Wahhabi radicalism of Saudi Arabia. What the Middle East lacks are robust institutions to regulate human rights, economics, and governance with resources and authority.

The United States has the resources and still some good will among the people of the Middle East. Much of that has been squandered since 2003 up till today. But that good will is there and the United States could seize this opportunity with a long-term Strategic Influence campaign that undermines the *oppression* narrative, deflates the *resistance* movement, and diverts *triumph* to other more "legitimate" values and goals. To do so, the United States must rethink its strategic posture, which entails redesigning its goals and strategies. It is to that that I now turn.

## Of Goals and Strategies

It is difficult to discern what the goal of U.S. strategy toward Iran is. This has been true for some years. It is, I think, unreasonable to believe that George W. Bush wanted to empower Iran by removing the Taliban and Saddam Hussein from power, even though that was the direct result of his policies. The Obama administration was equally confusing in terms of its desired end state with Iran. They signed a historic agreement with Iran, but one that only covered the nuclear question and only for a short period of time. The Trump administration had been rhetorically consistent: Iran is the leading state sponsor of terrorism, Obama's agreement with Iran was the worst deal ever, Iran will only respond to pressure. In fact, the Trump administration had crafted a "strategy" they call "Maximum Pressure." However, not one of these administrations had articulated an end state, a goal for their "strategies."

Without an end goal, of course, you cannot have a strategy. What you have is a course of action, or several course of action options. A strategy is a way to get to a goal. That goal must be articulated in terms of a particular distribution of resources, security balance, or something of that sort, a reasonable definition of what is good enough/close enough to that state, what timeline is and is not acceptable to reach the goal, and other such considerations. For some time, the U.S. goal toward the Soviet Union, for example, was to contain the spread of its ideology, influence, and hegemony. Reagan changed the end goal to defeating the Soviet Union, imposing regime change, and pursued strategies to achieve that goal.

What is the goal of U.S. strategy toward Iran? Is it regime change? Some say of course it is, we are just afraid to say so publicly. Is it containment? For how long, in what areas? Is it integration into the "community of nations?" That is, engagement. Why has no president clearly articulated what the end state is for our Iran strategy? (Or perhaps better, a regional strategy for peace and progress in the Middle East that includes the Iranian people.) Iran's end state is clear, they want to dominate the Gulf, eradicate the State of Israel, push the United States out of the Middle East, and, ultimately, be the regional hegemon with the concomitant global prestige and influence that would follow. It would help if the United States had such a clear end state in mind that was not simply a negation of Iran's goals.

The goal of strategic influence is to erode the will of the enemy. Economic sanctions and kinetic strikes alone have not and will not achieve that goal. As I wrote above, reliance on kinetic action and economic sanctions seems to make sense for a power that has plenty of both. However, since the ultimate goal is to erode the enemy's will, these approaches, although readily at hand, are contraindicated. Indeed, it goes a long way toward answering one of the most important questions strategists are asking. After twenty years of war against violent extremism why is it that we win every battle, but cannot win the war? Why is it that after over forty years of increasingly hard sanctions against Iran, its influence in the region is increasing? It is one of the driving contentions of this work that we are not "winning" because we are not fighting the right war, have not identified the right goals, and have no clear articulation of what "winning" is. In short, we have no national Strategic Influence strategy.

Lastly, the United States must be clear in what the goal of this particular Strategic Influence strategy is. It is extremely dangerous to engage in Maximum Pressure or Strategic Influence without having a clear goal in mind, understanding what milestones must be reached to achieve that ultimate goal, have clear metrics for measuring success, and so on. What was the goal of the Trump administration's Maximum Pressure? I accessed the State Department's Maximum Pressure on Iran webpage.[1] It is a collection of bullet-point tactical moves and successes of the campaign. They include things such as, "The United States will continue to apply maximum pressure on the Iranian regime until its leaders change their destructive behavior, respect the rights of its people, and return to the negotiating table." The problem here is that "destructive behavior" and "respecting rights" are ultimately unmeasurable and provide an opportunity for perpetually moving the goalposts. These are neither clear objectives nor are they the stuff of successful strategies. Removing IRGC forces from Syria, for example, is a key objective that is measurable. That point aside, there is a more far-reaching and dangerous problem, without a clear goal and clear methodologies for achieving those goals we run the risk of alienating another generation of Iranians. In the next section I discuss more specifically what Strategic Influence methodologies are and how they are constructed. In the following section I propose what that might look like applied to Iran.

## Strategic Influence Methodologies

Elaborating on the importance of goals, without a goal there can be no strategy but there are different types of goals. There are strategic goals. These are objectives in support of national interests, such as securing the right of free passage through the Persian Gulf. There are proximate goals. These are objectives that are necessary to support strategic goals, such as maintaining basing rights near the Persian Gulf. The proximate goal, by definition, is subordinate to the strategic goal and is more fluid. As long as the basing rights enable patrolling and effectively guaranteeing free travel in the Persian Gulf it does not matter where the base is. And there are functional goals. These are objectives that enable carrying out the other objectives, such as having mechanisms for targeting audiences for messaging. For example, "What we are seeking to do in this discussion is stock our toolbox with more appropriate tools, train the appropriate number of true craftsmen, and enable them with a strategy that is capable of producing and acting on the all-important set of plans requisite to build peace" (Cobaugh 2017, 1). Tools and craftsmen, the combination of which implies training, are functional. The need to acquire tools and people adequately trained to use those tools is an objective. When that is specified by type and timeline it becomes a goal. "We must hire and train 50 people skilled in Python Artificial Intelligence tools by this time next year" is a goal, but a functional goal. While I will spend very little time on functional goals for this work, it is important to bear in mind that any strategic effort will have to be articulated down to this level for cost and sustainability planning purposes.

Strategic and proximate goals are far more relevant to the purposes of this effort. For example, the need to understand the operational environment is critical to successful influence campaigns. "In particular, the joint force commander (JFC) and staff must attempt to understand what people think, how they perceive the operational environment, and why. It may require analysis of the informational and cognitive dimensions that shape the local social, political, economic, and information systems" (JCH-3-10 2010, 26). This is why this work began with a deep dive into the history, ideology, and structure of Iran's strategic culture. First, they look for opportunities to export those elements by understanding the operational environment and seeking similar narratives of oppression. But also, second, because the United States must understand Iran at that level, more so actually, to effectively counter them. This requires a dedicated cadre of trained experts and managers in Publicly Available Information (PAI) research and Open Source Intelligence (OSINT). It must be a top priority for the United States to create an OSINT domain and to properly train and equip this force technologically.

This is because influence involves, "the integration of designated information-related capabilities in order to synchronize themes, messages, and actions with operations to inform United States and global audiences, influence foreign audiences, and affect adversary and enemy decisionmaking" (FM-3-13 2013, 11). The Joint Commander's Handbook for Strategic communications specifies four proximate goals that are resonant with Strategic Influence, insofar as Strategic Influence is being used for crafting narratives, themes, and messages. They are "(1) Improve US credibility and legitimacy, (2) Weaken an adversary's credibility and legitimacy, (3) Convince selected audiences to take specific actions that support US or international objectives, and (4) Cause a competitor or adversary to take (or refrain from taking) specific

Actions" (JCH-3-10 2010, 62–63). There are two key differences in meaning between Strategic Influence and these definitions. The first is that current DOD doctrine has information operations in support of kinetic action, where Strategic Influence posits that kinetic action *is* messaging, just of another kind and as such integral to Strategic Influence. In other words, both narratives and kinetic action are components of Strategic Influence. The second is that the ultimate goal of strategic influence is to erode the will of the enemy through unified action. "Unified action is the synchronization, coordination and/or integration of the activities of governmental and nongovernmental entities with military operations to achieve unity of effort" (JCH-3-10 2010, 23). To achieve unity of effort, then, is to leverage the resources available to the U.S. government (USG) to produce a specific effect on a target. The proximate goal can be activating identities, mobilizing audiences, or battling a narrative, but the strategic goal is always eroding the will of the enemy.

There are two major impediments to this whole of government approach. The first is inadequate attention and resourcing for Strategic Influence. "A lack of sufficient government-wide guidance, resources, and capabilities hinders our ability to effectively coordinate and synchronize our activities and achieve unified action" (JCH-3-10 2010, 24). The lack of resources is a result of the lack of priority given to Strategic Influence. Even as the USG realizes that Russia, China, Iran, and others are waging these campaigns effectively and achieving effects in their respective theaters, the resources needed to effectively battle and win this war is still lacking. There remains an overwhelming preference for hardware and little understanding of the need for cognitive warfare waged through Strategic Influence. This must change.

The second impediment to the whole of government approach is that there is no unity of effort. Some policy is set by the Interagency Policy Committee for Global Engagement, which is chaired by the director for Strategic Communication of the National Security Council (JCH-3-10 2010, 30). That policy is then carried out by the Department of State's Global Strategic Engagement Center (GEC), an interagency organization that has representatives from the DOD, National Counterterrorism Center, the Intelligence Community, and other entities. The scope, staffing, and resourcing of this entity are not commensurate with its mission. And its mission since 2017 has been to focus on "counter foreign state and non-state propaganda and disinformation efforts" that threaten U.S. national security interests as well as the national security interests of U.S. allied and partner countries. This language indicates a much broader purpose for the new GEC than the original one, possibly encompassing counterterrorism communications but also expanding the GEC's coverage to include countering certain foreign communications from any source" (Weed 2017). But more, other entities, particularly the DOD, control larger budgets and staffs for messaging than the GEC does and because they are better staffed and resourced they are able to set their own policies. In effect, this makes the GEC a consulting and coordinating body more than an execution arm for uniting effort or action.

I strongly recommend that the NSC and GEC continue working to shape national priorities, providing unity of effort with the interagency community. However, the USG should look to SOCOM and the 1st Special Forces Command to provide unity of action. This recommendation rests on the fact that the DOD is further along in developing the necessary doctrine, experience, tools, skills, and personnel to carry this out globally in a structured and sustainable way. While SOF is a small community they can and should provide leadership to larger efforts and teams. Properly resourced they could execute or lead full spectrum Strategic Influence operations unlike any other community within the USG, particularly when it comes to narrative framing and kinetic action as twin pillars of Strategic Influence.

Since even kinetic action is messaging, the most important element to Strategic Influence is narratives. Yet it is the element the United States lacks the most. "Narrative (or rather lack of) is, in my opinion, one of the ... most tragically flawed aspects of our (if one actually exists) US communication strategy ... As narrative pertains to our strategy, the bottom line, as noted by Dr. Maan, is simply that we need a compelling narrative (story) to explain the meaning of our intentions and actions" (Cobaugh 2017, 17). I agree with Cobaugh that the United States fails consistently to produce a coherent and cohesive narrative, which speaks to a failure of unity of effort. The information space is more crowded than it used to be, but during the Cold War the narrative was fairly simple and effective. Since then, the United States seems to not be able to find a narrative that galvanizes supporters and works toward eroding the will of the enemy. Where Cobaugh is in error is in defining narrative as simply a compelling story.

The Joint Commander's Handbook takes a more Strategic Influence approach to the issue of narratives. Speaking to the perspective that sees the battle of the narrative as a battle to get audiences to buy a story is incorrect. "The battle is not merely to push aside, defeat or gain superiority over the enemy's narrative; it is to completely supplant it. In fact, upon our winning the battle of the narrative, the enemy narrative doesn't just diminish in appeal or followership, it becomes irrelevant" (JCH-3-10 2010, 41). They go on to say that the battle of the narrative is about dominating the cognitive domain the way armed forces dominate the physical domain. Combined you have the essence of Strategic Influence, because when you dominate both the physical and cognitive domains you erode the will of the enemy.

Narratives are broad-based and value-driven and to dominate a region must be customized to the audience(s) of that region. The information environment is region-specific although all messaging has the potential to go global (FM-3-13 2013, 7). Translating narratives to meet the specifics of the region is the responsibility of the commander and their staff. "Commanders synchronize messages and actions with overarching themes in operations to inform and influence audiences in their area of operations and area of interest . . . Synchronization of messages and actions promotes and shapes the attitudes and behaviors of the audiences in the area of operations while affecting adversary or enemy information efforts" (FM-3-13 2013, 11). This is where the experience of Psychological Operations and Civil Affairs SOF units, under the command of 1st Special Forces Command is particularly adept, particularly when you consider the various "actions" that constitute influencing. These obviously include messaging, but also symbolic messaging like a U.S. flag flying next to an Iraqi flag on the new schoolhouse built in Basra, and also kinetic action. All of these send a message, all of these are information.

Lastly, the execution of an effective strategy must be handed to practitioners for execution. While there are many important facets to Strategic Influence execution two merit special attention: 1) targeting and 2) lines of effort. Targeting allows the commander's staff to "synchronize limited resources in time and space to achieve the desired effects for the commander. The targeting focus of the G-7 (S-7) essentially answers the following for the staff: who are U.S. forces targeting, how will U.S. forces find them, what message will U.S. forces send them, and how effective was the sent message?" (FM-3-13 2013, 61) The effectiveness of an influence campaign must be measured against the strategic, proximate, or functional goals that are clearly articulated in the plan which includes the type of goal, the time horizon, and the relationship between narrative, theme, and message. These are all included in the lines of effort.

Lines of Effort (LOEs) are distinct paths to achieve strategic, proximate, or functional goals. While they each have their own staff, resourcing, targets, and measures of effectiveness they must, as a whole, support the commander's intent. Specific to supporting a narrative Cobaugh recommends the following five LOEs: (1) diplomacy, (2) relieve suffering, (3) grievance resolution, (4) capacity building, and (5) kinetic targeting (Cobaugh 2017, 23). These resonate well with Strategic Influence campaigns as they are whole of government, combine narrative and kinetic messaging elements, can be adapted to fit circumstances, and can be sustained over long periods of time. They also fit precisely in the skill sets of SOF. Psychological Operations can support diplomatic efforts with audience targeting and messaging in support of diplomatic efforts. More, they can inform diplomatic efforts by giving insights from local populations, not just the local government. This is strengthened by the participation of Civil Affairs troops who, in many cases, are leading efforts in LOEs 2 and 3 usually alongside other USG entities. They, too, often have a pulse on the population that national or provincial government officials do not. They are indispensable to diplomacy, relieving suffering, and resolving grievance.

Civil Affairs also supports building capacity, the 4th LOE. They, along with other USG entities, partner nations, and other SOF elements help identify need from the local population (a decidedly better approach than imposing solutions from above, particularly if the goal is influence) and direct efforts to build social, technical, economic, and other types of infrastructure. Another important facet of capacity building belongs to Special Forces (SF)—Green Berets. SF troops have several core missions, but foreign internal defense is one of their signature skills. We must surpass Iran's capability in this regard, and we have the skill and resources to do so.

Lastly, kinetic targeting must not lead our efforts to defeat the enemy because by itself it rarely erodes the will to fight. Theoretically, it is possible to so defeat a force through kinetic action that they totally surrender and never fight again. This is truer of large land and sea domains than it will likely ever be of Strategic Influence domains. For every terrorist or insurgent killed the risk is run of creating martyrs for the cause and opportunities for the enemy to recruit and perpetuate their narratives. This is not an argument for pacifism. It is an argument for understanding that kinetic action must be in service of the goals of Strategic Influence. This means messaging must prepare the operational environment for strikes, albeit indirectly and be ready to exploit the action when taken. Kinetic targeting is not just identifying targets for action, it is about targeting opportunities to support the overall strategic intent.

There are not enough SOF troops to support Strategic Influence campaigns across the globe. There are enough to work with the appropriate military, USG, and partner nation elements in the Middle East to impact Iran's efforts and erode their will to fight. There are enough SOF elements to lead efforts in the South China Sea and Eastern Europe as well. When the National Security of the United States requires combating near-peer and rogue state elements operating in the "Gray Zone" or Irregular Warfare, it is to Strategic Influence that they should turn as a means and SOF as the preeminent force to execute those campaigns.

## Iran

There is a need to develop and articulate a clear end state, a goal for U.S. strategy toward Iran. It is not unreasonable for the United States to want Iran to change its nuclear ambitions (assuming one believes they are looking to either develop weapons or reach breakout capability) and change its regional activities. But it is unrealistic to think that the current regime is going to do anything other than delay the nuclear question while they continue to develop dual use technology and expertise. It is doubly unrealistic to expect them to abandon their Strategic Influence operations when they continue to increase their influence. They believe deeply that they have history, ideology, and geography on their side; they are not likely, therefore, to give up their advantages and opportunities.

This leaves U.S. policymakers with limited choices. The first is to take limited action and wait, articulate no strategy, make no major strategic moves, and just let things play out as they will. The Sistani succession in Iraq, the role of the PMF, the future of Hizb'allah, and the fate of Assad will sort themselves out in time, after all, as will the fate of the current regime in Iran. Knowing when to do nothing is also good strategy. However, when your adversary is active and achieving effects that could potentially alter the strategic landscape for decades to come, which Iran is doing in its near abroad, then doing nothing is contraindicated. Further, it should be clear that the current LOEs, first attempting to diplomatically isolate Iran, now re-engaging diplomatically, then back and forth, while trying to cripple it economically, is not producing the effects successive U.S. administration claims to seek. Iran is ordering nuclear enrichment levels to increase to pre-JCPOA levels, and its regional activities have not abated at all. This is the result of the United States fighting the wrong war, using the wrong weapons.

But a corollary of fighting the wrong war is having the wrong goals and the wrong targets. The United States should not seek regime change in Iran as its strategic goal, per se. It should seek self-governance for the Iranian people as its strategic goal. Those who think regime change should be the U.S. goal should have to answer the following question: If the Supreme Leader is deposed, if the system implodes, what will emerge? It is, to my mind, a fantasy to believe that what replaces the *velayat-e faqih* is a liberal Western democracy. That flight of fiction is similar to the belief that the Iraqi populace would welcome the U.S. invasion of Iraq in 2003 as liberators. The most likely outcome is that the IRGC will assume power, impose order, and either establish a military dictatorship or, more likely, appoint a political figurehead to represent their government. They are too wealthy, too powerful, too organized to fold up and go away. If there is an accommodation between the IRGC and the network of Mosques, the *ulama*, the United States will be no better off than they are in dealing with the current system.

Regime change, per se, is inadequate as a goal because it fails to consider the day after. The driving question for U.S. strategy, and one which seems to get little attention in the media, among think tanks, and from the USG more broadly is this. Is there an alternative that is palatable to the Iranian people, will guarantee order, yet change Iran's strategic objectives? The answer is yes. I believe a U.S. Strategic Influence campaign can be designed that targets these elements within Iran, partners with the Iranian people and reformers, and move toward a shared goal of self-governance for the Iranian people. In Iran that means messaging in support (either indirectly or through legitimate proxies) of certain key actors, key principles, and preparing the ground for a transition to self-governance. There is no fast and easy path to this outcome. But it is the optimal long-term solution. This requires strategic patience, which is aided by having quantifiable metrics for reaching key milestones. However, any Strategic Influence policy in Iran must be in tune with the desires of the Iranian people, that means listening to them. If U.S. policies are in support of their ambitions for freedom and prosperity, then U.S. strategies have a greater chance of success.

Put another way, the only ones who can put maximum pressure on the regime are the Iranian people, and we should be their strong, consistent allies. The United States must seek out opportunities to ally themselves with the Iranian people against the Iranian government. The United States must eschew any policies that feed into the *oppression* narrative that feeds *resistance*. But more, the United States should have clear goals and specific Strategic Influence campaigns designed that strike at Iran's vulnerabilities. One key constraint the United States must overcome is having only limited and often indirect access to the Iranian people. The Iranian government works assiduously to try and block Internet access to their citizens. Iranians, especially the youth and urban populations, are tech savvy and find ways around that; the United States must find ways to help them. For example, there is technology that currently exists that broadcasts Wi-Fi over large areas for short periods of time. This technology must be invested in and its range and duration expanded.

For Iran, specifically, but also for the region more broadly, I am proposing a contemporary version of Radio Free Europe campaigns of the Second World War and the Cold War but heavily reliant on new forms of communication and technology. The Iranian people must be able to access applications, websites, radio, television, and other information outlets from the West. The coverage should also allow messaging from a dedicated Special Operations Forces unit with multiyear assignments to assure consistency. Every pertinent move by the Iranian government should be tracked and reported back to the Iranian people. Every pertinent move by the United States and its allies should likewise be amplified. Basic PsyOp tactics, techniques, and procedures that identify major themes and that must remain consistent over time, and messages that are tactical and supportive of the strategic themes need to be designed and approved so that messaging can be done in real time, but themes are consistent and long term.

For the moment, given our limited access to the Iranian people the above is the best, the minimum, we should be striving toward. This will require partnering with scientific labs and industry to develop the technology necessary to maximize the reach of these Strategic Influence campaigns. However, for this to be effective across Iran's near abroad we must do more than messaging. Strategic Influence is not just about winning hearts and minds, but it is about eroding the will of the enemy. A regional, long-term Strategic Influence campaign that goes beyond economic sanctions and the occasional kinetic strike will require a concerted effort, a unified command, and a programmatic tie-in to Congress and the National Security Council. This is not just to ensure accountability, but is to guarantee material and political support. This strongly recommends that the program be run by a joint task force, either in the National Capitol Region or at Fort Bragg, NC, with 1st SF Command elements working in unison with Special Operations Command in Tampa, the U.S. State Department, the Intelligence Community, other USG assets, and partner nations, with SOF leading the charge.

The United States is facing a steep long-term challenge in the Middle East because of Iran's activities, and elsewhere because of near-peer activity. Between the United States and Iran, as well as between the United States and Russia and China, goals are diametrically opposed, as are ideologies. A long-term strategy requires widespread support and must be managed by professional joint task force experts, not political appointees. Further, and this is just as important, using Special Operations Forces will get the United States more than just a focused, well-trained, well-equipped, and ready-to-operate toolkit with all the essential tools ready at hand, it will get the United States a model it could then deploy to other theaters to engage in Strategic Influence campaigns against near-peer rivals.

If the United States is serious about the near-peer and rogue state threat, a revisiting of the role of SOF is essential and Strategic Influence is the way in which they should be refocused. In fact, this would be a return to original intent. Special Operations was split from the Office of Strategic Services to focus on psychological operations and foreign internal defense. The main point of which was to weaken the will of the enemy. "Based on Donovan's vision, the OSS developed the SO [Special Operations] branch, clearly modeled on the British Commandos, to increase 'the enemies' misery and weaken his will to resist."[2] SOF is, was created to be, and should be understood to be, the preeminent Strategic Influence weapon in the world.

There are specific opportunities that are ripe for exploitation. If the United States seeks to target moderates, reformers, and the Iranian youth for messaging, the United States needs to articulate that strategy—Iranian self-governance, and then develop LOEs that exploit cleavages between the Iranian people and the regime. The first one that bears emphasizing, again, is that the *velayat-e faqih* system does not enjoy a great deal of legitimacy among the Iranian people, the majority of clerics in Iran, and even less so clerics and populations outside Iran. The ruling system in Iran does not enjoy a great deal of legitimacy among the majority of Iranians. This is a leverage point that is ripe for exploitation.

A critical factor that partly explains the rejection of the *nizam*—the system—by the Iranian people is that the majority of Iran's population is too young to remember the 1979 Revolution and a significant plurality barely remember, if at all, the Iran-Iraq War. According to Index Mundi 62 percent of Iran's population falls between the ages of fifteen and fifty-four.[3] Statista records that 69 percent of the population falls between fifteen and sixty-four.[4] The revolutionary generation is passing. In its stead, even among the current leadership, we see technocrats, those who seek more openness with the West, those who want progress, economic growth, and who believe that Iran's greatness is best achieved through science, education, and economic growth. The worst outcome of U.S. action would be to create another generation of Iranians who see the United States as oppressors and seek, therefore, to *resist*.

Another factor undermining public support for the *velayat-e faqih* system is that many who sought Islamic governance in 1979 did not necessarily want a theocratic government. Immediately after the revolution Michel Foucault traveled to Tehran to report on events. He asked members of the elite and general populace the same question, "What do you want?" "'During my entire stay in Iran, I did not hear, even once, the word 'revolution,' but four out of five times, someone would answer: an Islamic government'" (Crooke 2009, 104–105). According to Foucault's observations, however, rather than a "narrow" theocratic state an Islamic government was meant to enhance the spirituality of the people. Through this spiritual renewal, "Iranians could not only change the political order in Iran, they could change themselves, their way of being, their relationship with others, with things, with eternity, with God" (Crooke 2009, 105). Rather, the revolution produced a theocratic state with a narrowly construed and conservativistic view of Islam at its core.

Another important cleavage that is ripe for exploitation, closely related to the first, is the desire for the Iranian people to have true democracy—self-governance. Self-governance, then, requires particular types of knowledges such as mathematics, science, technology, and the ability to build social and technological infrastructure that enables and empowers specialization in service of the people. "Since the 1979 revolution, the essence of the concept *hokomate mardomi* (people's governance) has remained strong in Iran. . . . In the 1980's, the concepts *Mote'ahed* (committed) and *Motekhases* (specialist) became popular in Iran. . . . The dynamic of this debate led to the adoption of both terms by the state and other institutions—the idea that good citizens have (41) to be both *Mote'ahed* and *Motekhases*" (Rostami-Povey 2010, 42). In this sense, we see university students advancing science and technology and clamoring for more self-governance as well as self-identifying as Islamist.

That is, there is a strong belief in Islam and the need for Islamic governance, as Foucault reported, but it is not the strict conservativistic Islamic jurisprudence of the ruling clerics. As we saw in the section above on Islamic democracy, "Talibanism and Saudi-style conservatism has been engaged in a battle between conservative and democratic Islam, because the majority of the people believe in *Fiqh Poya* (dynamic jurisprudence), the idea that Islam is compatible with modernism. The conservatism of the state and institutions in Iran is based on the promotion of patriarchal attitudes on gender issues and the limiting of democratic rights and citizens' access to public spaces" (Rostami-Povey 2010, 43). Democracy is not contradictory to Islam in this view. They are not only compatible, but they are also complementary. This is why expanding access to "public spaces" technologically is so important.

Iran does not fear full-scale invasion by the United States or any regional power because of the way it has organized its homeland defense using IRGC and Basij forces. It does fear further erosion of support from the populace. It therefore builds defensive and offensive capability in the spiritual, psychological, and social domains, coupled with asymmetric military capability. The United States, conversely, mostly underplays the importance of these factors and builds overwhelming military and economic force and leverages that power to achieve strategic ends. This is disorientation at work.

While policymakers will articulate goals and professionals will craft the LOEs, narratives, themes, and messages to be deployed, below are a few principles and general thematic suggestions based on the concepts of Strategic Influence and the history and ideology and structure of the Iranian government and culture. These narratives and themes should stress Iranian nationalism, in contradistinction to international Shi'ism. Appeals to nationalism should stress the very elements that some among the nationalist factions also support. These are, among others, prowess in math, science, technology, and trade. Further, the Cylinder of Cirrhus provides a foundation and opportunity for discussing human rights in an Iranian nationalist and non-Western context. Assuming, the U.S. goal is to partner with the Iranian people to achieve self-governance by exploiting the cleavages that exist between the government and the people, such as the modernist/conservativistic and democratic/theocratic divides, the United States should articulate Strategic Influence campaigns using the LOEs framework suggested by Cobaugh; they are (1) diplomacy, (2) relieve suffering, (3) grievance resolution, (4) capacity building, and (5) kinetic action (2017, 23).

(1) Diplomacy, where official U.S. government communication channels are used to deliver consistent messaging that the regime in Iran is the enemy of progress, modernization, freedom, and the self-determination of the Iranian people. But also pressing allies into service to champion the cause of the Iranian people while isolating the regime. Further, the United States should have public diplomacy efforts wherever possible to show that the United States stands with the Iranian people but not the regime, this should include cooperating with Shi'a elements in Iraq and elsewhere. For example, a Cylinder of Cirrhus organization could be founded in Iraq that promotes modern, nationalist, human rights based on ancient non-Western texts. These messages, talks, pamphlets, and so on, could then be broadcast into Iran. Lastly, narratives, themes, and messaging from the psychological operations perspective should lead and sync with all diplomatic efforts.

(2) Relieve suffering, where suffering is understood to be both physical and psychological, the United States should be leading efforts to get the international community to support the Iranian people's access to information, vaccines and other medications, and support in their efforts to achieve self-governance. Here is a story that highlights the way the Iranian elite use this LOE to continue to show the United States as an enemy of the Iranian people. President Rouhani claimed that Iran attempted to purchase COVID-19 vaccines from the global COVAX system using funds they have in South Korea. They applied for and received a permit from the U.S. Office of Foreign Assets Control. "However, the US Treasury demanded the funds must first be transferred to an American bank before they could be transferred to Switzerland to make the purchase. . . . 'Wherever you found our money, you stole it. You are famed for stealing. How could we trust thieves?' Rouhani said . . . 'Not only in vaccines, medicine and foodstuffs, you will not find an instance where we want to purchase something from outside the country and we don't see the effects of the US's cruelty and knavery,' he said, referring to what Iran has identified as 'economic terrorism' by the US" (Motamedi 2020). Do the Iranian people believe this? How many see this as the Iranian elite blaming the United States for their own incompetence? How many see it as the United States trying to inflict pain and suffering on the Iranian people? With the ability to message the Iranian people directly, this would be a great opportunity to shape the narrative against the Iranian leadership. This also applies to (3) grievance resolution. Until the United States has direct access to the Iranian people this can only be done through messaging. However, great care must be taken to ensure that the messaging is addressing the grievances of the Iranian people and not those of the regime. This could include a thorough accounting of the Mossadeq affair, the accidental shooting of an Iranian airliner during the Iran-Iraq War, and other real and perceived grievances. Suffering cannot be understood to be only

physical and current, for a people who live their history ancient grievances are current grievances.

(4) Capacity building, where capacity is both physical and psychological the United States is somewhat limited by its lack of access. Therefore, it is imperative to increase direct access to the Iranian people by expanding their Internet access. But the United States can also work through partners to deliver information—the most important capacity of all. Whether or not the United States supports insurgent groups inside Iran and builds their capacity is a high-level strategic decision. However, care must be exerted to ensure that the United States and allies are not seen as the cause of massive Iranian government retaliation generating ire from the Iranian people. In everything the United States does it must encourage Iranian nationalism, where that would mean a modern state that respects human rights, the rule of law, and other such "universal" principles.

And, lastly, (5) kinetic targeting where IRGC and other designated terrorist actors are "legitimate" targets, this must be messaged before and after strikes. The United States must communicate to the Iranian people that these strikes are necessary to preserve the international order and that IRGC and Quds Force are not just oppressing the Iranian people, denying their basic human rights, but that they are attempting to establish similar systems in Lebanon, Iraq, Syria, and elsewhere. The Iranian government is imperialist and criminal. In other words, kinetic action against legitimate targets that limit Iran's reach and power is in service of the narratives, themes, and messages of the Strategic Influence campaign, not the other way around.

More broadly, the modernistic/conservativistic and democratic/theocratic divides provide opportunities for the United States to ally itself with the Iranian people. Other potential opportunities worthy of exploration for potential exploitation are the formal and informal divide, which could attempt to bring the Artesh and the Majles, as examples, closer to the people and farther from the *Rahbar*. Another possibility is exploiting the myths of origin of the revolution. This narrative could follow this logic: the revolution was not of the people, for the people, and by the people. It was coopted by the religious elite and they have exacerbated their hold on the people and perpetuated that initial theft of the will of the Iranian people by continually denying them their basic human rights.

These Strategic Influence campaigns, designed to continually strain the divide between the Iranian people and the Regime, will require technological effort, consistent messaging, material support, and kinetic action that perpetuates the narrative. The United States must have clear targets in mind for its messaging. The Iranian urban population and youth are more technologically savvy and more in line with modernity and democracy. The rural populations tend to be more traditional. Care must be taken not to lose the rural audience while focusing on the urban. Another advantage of this approach is that it could allow the Iranian government to focus more resources domestically, further challenging their capacity to export their ideology and materially support their proxies. Further, these Strategic Influence campaign narratives and themes could be modified to combat and defeat Iran's Strategic Influence efforts in its near abroad.

## Iran's Near Abroad

The above describes a framework for a Strategic Influence campaign aimed at exacerbating the divide between the Iranian people and the Iranian government. The overall goal, as is the case with every Strategic Influence campaign, is to erode the will of the adversary, in this case the Iranian leadership. Division between the leadership and the people must be exploited to achieve this end. Simultaneously, the United States must wage a regional Strategic Influence campaign to defeat Iranian narratives and create similar divides among the peoples of the region and the Iranian leadership.

There are great opportunities and significant constraints in executing a successful campaign. Across the Middle East there is a desire for self-governance, security, economic prosperity, modernization (to some degree)—to live a life of dignity and peace. I have long been an advocate for a regional human rights, self-governance, and economic development plan—a Middle East Marshall Plan—The Middle East Peace and Prosperity Initiative. The United States, leading European and Asian allies, along with international organizations, should work to establish *inclusive* regional institutions that promote and enforce government transparency, respect for human rights, and trade that enables economic, not just political, self-governance. Lifting people out of poverty, empowering them, and honoring their history and identity is the best way to break the will of a *resistance* that is built on narratives of *oppression*. The effects of the pandemic present opportunities for such a regional campaign.

However, the constraints are significant. Such a strategy or any proximate goals of such a strategy will take time, money, and patience, things that are not strong suits of the United States. Take, for example, this analysis, "Iran's quest to maximize its influence in Iraq met with some successes; it reached its peak around 2006-7, after which it plateaued and initiated a gradual decline" (Juneau 2015, 9). The timeframe for that analysis may have led to some dangerously wrong conclusions. Relatedly, the U.S. foreign policy establishment must embrace innovation and not immediately reject ideas as grandiose or fantastic. Reshaping the operational environment of the Middle East will require reshaping the information environment. This is not a small task and requires deep, long-term strategic thinking and a lot of imagination with some risk taking. Further, the United States must rethink the way it formulates strategy, develop joint efforts that are insulated from political change, and have high-level support from the requisite bodies as outlined above. To fight the right fight is to understand that the war is a long war, the battles temporary. This also means taking care to measure effectiveness against strategic and proximate goals. So that what may appear to be setbacks do not derail plans that are on a trajectory to success.

Another significant constraint on U.S. Strategic Influence campaigns meant to defeat Iranian narratives is the perception of hypocrisy that results from U.S. ties to regional powers that are seen to be as guilty as Iran of human rights abuses, lack of democracy, and economic self-determination. The United States must bring allies into this vision and encourage reform. As of this writing, for example, Saudi Arabia, arguably the most conservativistic state in the Middle East has been making strides in modifying its domestic policy, allowing for some elections, reforming governance, and diversifying its economy and education systems. These are examples that must be trumpeted throughout the region, and encouraged to continue and increase in scope.

But what is perhaps the greatest constraint is the perception of the United States as a "hegemonistic," "arrogant," "colonialist," and "imperialist" power. This is the perception of the United States that Iran perpetuates, and they retell the stories of Mossadeq, sanctions that hurt the average Iranian, shooting down of a passenger airliner, supporting Saddam Hussein during the Iran-Iraq War while he used chemical weapons against Iranians and violently suppressed the Shi'a of Iraq, invading Iraq in 2003, exacerbating the suffering of the Shi'a, and so on. In 2016 the U.S. State Department commissioned a report that found 40 percent of Iraqis believed that the United States was "working to destabilize Iraq and control its natural resources" (Campbell 2016). They also blamed "'active disinformation campaigns,' supported by Iraqi media," in other words the Iranians, for convincing nearly one-third of Iraqis to believe the United States created Daesh as an excuse to keep troops in Iraq and take control of their oil (Campbell 2016).

Another poll conducted in Iraq and Syria found even greater numbers believing this narrative. "When posing this question, the surveyors used an Arabic word that translates to literal creation, not, for example, a byproduct of U.S. policies or complicity in allowing for the Islamic State group to rise. . . . The belief of U.S. involvement in the extremists' rise also leads public perception in Iraq where 85 percent agree with that assessment, more than the 71 percent who agree it was created by poor central government policies, 71 percent who believe it was caused by another Arabic system, and 42 percent who believe it's the result of Iran's meddling" (Shinkman 2015). That same poll found that 82 percent of Syrians believed the United States created Daesh. This included 86 percent in government-controlled areas, those who are most susceptible to government messaging, "but also in opposition-controlled areas and regions controlled by the Kurds, where 83 percent and 81 percent agree, respectively. Even in Islamic State group-controlled regions, 62 percent believe this to be true" (Shinkman 2015). What should be clear from this, even if Iranian authorship of these narratives is in doubt, is that the United States is not successful in shaping popular narratives that promote U.S. strategic goals.

The United States must defeat Iranian narratives, supplant them, but to do so they must generate narratives that achieve strategic goals, which means the United States must have strategic goals. Regionally, the United States should be pursuing a plan that is inclusive, promotes human rights, the rule of law, political and economic self-governance, and economic opportunity. This will require creating and strengthening institutions in the region that are inclusive and have economic and political power such that all nations of the region can be held accountable. This will take a very long time to build, and it will be very difficult to achieve; and given how these things will be defined by Iran versus Saudi Arabia makes it almost a non-starter. But this challenge is the point. Striving toward regional peace and prosperity can be leveraged inside Iran as evidence of U.S. good will and support continuous efforts to increase the divide between the Iranian people and the *velayat-e faqih* system. While the creation of such regional institutions is a long-term goal it is still what I define as a proximate goal because it is in service to the strategic goal of creating systems that promote the values and practices that will create stability, peace, and prosperity for the people of the region, cleavages with the Iranian elite, and ultimately an erosion of the Iranian leadership's will to continue their Strategic Influence campaigns.

While that is being considered and the enormity of the effort processed, the United States can begin working on building up nationalism in the region. Nationalism and international institutions need not be in conflict, that is entirely a function of power and how resources are controlled and distributed. That there are many theories concerning nationalism is also true and beyond the scope here. By nationalism I mean building up a national identity for Iranians, Lebanese, Iraqis, and Syrians. Admittedly, there is less "national" identity in Syria than in the other states and that is true both historically (as we saw above) and due to the current Civil War, which exacerbated ethnic and confessional divides. Nevertheless, one of the great divides in Iranian history, ideology, and structure is the divide between a modern state that promotes self-governance versus a conservativistic state ruled by or heavily influenced by clerics. This divide resonates with the people of the region who have dealt with military dictatorships, imposed monarchies, and other forms of non-self-governance. The United States must take on this battle of the narrative and it must win.

The main narrative Iran uses in its near abroad is that shared *oppression* has been overcome by *resistance* that led to *triumph*. This has resonated with many Shi'a in Lebanon, Iraq, and Syria. The United States must displace the *oppression* theme and project it onto the *Velayat* system; coopt the *resistance* theme to show U.S. arms defeated Saddam Hussein and Daesh and are now being used to defend the sovereign rights of the peoples of Lebanon, Iraq, and Syria; lastly the United States must coopt the *triumph* narrative, partly by showing that it was the United States that acted to defend the Shi'a, Kurds, and others in the region, but also that *triumph* now means responsibility to govern, not delay justice and progress to the peoples of the region. Strategic Influence campaigns promoting nationalism—One Lebanon, One Iraq, One Syria—can be designed that (1) respect the history, culture, and particular circumstance of each state, (2) builds state capacity, (3) reduces dependence on militias, (4) reduces foreign interference, and (5) guarantees national and individual security. Again, the particularization of such a plan is to be designed and implemented by professionals, preferably led by SOF units as articulated above. However, here I offer a general framework for such campaigns.

When policymakers and practitioners, scholars and scientists use terms like "Middle East," is it clear what they mean? Is the term Middle East a geographical marker? What are its true boundaries? How far west does that go before it becomes the "Middle East and North Africa?" Is Libya part of the Middle East? How far east before it is Asia? Are Afghanistan and Pakistan part of the Middle East? Is it a cultural designation? If so, it is a mix of Arab, Kurd, Persian, Yazidi, and many others. It is also a mix of Sunni, Shi'a, Jew, and Christian. Perhaps it is time for the term to be retired or redefined. For the purposes of this work the United States should reconceptualize the Middle East as the cradle of civilization, the birthplace of the three great monotheistic religions, the land of Moses, Jesus, and Mohammed. Then it should get to work building modern states where once stood empires.

Each state in the region, however defined, has its own history, culture, and particular circumstances. This work began with a historical sketch of Iran and for each state considered as targets of Iranian Strategic Influence campaigns it did the same. One cannot do Strategic Influence without a deep and abiding knowledge and respect for the histories of the peoples in these states. Symbols, tropes, and messages that are meant to evoke emotion, to move the masses toward a renewed sense of nationalism redefined to mean it is they who govern, must acknowledge the *oppression* but the pivot is to redirect the narrative to show Iran as the oppressor, the bringer of a foreign system, force of arms, and corruption. This perception already exists among certain populations in the region, the effort must now be leveraged targeting the Shi'a population. Such a theme could use language like this. "The Shi'a overcame oppression in Iraq with the help of the U.S. and you are now free. The U.S. defeated Saddam and turned him over to you, the Iraqi people, for justice. We brought you elections. We brought you self-governance and independence. We fought with you to defeat Daesh. You fought a great resistance, but not for the sake of resistance alone, but for the sake of living in peace, prosperity, and justice. You must rise now and see what your neighbors are trying to do to your country. How they manipulate you to create strategic power for themselves. You must say no to foreign interference, even as you have friendly relations with all your neighbors and the international community." Or other words, tropes, and narratives that appeal to these themes.

These words, or others, are meant to evoke a sense that *resistance* was *for* something greater than Iranian strategic goals. It was so that the people of Lebanon, Iraq, and Syria could live in peace and dignity. The guarantor of this peace and dignity, historically has not been the state government. State governments have been sites of oppression and corruption, Assad, Saddam, decades of malfeasance in Lebanon. Nationalism is about a people's identity, but it must also be about governance. Roads, schools, and hospitals must be built, staffed, and maintained; garbage hauled away; security in neighborhoods in every province must be provided; social services can be in the hands of local religious organizations partnering with the state who brings supplies and in cases of emergency labor, soldiers, engineers, or whatever is needed. For this idea of nationalism to take hold the United States must revitalize its efforts to build state capacity, reduce corruption, and help create modern states. One Lebanon, Iraq, and Syria ultimately must mean for each: one state, one government, one people, one united effort toward peace and prosperity. Regional institutions can support by sharing best practices in governance, reducing corruption, and so on. International institutions have failed for not being organic. Regional institutions must be legitimately regional, recognized as such, and given authority as such.

If the state is functioning as a modern state, providing services, guaranteeing security, policing itself for corruption, and so on, the justification for the militias begins to evaporate. The state is providing for widows and orphans, through Mosques and religious organizations, sure, but those without militia affiliation. In Iraq that would be the Sistani network, they have followers in Lebanon as well. The end to building state capacity is not just to get the trains running on time, although trains should run on time, it is to build trust with the people. It is so that the people turn to the state and not local militias for representation, solutions, alms, and pride. Re-centering the locus of identity, as it were, is neither an easy nor short-term task. It is however the only way to reduce the power of militias whose primary source of power is popular support.

As of this writing there is movement along this front, not surprisingly, led by Sistani. "Four brigades close to top Shiite cleric Grand Ayatallah Ali al-Sistani held a Dec. 2–4 conference on supporting the state against opposition movements from some militias close to Iran" (Saadoun 2020). In October 2020 Sistani called for the disbanding of all militias, which would include the PMF militias. According to Abdul-Hussain, this is partly motivated by the power accumulation of Kataib Hizb'allah (KH), "Kataib Hezbollah has been busy building a 'statelet' within Iraq. If the government does not act quickly, it will soon become stronger than the Iraqi state itself; it will dominate Iraq in the way Hezbollah dominates in Lebanon and will seal Iraq's slide into failure as a client state of Iran" (2020). The cleavage being exploited here is that KH, although Iraqi, is not serving Iraqi interests but the interests of Iran. Further, the only legitimate use of arms is that sanctioned by the state. Readers will recall that it was a fatwa from Sistani that was used to justify the creation of the PMF, even though his office pushed back on that interpretation early. He is now taking an active role in arguing for their disbandment. The United States must have an active, strong, and continuous narrative in support of these themes, with messaging—the purview of psychological operators—and material support—the purview of Civil Affairs troops, with building state capacity to provide security—the purview of SF, and where necessary and in support of these strategic objectives kinetic strikes—the purview of special mission units.

It would be a mistake to think that social services and such are the only roles these militia play. The *triumph* narrative is still being used today. In Lebanon Hizb'allah forced the Israeli withdrawal in 2000 and fought them to a standstill 2006. They claim that Israeli aggression makes it necessary that they continue to bear arms. In Iraq, the PMF emerged as the "Sacred Defense" because the regular army and local police fled as Daesh marched toward Baghdad. In Syria, the "imperialists" used "terrorists" to try to break the Arc of Resistance by fomenting rebellion and trying to topple Assad, but the Iranians came to their defense and Assad is in power to this day because of Iran's militias. In other words, Iranian militias are the only force in the region that has successfully stood up to the imperialist and won. But more, Iran defended the Lebanese, Iraqi, and Syrian people.

They go on to paint a picture of how the United States continues to attack the resistance, that the United States is the world's leading terrorist. I noted above that the U.S. strike that killed Soleimani also killed Muhandis the leader of KH but also the deputy commander of the PMF. That is, the United States killed an Iraqi official on Iraqi soil. The immediate response to that from the Iraqi Militia side was to launch a rocket attack that was more symbolic than deadly, but also to use the parliament to insist that the Iraqi government force the Americans to leave. The militias are still active, the

U.S. military is still operating in Iraq. Neither side achieved anything, in other words. Except that the view of the United States as an occupying force is now documented and legitimated by a non-binding resolution of parliament. This strengthens the *oppression* narrative and fuels *resistance*. Part of the problem is that the United States did not message prior to attacking in an effective way. Targets should be known, kinetic action against them proof of the long reach of U.S. power is service of justice—preferably Iraqi justice. Immediately after a kinetic strike a unified message across all channels should list the crimes for which the culprit was killed. That Muhandis was conspiring with Soleimani is evidence that he and his militia are puppets of Iran and not loyal to Iraq. These narratives, or others like them, must be crafted so that they are in service of the strategic goal yet support proximate goals of targeted kinetic action.

Overall, Iranian narratives of *oppression, resistance,* and *triumph* are very effective; they must be taken on directly and totally defeated. To do so the United States must redouble its efforts in foreign internal defense—the purview of SF (Green Berets)—and increase the training and supplying for the Lebanese and Iraqi armed forces. Further, campaigns need to be launched that make these armed forces main symbols of national unity. This must show the hard, military side the armed forces, and some successes would not hurt. The United States must endeavor to change the security calculus in these states. First, the United States must get Israel to make security guarantees to Lebanon. These guarantees should include using the Lebanese Armed Forces to patrol the Lebanese-Israeli border. This serves multiple proximate goals: legitimizing the Lebanese Armed Forces, strengthening the central government, creating a buffer zone between Hizb'allah and Israel, weakening Hizb'allah arguments for maintaining their arms.

In Iraq the United States must pledge to work with the Iraqi military to develop elite anti-terror units to secure the borders and to suppress any insurgency and/or terrorist uprising. In 2008 Maliki's government took on al-Sadr with U.S. support and defeated him. This broke the back of the Mahdi Army and forced al-Sadr off of the political stage for years. When he re-emerged, it was not as a militia leader but as a social service provider and political figure. A similar war today against KH could provide a similar or better outcome.

Syria is a different case because as of this writing the Civil War has not ended. The U.S. position on Syria is also unclear. The United States could easily withdraw forces and allow the Russians, Turks, and Iranians to hash it out for years. Assad supports the Kurds, the Turks support Sunni groups, Russia and Iran support Assad—out of convenience if not love—and this could go on for years. Syria is critical to Iran's regional ambitions. The United States can still impact outcomes in Syria, and probably should before things settle in Iran's favor. Again, if the United States is serious about the near-peer fight and the fight against Iran, it should probably not concede Russian privileges in Syria. Forcing the Russians to abandon their bases and ally would be the kind of humiliation Putin would hate. Forcing the Iranians out of Syria would give them a stunning defeat that would deflate the *triumph* narrative. The problem is that there is no real U.S. strategy in Syria, just like there is none across the region.

The United States has virtually no influence in Syria. From the Obama administration's declaration that Assad must be brought to justice, which translates into Assad must fight until the bitter end because death awaits him otherwise, to the Trump administration's fracture over Trump's Tweeted policy to withdraw from Syria. To put it simply, the United States not only has no influence in Syria, it also has no strategy or even strategic interests in Syria; Syria long having been in the Russian camp. However, if the United States is going to engage Iran, check its hegemonic ambitions, and counter its Strategic Influence campaigns, then it cannot ignore Iran's activities in Syria. Syria also provides a testing ground for challenging Russia.

For the United States, the questions are: What is the end state of our policies in Syria? Do we have this articulated? The United States should be clear that it has no intention of opposing Assad, now or in the future. Or, far better, that the only acceptable outcome for Syria is a transition to self-governance. It should be clear, consistent, and expend resources in support of that goal. Other proximate goals should make clear that the long-term stability of Syria is critical to the region and that that stability is only possible through self-governance. Further, that the suppression of all terror networks in Syria must be agreed upon, but there is the rub. The Turks will say that it means the elimination of the PKK—the Kurdish Worker's Party—that Turkey lists as a terror organization and who allegedly operate in Northern Syria, occasionally with U.S. help; for the Israeli's and the United States, Hizb'allah and Iran's IRGC are terror organizations, therefore they would have to leave; and for the United States and Syria, al-Qaeda is another such organization. In other words, here the old adage that one man's terrorist is another man's freedom fighter is most eminently clear. Clearing the Kurdish region of Syria of PKK elements is in the U.S. interest, but so is ensuring that the Kurds are guaranteed security for cooperating with Turkey. All other groups should be expelled from the country as part of the transition to self-governance.

In the meantime, Syria presents an interesting laboratory for the more lethal kinetic action options that SOF offers. Should the United States begin targeting Iranian IRGC and Quds Force operatives in Syria? I do not mean the militias that are part of the Syrian regime, but actual Iranian officers. Such a move would escalate the tension but could prove beneficial in the long term. One benefit would be to send a signal to Iran that the rules of the game have changed. The killing of Soleimani could be interpreted that way, but there is an opportunity here to make a statement that the incident was not a one-off but a long-term official U.S. position. The message would be: the IRGC is an expeditionary military organization hostile to the United States and they will not be permitted safe harbor anywhere. With every such strike advertised across Syria, Iraq, Lebanon, and Iran the *triumphalist* narrative will begin to weaken.

I noted above that it is part of Iran's methodology not to go beyond what the United States will tolerate. In Iraq during the U.S. invasion, they killed U.S. troops with virtually no reprisals. Some think that Soleimani's killing was partly revenge for the American blood he had on his hands. That strike occurred too long and far apart from attacks on U.S. soldiers to serve any strategic purpose, however. Rather, the Trump administration seems to have been saying that any attack, however small, by any Iranian proxy will be cause for action against Iran itself. That is an escalatory course of action, but not one policymakers should reject out of hand. If Iran knows that IRGC officers in Syria are fair game for SOF troops, how would they react? This bears consideration.

However, the main effort of U.S. kinetic action as part of a broader Strategic Influence campaign against Iran in Syria, must be to destroy Iran's logistics chain. Iran wants, needs, an uninterrupted supply chain that goes from Tehran to the Israeli border. The United States from both the Syrian and Iraqi side should make the cost of that supply chain too high for Iran to maintain. Again, this must be part of a bigger strategy; it must be worked out with the National Security Council, the Intelligence Community, and Congress. Like the Cold War, a Strategic Influence campaign must cross U.S. administrations. Iran will think that the U.S. commitment to defeating them in their near abroad is temporary, that they can wait it out, the strategy must be clearly articulated and palatable to both political parties to ensure long-term survival of the strategy. In the meantime, successes using this approach will feed acceptance of this approach.

But Syria, like Lebanon and even Iraq, is not monolithic in ethnic or religious make-up. A long-term solution to the Syria question must look to regional dynamics as well. Put simply, if the United States wants to maintain hegemony, defeat Iran's Strategic Influence campaigns, create peace and prosperity, Assad must be made to quit Syria. Peace in Syria means something different than it does in Iraq and Lebanon, however. In Syria the majority are Sunni Muslims, long dominated by an Alawi sect that only recently was recognized as Shi'a. Could a peaceful solution be found that does not increase the need for Shi'a militias? That is a difficult challenge. Guaranteeing Shi'a and other minorities protection under the law, security, dignity, self-governance, and economic prosperity will be a tall order when a majority that has been oppressed comes to power, as we saw in Iraq after the defeat of Saddam Hussein. Yet without such guarantees in writing and in practice Syria could be doomed to more cycles of violence.

Each country where Iran is executing its Strategic Influence campaigns the United States must counter with similar LOEs. Recalling the LOEs from above, they are (1) diplomacy, (2) relieve suffering, (3) grievance resolution, (4) capacity building, and (5) kinetic action (Cobaugh 2017, 23). (1) Diplomatic efforts by the United States and its allies must stress the basic principles of self-governance; these include rule of law, economic opportunity, respect for human rights, among others. The United States cannot champion human rights against rivals and turn a blind eye toward similar abuses among allies. The United States must help stand up regional institutions that have some authority, supported by the UN, the EU, and others. Militias must be delegitimized and outlawed across the region. Iran must be part of these organizations and the rights of Iranian citizens must be guaranteed as well. These diplomatic efforts must take on security questions as well, perhaps including the nuclear question as well as the activity of proxies.

To (2) relieve suffering and (3) resolve grievances is partly to take ownership of the errors and positive things the United States has done. They also present opportunities to clarify Iran's role in the current troubles. Conflict perpetuation does not serve the interests of the peoples of Lebanon, Iraq, and Syria; it serves Iran's interests. Militias in these places no longer serve the interests of justice and security. (4) Building state capacity is the way the United States can help citizens in these states to relive suffering and resolve grievances. The state is the provider of services and justice. The But only a state with the capacity to deliver these things consistently, without bias, and without corruption will gain the support of the people. And lastly (5) kinetic action is in support of these goals. When a militia leader is targeted the locals know why they understand that this is part of a larger campaign to bring order and self-governance. They understand that the United States is working to bring a modern state into being and that a modern state must have a monopoly on the use of force.

This framework is deliberately vague so as to provide the outlines, the targets, the methods, and the goals. Actual campaigns would be far more specific in these aspects and also in terms of resources and time frames. One key point here is that having a strategy and narrative in place will make messaging faster and easier. This is because messaging is an extension of already approved policy—the narrative. Delays in messaging, because there is no clear strategy in place, often results in lost opportunity as many who have working in psychological operations know. These LOEs are good, but not necessary, others can work as well or better. They, too, were chosen to support the framework of an idea. The bottom line, however, is firm. Iran is fighting a Strategic Influence campaign in Lebanon, Iraq, and Syria and the United States is not. The United States should learn how to counter and fight such a fight against Iran, and further develop those skills for application against near-peer states Russia and China.

## SUMMARY

From the background chapters, through the empirical chapter, to the conclusion, I have tried to articulate what Iran is doing and why. But I have also laid the groundwork, I believe, for how the United States should respond. I believe the United States is failing in its contest with Iran because it is fighting an Anti-Terror War using relatively rare kinetic strikes and a lot of diplomatic and mostly economic pressures. These will have limited short-term effects. But there are very significant portions of the population in Lebanon, Iraq, and Syria that are more loyal to Iran and believe more firmly in Iran than they do in the United States. The United States cannot win this fight because it is fighting the wrong fight. A Strategic Influence campaign does not just seek to erode the resources of the enemy, at best that delays the enemies plans and forces the enemy to find other means to fund, supply, and so on. The end must be an erosion of the will to fight.

That is not an abstract, touchy-feely, version of winning hearts and minds. It is not just messaging. It involves kinetic action, economic pressure, diplomatic pressure, but it involves all of these things in a concerted effort to erode the will of the Iranian political elite to continue down this path. So far as this observer can tell the Trump administration's Maximum Pressure campaign was somewhat successful in limiting Iran's oil revenue and making it hard for them to move freely in the area. But India and China have signed deals to increase their purchasing of Iranian oil. And China and Iran have signed a "25 Year Strategic Partnership Plan." One that they have been working on for years. So, Maximum Pressure, like engagement before it, has not produced, in the short-term tangible positive effects for the United States.In Iraq, for example, KH, is far stronger now than it was four years ago. And if Iran is successful in the Sistani succession question, the United States may lose Iraq for two generations or more. But, more importantly, the "Maximum Pressure" campaign, like the engagement before it, failed at eroding the will of Iran's political elite. But, then again, that has been the case since the 1979 Islamic Revolution.

A holistic Strategic Influence campaign moves across theaters, assesses opportunities and challenges, consistently messages the core themes of the campaign, and uses economic, diplomatic, and kinetic assets *in support of influence*. In other words, we should borrow Iran's playbook to defeat Iran. But more, we should be very clear that we are developing our own *New Way of War.* And that we will be using this model in our near-peer competition in Eastern Europe and the South China Sea, for example. It is for this reason that I suggest that SOF be the principal tool for this endeavor.

SOF is known as the tip of the spear. It is the first in and the last out. The three brigades that make up SOF, the Green Berets (SF), Civil Affairs, and psychological operations have the type of specialized skills that the United States needs to deploy in Iran's near-abroad and in Iran itself. SOF has the capability and the experience necessary to design and execute this strategy. That it requires joint coordination with allies, the Intelligence Community, State, and other USG entities is clear and that suggests that the SO Command in Tampa and the 1st SF Command on Ft. Bragg should take the lead on designing and executing. It is my firm belief that without this type of holistic approach, Iran will continue to be a source of instability in the region for decades to come.

Finally, I want to close with an ambitious thought. The answer to the question what should be the end state that a Strategic Influence campaign seeks is simply this: A U.S.-Iranian partnership. With a population of over seventy million people, the average age of which is in their late twenties to thirties, with a large middle class, with a vibrant diaspora, with great education in math and science, with a strategic location that makes it the gateway to the Central Asian States, a chokepoint of the Persian Gulf, and a bridgeway to the greater Middle East, Iran was and should be again a U.S. partner and ally. The Iranian people are not our enemy. The regime in Tehran is. That regime is already giving way because of age and death to a younger generation whose views of the United States are more nuanced. The United States should be playing to the younger population that think so highly of American culture, music, technology, and education. The United States can help Iran emerge from the shadows of the *velayat-e faqih* system and unleash the power of their people. Come trade with us. Come travel here. Let us travel there. Let us study together. All of this should be what the United States should be striving for and should be working to avoid any actions that threaten this relationship. If this can come from the renewed JCPOA negotiations, that would be ideal. This should be the long-term U.S. strategic goal.

In the meantime, the current regime must pay heavily for their actions. But great care must be expended so that we do not make enemies of those who will be instrumental in the transition. What sort of security guarantee would make the next generation of rulers feel safe in dealing with the United States? What sort of trade deal could we emplace once the nuclear and the support for guerillas are settled? What sort of guarantee can the United States and partner nations give that the Shi'as of the Middle East will be treated like full citizens and their religious rights respected? What sort of rapprochement could the United States broker between Iran and Saudi Arabia? The answers to these questions are the proximate targets the United States must achieve to reach the end state.

The one question that will take longer to answer and may not fully satisfy anyone is what to do about the Israeli-Iranian relationship. The animosity goes deeper than just the ruling elite and mutual recognition and respect would take generations to achieve. What is good enough here? A security agreement? A simple non-hostility pact? Perhaps more is possible with the next generation of leaders, and it is certainly possible with Saudi Arabia, especially as the Desert Kingdom modernizes its economy and political structures. And, this observer believes that Saudi Arabia has blessed the agreements between the United Arab Emirates and Bahrain and Israel. Whether this is a movement toward peace or an alliance against Iran remains to be seen. An Iranian-Israeli rapprochement, however, for the time being, is a bridge too far.

The key for U.S. strategic designers is to recognize that this is an intergenerational influence campaign. It is not about quick wins. It is about fundamentally transforming a contentious relationship into a cooperative one. The young in Iran generally admire U.S. wealth, technology, education, and, in principle, our rights and liberties. They aspire to achieve those things for Iran, and we should encourage that. But we should make it clear that rejecting the *Velayat* revolutionary mission is central to that. We should make it clear that as long as they are willing to join the "community of nations" and modify their militancy, that the world will support them economically, technologically, and in other ways.

For this to be successful, of course, the United States must work with partners to weaken the power of the IRGC. Sanctioning IRGC officers and companies helps, but it is not enough. Also care must be taken that these sanctions are not punishing the Iranian people unless we are messaging them directly to mitigate those effects. Targeted kinetic action, strikes against IRGC assets, should also be considered. Capturing and trying IRGC officials should also be considered. The IRGC must be degraded if the Iranian people are to achieve self-governance. Otherwise, any transition in leadership will likely result in the IRGC taking more power.

Republican and Democratic administrations and national security officials should be able to design and endorse such a plan, believe in such an end state, and work toward such a goal. For this to be a multiyear effort will require buy-in from leadership in both parties, in the Congress, and the national security establishment more broadly. There has been no clear strategy articulated for Iran or for the Middle East more broadly, only proximate goals like keeping shipping in the Persian Gulf free and open. Without a clear strategic goal, the United States cannot achieve success. Further, without a clear strategic goal, the United States cannot clearly articulate the strategy for getting "there." I have endeavored to provide both an end goal and the means to achieving it. Strategic Influence is the strategy to get us to the admirable and desirable end state of a partnership between the U.S. and the Iranian people. And I believe I have shown why these efforts matter, how they can be executed, and by whom they should be executed.

Here's to the day when flights from L.A. to Tehran are frequent, cheap, and safe!

# Notes

## INTRODUCTION

1. A word on nomenclature: I use the terms Iran, the Islamic Republic of Iran, IRI, interchangeably and always in reference to the political elite, those responsible for and implicated in Iranian strategic policymaking.
2. www.gecforum.org

## CHAPTER 2

1. In their defense these typologies are used in Iran's domestic discourse, although once ported to the West these terms cannot be assumed to mean precisely the same thing.
2. It would be a mistake to think of Ahmadinejad as simply a former president. He is the leader of a powerful faction and given how important informal institutions are he remains a very important player in Iranian politics.

## CHAPTER 4

1. We will see these elements at play in chapter 7 on Lebanon.

## CHAPTER 5

1. It should also be noted that terror in this sense has a religious meaning. To strike terror in the hearts of the enemies of God is a fairer reading than thinking of terror in the contemporary U.S. lexicon.

## CHAPTER 6

1. With greater amounts of oil coming from various actors including the United States and as global markets shift to renewables, this is becoming less true by the day.

## CHAPTER 8

1. Note here the similarity to Sederberg's point regarding behavioral expectations as part of normal civic engagement before the breakdown of social cohesion that requires engaging in the political.
2. There is similar talk about the succession of Iran's Khameini.

## CHAPTER 9

1. This is a pattern we saw play out in Iran's history as well. From the earliest days of Iran's history, the Shahs sought legitimacy from the clerics and the clerics used that to increase their power, which in turn warranted suppression of the clerics by the Shahs. This long-lasting conflict culminated in the merging of Mosque and State in the 1979 Islamic Revolution.
2. https://www.treasury.gov/press-center/press-releases/Pages/hp271.aspx

## CHAPTER 10

1. www.state.gov/advancing-the-u-s-maximum-pressure-campaign-on-iran/
2. www.soc.mil/OSS/special-operations.html
3. www.indexmundi.com/iran/age_structure.html
4. www.statista.com/statistics/294213/iran-age-structure/

# Bibliography

Abdul-Hussain, Hussain. 2020. "Why Iraq's PM Should Heed Al-Sistani and Disband Iranian Militias." *Arab News*, October 16, 2020. https://www.msn.com/en-ae/news/other/why-iraq-s-pm-should-heed-al-sistani-and-disband-iranian-militias/ar-BB1a6QOb.

Abrahamian, Ervand. 2008. *A Modern History of Iran*. Cambridge, UK: Cambridge University Press.

AFP. 2016. "Iran's New Parliament Has More Women than Clerics," May 1, 2016. https://www.dawn.com/news/1255639.

Algar, Hamid. 1981. *Islam and Revolution: Writings and Declarations of Imam Khomeini*. Berkeley, CA: Mizan Press.

Alrumaithi, Mohamed. 2010. "Iran's Strategy of Influence in the Middle East." Naval Postgraduate School.

Al-Tamimi, Aymenn Jawad. 2019. "Reconstruction in Syria: Interview with Jihad al-Bina'." *Aymenn Jawad Al-Tamimi*, January 4, 2019. http://www.aymennjawad.org/2019/01/reconstruction-in-syria-interview-with-jihad-al.

Ansari, Ali M. 2003. "Continuous Regime Change from Within." *The Washington Quarterly* 26 (4): 53–67.

Aramesh, Arash. 2011. "Clerics and IRGC Find Common Ground in Attacking Ahmadinejad." InsideIRAN.Org, June.

Arjomand, Said Amir. 2009. *After Khomeini Iran Under His Successors*. Oxford: Oxford University Press.

Baer, Robert. 2008. *The Devil We Know: Dealing with the New Iranian Superpower*. New York: Three Rivers Press.

Beeman, William O. 2008. *The "Great Satan" vs. the "Mad Mullahs:" How the United States and Iran Demonize Each Other*. Chicago: University of Chicago.

Blanford, Nicholas. 2006. "Shia Crescent Pierces Heart of Arab World: Sunni Governments Are Nervously Eyeing a Militant Alliance Capable of Taking on Israel." *The Times*, 2006.

Boroujerdi, Mehrzad. 1992. "GHARBZADEGI: The Dominant Intellectual Discourse of Pre- and Post-Revolutionary Iran." In *Iran: Political Culture in The Islamic Republic*, edited by Samih K. Farsoun and Mehrdad Mashayekhi, 205. London and New York: Routledge.

Buchta, Wilfried. 2000. *Who Rules Iran? The Structure of Power in the Islamic Republic*. Washington, DC: The Washington Institute for Near East Policy and the Konrad Adenauer Stiftung.

Buzan, Barry, Ole Waever, and Jaap de Wilde. 1998. *Security: A New Framework for Analysis*. Boulder, CO: Lynne Rienner Publishers.

Cafiero, Giorgio, and Maysam Behravesh. 2020. "Iran's Fatemiyoun Forces: A Challenge to the US Mission in Afghanistan?" *Inside Arabia*, February 2020. https://insidearabia.com/irans-fatemiyoun-forces-a-challenge-to-the-us-mission-in-afghanistan/.

Calder, Norman. 1982. "Accommodation and Revolution in Imami Shi'i Jurisprudence: Khumayni and the Classical Tradition." *Middle Eastern Studies* 18 (1): 3–20.

Campbell, Andy. 2016. "One-Third Of Iraqis Believe America Supports Terrorism." *Huffington Post*, April 7, 2016. https://www.huffpost.com/entry/iraq-america-terrorism_n_5706bbfae4b0b90ac271ab14.

Cobaugh, Paul. 2017. "Soft Power in the Lead." In *Soft Power on Hard Problems: Strategic Influence in Irregular Warfare*, edited by Ajit Maan and Amar Cheema, 133. London: Hamilton Books.

Cordesman, Anthony H., Bradley Bosserman, and Jordan D'Amato. 2011. *U.S. And Iranian Strategic Competition*. Washington, DC: Center for Strategic and International Studies.

Cordesman, Anthony, and Martin Kleiber. 2007. *Iran's Military Forces and Warfighting Capabilities*. Westport, CT: Center for Strategic and International Studies.

Crooke, Alastair. 2009. *Resistance: The Essence of the Islamist Revolution*. Pluto Press.

D'andrade, R. G. and M. Wish. 1985. "Speech Act Theory in Quantitative Research on Interpersonal Behavior." *Discourse Processes* 8: 229–59.

Daniel Brumberg. 2010. *Iran Primer: Iran and Democracy*. Frontline: Tehran Bureau.

Dehghanpisheh, Babak, 2012. "Meanwhile, Inside Iran" Khamenei Consolidates his Power," *Time*.

EIA. 2019. "Iran: Executive Summary." U.S. Energy Information Agency.

Eisenstadt, Michael. 2015. "The Strategic Culture of the Islamic Republic of Iran Religion, Expediency, and Soft Power in an Era of Disruptive Change." *Middle East Studies Monographs*. Marine Corps University.

Erdbrink, Thomas. 2016. "China Deepens Its Footprint in Iran After Lifting of Sanctions." *The New York Times*, 2016.

Farhi, Farideh. 2008. "Crafting a National Identity amidst Contentious Politics in Contemporary Iran." In *Iran in the 21st Century*, edited by Homa Katouzian and Hossein Shahidi, 317. London and New York: Routledge.

Farsoun, Samih K., and Mehrdad Mashayekhi. 1992. *Iran : Political Culture in the Islamic Republic*. London; New York: Routledge.

FM-3-13. 2013. *Inform and Influence Activities.*
FM-3-13, and Department of the Army. 2013. *Inform and Influence Activities.*
Fulton, Will. 2011. *A Window into the Foreign Policy of Iran's Supreme Leader Ali Khamenei.* Washington, DC: American Enterprise Institute Iran Tracker.
Fulton, Will, and Sam Wyer. 2013. *Iranian Strategy in Syria.* American Enterprise Institute and the Institute for the Study of War.
Gleave, Robert. 2007. "Conceptions of Authority in Iraqi Shi'ism: Baqir al-Hakim, Ha'iri and Sistani on Ijtihad, Taqlid and Marja'iyya." *Theory, Culture and Society* 24 (2): 59–78.
Gough, LTC Susan L. 2003. *The Evolution of Strategic Influence.* Carlisle Barracks, PA: U.S. Army War College.
Green, Jerrold D., Frederic M. Wehrey, and Charles Wolf. 2009. *Understanding Iran.* Santa Monica, CA: RAND.
Harb, Mona and Reinoud Leenders. 2005. "Know Thy Enemy: Hizbullah 'terrorism' and the Politics of Perception." *Third World Quarterly* 26 (1): 173–197.
Harik, Judith Palmer. 2004. *Hezbollah: The Changing Face of Terrorism.* London and New York: I.B. Tauris.
Hourcade, Bernard. 2008. "The Rise to Power of Iran's 'Guardians of the Revolution.'" *Middle East Policy* 16 (3): 58–63.
ICRO. 2019. "The Islamic Culture and Relations Organization." ICRO. http://en.icro.ir/index.aspx?fkeyid=&siteid=257&pageid=9641.
Jamal, Ahmad Shuja. 2019. "The Fatemiyoun Army: Reintegration into Afghan Society." United States Institute of Peace. https://www.usip.org/sites/default/files/2019-03/sr_443-the_fatemiyoun_army_reintegration_into_afghan_society-pdf_0.pdf.
JCH-3-10. 2010. "Commander's Handbook for Strategic Communication and Communication Strategy v 3.0." US Joint Forces Command; Joint Warfighting Center.
JDN-2-13, and Joint Chiefs of Staff. 2013. *Commander's Communication Synchronization.*
Joint Chiefs of Staff. 2017. "The National Security Strategy of the United States of America 2017."
Juneau, Thomas. 2015. *Squandered Opportunity: Neoclassical Realism and Iranian Foreign Policy.* Stanford, CA: Stanford University Press.
Kagan, Frederick W. 2012. "Iranian Influence in the Levant, Egypt, Iraq, and Afghanistan." A Report by the American Enterprise Institute and the Institute for the Study of War.
Karadeniz, Tulay. 2019. "Turkey Looking at New Trade Mechanisms with Iran to Avoid U.S. Sanctions." *Reuters*, April 17, 2019. https://www.reuters.com/article/us-usa-iran-sanctions-turkey-idUSKCN1RT15N.
Kaufman, Stuart J. 2001. *Modern Hatreds the Symbolic Politics of Ethnic War.* Ithaca, NY and London: Cornell University Press.
———. 2006. "Symbolic Politics or Rational Choice? Testing Theories of Extreme Ethnic Violence." *International Security* 30 (4): 45–86.
———. 2015. *Nationalist Passions.* Ithaca, NY: Cornell University.
Keddie, Nikki. 2003. "Better than the Past: What Recent History Taught Iranians." *The Iranian.*

Kenneth M. Pollack. 2005. *The Persian Puzzle: The Conflict Between Iran and America.* New York: Random House.

Khalaji, M. 2007. "Iran's Revolutionary Guard Corps, Inc." The Washington Institute for Near East Policy.

Knights, M. 2011. "Iran in Iraq: The Role of Muqtada al-Sadr." The Washington Institute for Near East Policy.

Latifi, A. 2017. "How Iran Recruited Afghan Refugees to Fight Assad's War." *The New York Times--Sunday Review*, 2017.

Laura Secor. 2007. "Whose Iran?" *The New York Times Magazine*, January 28, 2007.

Lesch, David W., and James Gelvin, 2017. Assad Has Won in Syria. But Syria Hardly Exists, *The New York Times*. https://www.nytimes.com/2017/01/11/opinion/assad-has-won-in-syria-but-syria-hardly-exists.html.

Levitt, M.P.S. 2015. "Kataib Al-Imam Ali: Portrait of an Iraqi Shiite Militant Group Fighting ISIS." The Washington Institute for Near East Policy.

Lt. Col. Davis, Daniel L. 2020. "A Deal between Iran and China Shows That 'getting Tough' Doesn't Solve the US's Problems." *Business Insider*, July 22, 2020. https://www.businessinsider.com/iran-china-deal-shows-getting-tough-doesnt-solve-us-problems-2020-7?amp=.

Mahmoud, M.M.C. 2013. "Syrian War Widens Sunni-Shia Schism as Foreign Jihadis Join Fight for Shrines." *Guardian*, 2013.

Majidyar, A. 2017. "Iran-Backed Iraqi Militia Group Launches New Brigade to 'Liberate' Golan Heights." The Middle East Institute.

Majlis Monitor. 2016. "Analysis: 2016 Iranian Parliamentary & Assembly of Experts Election Results." Majlis Monitor.

Malici, Akan, and Stephen G. Walker. 2017. *Role Theory and Role Conflict in U.S.-Iran Relations: Enemies of Our Own Making.* London, New York: Routledge.

Mattern, Janice Bially. 2005. "Why `Soft Power' Isn't So Soft: Representational Force and the Sociolinguistic Construction of Attraction in World Politics." *Millennium - Journal of International Studies* 33 (3): 583–612. doi: 10.1177/03058298050330031601.

McAdam, Doug; Tarrow. 2004. *Dynamics of Contention.* Cambridge: Cambridge University Press.

MEHR News. 2011. "Principlists' Largest Gathering Held." *MehrNews.Com*, November 18, 2011.

Milani, Abbas. 2010. "The Shah's Atomic Dreams." *Foreign Policy*.

———. 2011. "Is Ahmadinejad Islamic Enough for Iran?" *Foreign Policy*, April 29, 2011.

Molavi, A. 2006. *Soul of Iran.* New York: Norton.

Motamedi, Maziar. 2020. "Rouhani Defends COVID Vaccine Efforts amid US Pressure." *Aljazeera*, December 26, 2020.

Murray, W. K. 2014. *The Iran-Iraq War: A Military and Strategic History.* Cambridge: Cambridge University Press.

Nasr, Vali. 2006. *The Shia Revival: How Conflicts within Islam Will Shape the Future.* New York and London: W. W. Norton & Company.

Noe, Nicholas. 2007. *Voice of Hezbollah: The Statements of Sayyed Hassan Nasrallah.* London and New York: Verso.
Norton, Augustus Richard. 1985. "Changing Actors and Leadership among the Shiites of Lebanon." *Annals of the American Academy of Political and Social Science* 482: 109–121.
Nye, J.S. 2008. "Public Diplomacy and Soft Power." *AAPSS* 616: 94–109.
Ostovar, Afshon. 2016. *Vanguard of the Imam.* New York: Oxford.
Polk, William R. 2009. Understanding Iran. New York City: Palgrave.
Pollack, Kenneth M. 2005. *The Persian Puzzle: The Conflict Between Iran and America.* New York: Random House.
Rajaee, Bahram. 2004. "Deciphering Iran: The Political Evolution of the Islamic Republic and U.S. Foreign Policy After September 11." *Comparative Studies of South Asia, Africa and the Middle East* 24 (1): 159–172.
Rakel, Eva Patricia. 2009. "The Political Elite in the Islamic Republic of Iran: From Khomeini to Ahmadinejad." *Comparative Studies of South Asia, Africa and the Middle East* 29 (1): 105–125.
Rivera, W. A. 2016. "Discursive Practices of Honor: Rethinking Iran's Nuclear Program." *Foreign Policy Analysis* 12 (3): 395–412.
Roggio, B. 2016. "Iraq Prime Minister Establishes Popular Mobilization Forces as a Permanent 'independent Military Formation." *FDD's Long War Journal.*
Rose, J. 2011. *Zoroastrianism: An Introduction. I.B. Tauris Introductions to Religion.* New York: Tauris.
Rostami-Povey, Elaheh. 2010. *Iran's Influence: A Religious-Political State and Society in Its Region.* London and New York: Zed Books.
Saad-Ghorayeb, Amal. 2002. *Hizbu'llah: Politics and Religion.* London: Pluto Press.
Saadoun, Mustafa. 2020. "Shiite Factions Close to Sistani Move to Separate from Iran-Backed Militias." *Al-Monitor*, December 6, 2020. https://www.al-monitor.com/pulse/originals/2020/12/iraq-iran-pmu-sistani.html.
Sachedina, Abdulaziz. 2001. *The Islamic Roots of Democratic Pluralism.* Oxford: Oxford University Press.
Salhy, S. al-. 2012. "Iraqi Shi'ite Militants Fight for Syria's Assad." *Reuters*, 2012.
Sankari, Jamal. 2005. *Fadlallah: The Making of a Radical Shi'ite Leader.* London: SAQI.
Sederberg, Peter C. 1984. *The Politics of Meaning: Power and Explanation in the Construction of Social Reality.* Tucson, AZ: University of Arizona Press.
Shanahan, Rodger. 2005. *The Shi'a of Lebanon: Clans, Parties and Clerics.* London and New York: Tauris Academic Studies.
Shinkman, Paul D. 2015. "Poll: Syrians, Iraqis Believe U.S. Created ISIS, Don't Support War." U.S. News and World Report, December 18, 2015. https://www.usnews.com/news/articles/2015-12-18/poll-majority-of-syrians-iraqis-dont-support-obamas-anti-isis-war-believe-us-created-extremists.
Sowell, Kirk H. 2014. "Iraq's Second Sunni Insurgency." *Current Trends in Islamist Ideology* 17: 40–69.
Tarrow, Sidney. 1998. *Power in Movement: Social Movements, Collective Action and Politics*, 2nd ed. Cambridge: Cambridge University Press.

Tarrow, Sidney, and Charles Tilly. 2007. *Contentious Politics*. Boulder, CO: Paradigm Publishers.

Thaler, David E., Alireza Nader, Shahram Chubin, Jerrold D. Green, Charlotte Lynch, and Frederic Wehrey. 2010. *Mullahs, Guards, and Bonyads An Exploration of Iranian Leadership Dynamics*. Santa Monica, Arlington, and Pittsburgh: Rand Corporation.

The Guardian. 2011. "Medvedev Threatens US over Missile Shield." The Guardian.

Tibi, Bassam. 2008. "Islamist Parties: Why They Can't Be Democratic." *Journal of Democracy* 19 (3): 43–48.

Tilly, Charles. 2001. "Mechanisms in Political Processes." *Annual Review of Political Science*, 4 (1): 21–41.

Toumaj, A. 2017. "Qassem Soleimani Boasts of Tehran's Expanded Footprint throughout Middle East." *FDD's Long War Journal*.

Truzman, Joe. 2020. "Iranian-Backed Organizations Establish a Foothold in the Gaza Strip." *FDD's Long War Journal*. https://www.longwarjournal.org/archives/2020/05/iranian-organizations-establish-a-foothold-in-the-gaza-strip.php?utm_source=feedburner&utm_medium=email&utm_campaign=Feed%3A+LongWarJournalSiteWide+%28FDD%27s+Long+War+Journal+Update%29.

US Energy Information Administration. 2019. "The Strait of Hormuz Is the World's Most Important Oil Transit Chokepoint." https://Www.Eia.Gov/Todayinenergy/Detail.Php?Id=39932, June 20, 2019.

Verma, Nidhi. 2018. "Indian Oil Imports from Iran Surge to Highest since 2016 -Trade." *Reuters*, June 12, 2018. https://www.reuters.com/article/india-oil/indian-oil-imports-from-iran-surge-to-highest-since-2016-trade-idUSL4N1TE4HY.

Wastnidge, Edward. 2015. "The Modalities of Iranian Soft Power: From Cultural Diplomacy to Soft War." *Politics* 35 (3–4): 364–377.

Weed, Matthew C. 2017. "Global Engagement Center: Background and Issues." *CRS Insight*, August 4, 2017. https://fas.org/sgp/crs/row/IN10744.pdf.

Wehrey, Frederic M. and Theodore W. Karasik. 2009. *Saudi-Iranian Relations Since the Fall of Saddam: Rivalry, Cooperation, and Implications for U.S. Policy*. Arlington: RAND Corporation.

Wiktorowicz, Quintan. 2004. "Introduction: Islamic Activism and Social Movement Theory." In *Islamic Activism: A Social Movement Theory Approach*, edited by Quintan Wiktorowicz, 1–33. Bloomington, IN: Indiana University Press.

Wilson, S. 2011. "All US Troops to Leave Iraq by the End of 2011." *The Washington Post*, 2011.

Wright, Robin B. 2010. *The Iran Primer : Power, Politics, and U.S. Policy*. Washington, DC: United States Institute of Peace: Published in collaboration with Woodrow Wilson International Center for Scholars.

# Index

Abadi, Haider, 115, 123, 126–27, 136–40, 148, 184
Abu al-Fadhil al-Abbas Brigade, 170–73
adaptive resistance, 2–4, 29–30, 46, 51, 68, 70, 72–73, 127, 128, 143, 157, 175–76, 186, 189, 194
Amiri, Hadi, 120, 139–42
Asaib Ahl al-Haq, 144, 167, 172
Assad, Bashir, 6, 8, 145, 153–58, 160–66, 168–70, 172, 174, 176–78, 181, 185, 187, 190–93, 204, 215–19
Assad, Hafez, 154–56, 159–63, 165–67, 176, 185

Badr Brigades (organization), 120, 129, 140, 147

Daesh (ISIS), 13, 82, 107, 115, 120, 123–26, 129, 135, 138–39, 142–44, 148, 153, 155, 157, 168, 169, 181, 184, 212–16
designed redundancy, 2–4, 13, 41, 43, 44, 46–47, 50–51, 68, 70, 75, 127–28, 134, 137, 142–43, 157, 167, 173, 176, 185, 189, 194

factions, 3–4, 10, 12–13, 32–37, 39, 41, 43, 46, 48–51, 74–75, 125, 129, 136, 187, 208

Fatemiyoun Division, 174–75

Harakat Hezbollah al Nujaba, 168–70
hard power, 54–55, 59, 60, 67–68, 183
Hizb'allah, 4, 25–26, 66, 69–70, 77–79, 81–88, 90–92, 94, 99–106, 109, 117, 127–29, 132, 134–35, 137, 142–43, 146, 150–51, 153–54, 166–67, 170–73, 176, 184–91, 194, 204, 216–18, 226
Hussein, Saddam, 6, 12, 25–26, 72, 81, 108, 113, 115, 117, 123–25, 129–30, 135, 139–40, 142, 146, 153–55, 197, 214–15, 220, 222

Jaysh al-Mahdi, 129, 146
Joint Comprehensive Plan of Action (JCPOA), 4, 5, 9, 12, 38, 45, 204, 222

Kataib al-Imam Ali, 173
Kata'ib Hizb'allah, 81, 124–25, 129, 141, 143, 167
Khamenei, Ali, 37, 39–40, 45, 47, 50, 72, 97–99, 105–6, 110–11, 117, 119–20, 122, 127, 134, 136–41, 144, 145, 150–51, 168, 171, 176–77, 188, 190
Khomeini, Ruhollah, 11, 24, 25, 29–32, 37, 39–40, 46, 70, 73–74, 89, 90, 92,

94–99, 103, 105, 107, 108, 111, 115, 117, 131–33, 145, 154, 156, 188

Maliki, Nouri, 27, 123, 126, 136, 141, 143–45, 147–48, 184, 189, 217
al-Muhandis, Abu Mahdi, 125, 127, 138, 143, 150, 173, 189–90, 216, 217

Nasrallah, Hassan, 86, 90, 100–101, 105, 117, 130, 171

oppression, 4, 29–30, 33, 69, 76, 82, 84–85, 87, 89–90, 113, 117, 123, 129, 138, 140–41, 146, 173, 181–82, 184, 189, 195–96, 199, 205, 211, 214–15, 217

resistance, 2–5, 8, 11, 13, 15–17, 19, 21, 23–25, 27, 29–32, 35, 37, 39, 41, 43, 45–47, 49–51, 53, 68–74, 76–78, 81–84, 86, 88–90, 100–101, 104–5, 122–24, 127–30, 132, 134–35, 137–43, 147, 151, 153, 155–57, 163, 165–67, 169–73, 175–76, 180–82, 184–87, 189, 191–92, 194–96, 211, 214–17
Rouhani, Hassan, 35–39, 45, 74, 98, 133, 209
al-Sadr, Moqtada, 27, 109, 117, 118, 129, 136, 139–50, 156, 171, 173, 190, 217

Sistani, Ali, 99, 105–30, 135–38, 140, 145, 148–51, 187–90, 204, 215–16, 221

smart power, 59–60, 67, 183
social mobilization, 63, 66, 83, 85, 88, 128–29
soft power, 55, 59, 67, 68, 74, 183
Soleimani, Qasem, 12, 78, 124–25, 127, 130, 132, 136, 141, 143–44, 150, 173, 189–90, 216–19
spectacle theory, 162–64
strategic communication, 53–54, 57–58, 71, 200
strategic culture, 2–3, 12, 53, 179, 189, 195, 199
strategic influence, 1–4, 10, 12–13, 19, 25–26, 33, 41, 51, 53, 55–63, 65–74, 77–79, 82, 86–87, 92, 101, 106–8, 111, 122–23, 128, 131, 139, 157, 162–63, 165–66, 169, 173, 176, 178–79, 181–87, 189–91, 193–206, 208, 210–14, 218–22
strategic policy, 1–4, 9, 13, 15, 43, 47–48, 72, 186, 225

*triumph (triumphalism)*, 44, 69, 72–74, 77–78, 82, 85–86, 89, 122–23, 128–29, 135, 138, 140, 145, 147, 151, 166, 169, 173, 180–82, 184–85, 189, 195, 214, 216–19

*velayat-e faqih,* 11, 16, 25, 29–32, 34, 35, 38, 40, 43, 44, 47, 49–51, 70, 86, 89, 95, 97, 107–8, 111, 119, 122, 126–28, 131, 134–37, 140–41, 143–45, 150, 168, 179–80, 185, 196, 204, 207, 213, 222

# About the Author

**Dr. W. A. Rivera** is the Senior Enterprise Architect and Strategic Designer for CSS-LUCAS, a computational security studies and digital transformation company, and founding director of the Laboratory for Unconventional Conflict and Simulation (LUCAS). Dr. Rivera has been grappling with the complex issues of strategic culture since 2010 while at the University of Chicago's Computation Institute. His doctoral dissertation, "The Complexity of Iranian Foreign Policy: The Politics of Fear, Interest, and Honor," used Social Network Analysis to foreground the role of honor in foreign policy preference formation. Since then, Dr. Rivera has been working to advance the philosophical and theoretical understanding of strategic culture and the role of emotions and ideational frames, while developing software that enables both expression of theoretical insights and analytic rigor.